PRENTICE HALL

Realidades

Pre-AP*
Resource Book

Marcia L. Wilbur

Janice Hendrie

*Advanced Placement, Advanced Placement Program, and AP are registered trademarks of The College Board, which was not involved in the production of and does not endorse, this book.

PEARSON

Prentice
Hall

Boston, Massachusetts
Upper Saddle River, New Jersey

Pearson Prentice Hall™ is a trademark of Pearson Education, Inc.
Pearson® is a registered trademark of Pearson plc.
Prentice Hall® is a registered trademark of Pearson Education, Inc.

ISBN 0-13-166026-8
9 10 V004 11 10

Table of Contents

Preparing for the AP* Spanish Language Exam with *REALIDADES* 1

An Introduction to Pre-AP* Spanish Strategies 6

Listening

Preparing Students for Listening to Dialogues 9

Preparing Students for Listening to Narrations 13

Reading

The Role of Pre-Reading 18

Teaching Beginning Reading 19

Teaching Intermediate and Advanced Reading 21

Writing

Journal Writing 25

The Writing Process 27

Evaluating Students' Compositions 30

Preparing for the Grammar Fill-ins 32

Preparing for the Cloze Passage Completion 33

Speaking

Preparing for the Formal Presentation 36

Preparing for Timed Interactive Responses 37

Recording and Evaluating 40

Vocabulary

Effective Methods for Studying Vocabulary 47

Classroom Vocabulary Practice 50

Testing Vocabulary 53

Levels A/B/1 Resource Support 55

Level 2 Resource Support 95

Level 3 Resource Support 133

Pre-AP* Resources 164

Preguntas rápidas 166

Answer Key 169

Preparing for the Advanced Placement* Spanish Language Exam with *REALIDADES*

The integration of language, communication, culture, and critical thinking throughout all levels of *REALIDADES* provides a strong foundation for building the skills needed for success on the Advanced Placement* Language Examination. Teachers will find a wide range of activities and strategies within the Student Editions, Teacher's Editions, and program ancillaries (print and technology) to support pre-AP* skills development.

The sequence of instruction within each thematic chapter in the Student Edition is specifically designed to build language skills and communicative proficiency. The first section, *A primera vista*, provides comprehensible input through listening and reading with language presented in a cultural context. The second section, *Manos a la obra*, gives students a wide range of activities that progress from concrete to transitional to open-ended. This careful progression of activities is key to developing AP* language proficiency while building vocabulary and grammar mastery. Many of the activities practice the integration of language skills that students will find on the AP* Examination. In addition, many integrate culture through the use of articles, surveys, advertisements, art, photographs, and *realia*. The third section, *¡Adelante!* applies the different language skills and expands cultural understanding. The last section, *Repaso*, summarizes what students have learned in the chapter (vocabulary and grammar) and prepares students for the proficiency tasks found on the chapter test.

The Teacher's Edition provides extensive support and strategies that focus on building pre-AP* skills. The teaching support for each activity is conveniently contained within a "tab" in the side-margin wrap. The "Extension" ideas within this tab will be useful for teachers looking to expand and integrate more skills after completion of the initial activity. Across the bottom of the page, the section labeled

"Differentiated Instruction" has teaching suggestions for diverse learners and the teacher looking for pre-AP* activities will want to focus on the ideas for Multiple Intelligences, Advanced Learners, and Heritage Learners. In addition, the different print and technology components found in the program are referenced at point-of-use and many support building AP* skills.

Using *REALIDADES* to Prepare for AP* Spanish Listening Comprehension

The Video and Audio Programs for each level provide a wealth of listening opportunities. Each chapter has multiple activities that provide listening practice. These activities can be found in the Student Edition and the Writing, Audio & Video Activities Workbook. Students can access audio files and listening activities through the *REALIDADES* Companion Web Site at PHSchool.com and through the Interactive Textbook. The *Videohistoria* (found in *REALIDADES* A, B, 1 & 2) and the *Videomisterio* (found in *REALIDADES* B, 1 & 2) give extended contextualized listening opportunities with comprehension checks.

Using *REALIDADES* to Build Cultural Understanding

An inherent expectation of the AP* Spanish Language Examination is an understanding of cultural perspectives and practices. *REALIDADES* offers multiple opportunities throughout the chapter for students to consider cultural aspects of the Hispanic world that will prepare them to understand linguistic inferences and a wide variety of cultural viewpoints. Each chapter has a cultural backdrop that holds the chapter together, seen first in the opening pages of the chapter where a work of fine art introduces the theme. The Fine Art Transparencies that accompany *REALIDADES* provide teachers a way to make this culture come alive to students

*Advanced Placement, Advanced Placement Program, and AP are registered trademarks of The College Board, which was not involved in the production of and does not endorse, this book.

while integrating ways for students to practice with and produce Spanish. Throughout each chapter you will find, and be able to use daily, appropriate cultural notes (*Fondo cultural*) and activities that integrate culture into language practice. In addition, each chapter includes cultural projects and readings that help students understand the products, practices, and perspectives of the cultures of the Spanish-speaking world (*Perspectivas del mundo hispano* and *La cultura en vivo*). On the chapter test, students are asked a specific question that focuses on a cultural aspect developed in the chapter.

Using *REALIDADES* to Prepare for AP* Spanish Reading Comprehension

Read, read, read. Then read more. With the traditionally valued emphasis on interpersonal speaking skills, teachers often forget that printed texts provide rich sources of comprehensible input that can lead to acquisition. *REALIDADES* offers level-appropriate reading selections throughout the program. From the beginning of each chapter through the practice activities, the *¡Adelante!* section, and the test preparation, reading is emphasized. In the *A primera vista* section, students are led to understand new words and phrases in context in paragraphs and dialogues. In many *Manos a la obra* activities, students are called upon to not only practice vocabulary and grammar but also to read for meaning. For instance, activities that require students to choose words from a word bank to complete a paragraph or that have them pick between two verbs before completing the correct grammatical form emphasize reading comprehension. Many *Manos a la obra* activities are based on *realia* that not only bring culture into the activities but also require reading. Extended readings throughout *REALIDADES*, like the *Videohistoria* text pages and *¡Adelante! Lectura*

readings, provide strategy boxes on the student page. The teacher's wrap-around notes on these pages combined with the strategies presented in the Student Edition, when used consistently, equip students with a variety of tools for decoding texts. Pre-AP* teachers should consider lesson planning that allows for ample time to engage in the pre-reading activities that *REALIDADES* suggests, to complete the reading process, and to do the comprehension activities that cause students to engage in higher-order thinking like inference and interpretation. For heritage speakers of Spanish, who often need to be challenged to improve their reading skills, additional reading materials are provided in the *REALIDADES para hispanohablantes* Workbooks and *Lecturas para hispanohablantes* Readers.

Using *REALIDADES* to Prepare for AP* Spanish Informal Writing

Throughout *Manos a la obra*, a plethora of opportunities exist for students to write individual words and phrases, sentences, brief notes, letters, personal opinions, and reactions. These activities are labeled as *Escribir*. In addition, components of the *REALIDADES* program—the Practice Workbook; the Writing, Audio & Video Workbook, *REALIDADES para hispanohablantes*, the Interactive Textbook, the GoOnline Companion Web Site activities, and many more—offer students writing practice outside the text. The *Escribir* sections of the assessment program provide excellent examples of opportunities to write in an informal way. Encourage students to provide rich responses, going beyond a standard, bare-bones vocabulary, and expanding on their basic ideas. The tone of these writing pieces can be personal and interactive rather than based on formal conventions.

*Advanced Placement, Advanced Placement Program, and AP are registered trademarks of The College Board, which was not involved in the production of and does not endorse, this book.

Using *REALIDADES* to Prepare for AP* Spanish Formal Writing

Across the levels of *REALIDADES,* there are multiple opportunities for writing formal compositions. Each *Presentación escrita* or *Para escribir* task offers a process for planning, preparing for, executing, and evaluating the writing task. In order to provide thorough AP* preparation, students should be encouraged to engage in these formal writing situations as developed in *REALIDADES* A, B, 1, 2 and 3. Across the lessons, there are many strategies given for pre-writing exercises as well as ideas for making revisions. Pay attention to these and again, remind students to use the suggested tools to improve writing. The writing process is evident in all of the formal writing tasks set forth in *REALIDADES* and culminates in the writing experiences in *REALIDADES* 3. A key element in that process is the revision phase—creating opportunities for students to improve upon their work both by expanding on ideas and correcting potential errors.

Using *REALIDADES* to Prepare for AP* Spanish Paragraph Completion

In order to succeed on this portion of the AP* Exam, students need to understand a written passage well enough to make a grammatically appropriate sentence completion. Building reading comprehension skills will help improve student performance on this type of question. Additionally, throughout *REALIDADES,* teachers will find numerous *Leer/Escribir* activities that offer a similar task—make a choice based on what is read and understood. There are also many cloze passage activities in the textbook, workbook, and assessment program geared towards making appropriate word choices. All these help students learn to make linguistically appropriate completions.

Using *REALIDADES* to Prepare for AP* Spanish Informal Speaking

Verbal interaction is the key to success in this interpersonal arena. Students need both the ability to speak and to understand what is said to them so that an appropriate response can be formulated. Activities in *REALIDADES* always progress from a mechanical level, in which students produce a word or phrase, to paired activities to open-ended language. *REALIDADES* gives students many opportunities to communicate, and partner or paired work is the easiest way to achieve this sort of practice. Interpersonal speaking tasks are labeled *Hablar* and contain a two-person or group icon. In addition to the text activities, additional Communicative Activities and Situation Cards are found in the Teacher's Resource Book.

Using *REALIDADES* to Prepare for AP* Spanish Formal Speaking

Interpersonal speaking is developed throughout each chapter. These frequent opportunities enable students to perform successfully on the formal speaking tasks that are found at the end of the chapter in *¡Adelante!* section. The *Presentación oral* provides students a step-by-step performance-based task. Students are given strategies for planning and preparing their ideas and then are expected to perform a formal speaking task without the help of notes or a script. In addition, any activity in *REALIDADES* designed to be a formal writing exercise, poster presentation, and other such activities can serve as the basis for making formal speaking presentations. Whenever possible, it is important to move students from a heavy reliance on written notes with lengthy preparation time to allowing just enough preparation time to outline the main and supporting ideas followed by an opportunity for spontaneous speech.

*Advanced Placement, Advanced Placement Program, and AP are registered trademarks of The College Board, which was not involved in the production of and does not endorse, this book.

Using Rubrics and Scoring Guidelines with *REALIDADES*

Because nearly 50% of the AP* Spanish Language Exam is scored with scoring guidelines or rubrics, teachers should take advantage of the many sets of rubrics designed to evaluate specific writing and speaking activities found in the textbook. Each Theme Project (found in the Teacher's Edition interleaf pages), *Presentación oral*, and *Presentación escrita* has an accompanying rubric. Speaking and writing tasks in the assessment program also have accompanying rubrics. It is always important to provide students with these rubrics as they prepare for the performance-based tasks so that they know what is expected of them from the beginning. Time used in class to allow students to critique each others' work in groups using scoring guidelines is time well spent. Once students are familiar with this sort of evaluation, the teacher can assign and collect a task for formal grading, using the same types of scoring guidelines. For level 3 students, teachers might consider using the rubrics included in *REALIDADES* along with the scoring guidelines used for the various sections of the Free Response section of the AP* Spanish Language Exam found at apcentral.collegeboard.com/spanlang. Familiarizing students with AP*-level expectations in level 3 serves to build the rigor necessary for success on the AP* Exam.

Using *REALIDADES* to Develop Vocabulary

For students to be successful on the AP* Spanish Language Examination, they need a rich and varied vocabulary. *REALIDADES* does an excellent job developing vocabulary through its thematic, contextualized, and visualized approach to vocabulary in the *A primera vista* section. Comprehensible input is used to present vocabulary which is reinforced with visuals, reading, hands-on activities with clip art and gestures, TPR Storytelling, and video. The vocabulary presented in each

chapter is tightly connected to the theme and presented in manageable amounts. The presentation is followed by the systematic build-up of mechanical to paired to open-ended activities using new and recycled vocabulary. Students are given a number of practice opportunities to learn and retain vocabulary in the Practice Workbook and Guided Practice Workbook, GoOnline activities, electronic flash cards on the Interactive Textbook, the QuickTake quizzes on PresentationEXPRESS™ CD-ROM, and the MindPoint® Quiz Show game.

REALIDADES has included a section called *Exploración del lenguaje* and *Ampliación del lenguaje*. The section exposes students to language patterns like cognates, prefixes, root words, suffixes, and word families. Students learn the connections between English and Spanish as well as Latin, Greek, and Arabic. *REALIDADES* uniquely gives students the tools to learn about language, to make informed guesses about words, and ultimately, to empower students with strategies when they encounter unknown words on the AP* Language Examination or other standardized tests.

Using *REALIDADES* to Develop Grammatical Accuracy

Throughout the speaking and writing sections of the AP* Spanish Language Exam, a strong command of grammar is essential, in addition to the message conveyed. While the focus of the classroom activities in *REALIDADES* is on communication, helping students use language in syntactically appropriate ways can make communication clearer. In *REALIDADES*, students are provided grammatical input models in *A primera vista*. This input is followed by clear explanations in *Manos a la obra*. Since most students are not motivated by grammar study, each grammar point of *REALIDADES* A, B, 1 and 2 has an accompanying engaging *GramActiva* video segment available for classroom use and on the Interactive textbook. As mentioned earlier,

*Advanced Placement, Advanced Placement Program, and AP are registered trademarks of The College Board, which was not involved in the production of and does not endorse, this book.

the sequence of activities in *REALIDADES* always leads students to move from mechanical grammar activities to paired and open-ended activities in which students create language, applying accurate grammatical concepts. Laminated Grammar Study Guides help students to "see" the entire Spanish grammar system come together. Correct structural usages can be practiced and built by drawing students' attention to the practice activities in the Student Edition and Interactive textbook. Activities outside the text in the Practice Workbook, Guided Practice Workbook, and *REALIDADES para hispanohablantes* workbook plus the GoOnline website activities give students additional grammatical practice. The QuickTake quizzes on PresentationEXPRESS™ CD-ROM and the MindPoint™ Quiz Show CD-ROM give a fun way for students to test their vocabulary and grammar knowledge and then receive a review of their performance.

The newly revised AP* Spanish Language Exam format is intended to serve as an instrument for providing the evidence needed to support claims about what a student knows and can do in Spanish at the fifth- or sixth-semester level in college. The claims state that a student who receives a score of 3, 4, or 5 on the AP* Exam is capable of: communicating accurately and fluently in the interpersonal, interpretive, and presentational modes; understanding and being understood by a variety of speakers and in different settings; and acquiring information from authentic sources, remaining aware of cultural perspectives.

AP Spanish Language 2007 Exam Format

Section	Item Type	Number of Questions and % Weight of Final Score	Time	
Section I	**Multiple Choice**	**70-75 questions**	**50%**	**85-90 min.**
Part A: Listening	Short and Long Dialogues and Narratives	30-35 questions	20%	30–35 min.
Part B: Reading	Reading Comprehension	35-40 questions	30%	50-60 min.
Section II	**Free Response**		**50%**	**Approx. 100 min.**
Part A: Writing	Paragraph Completion (With Root Words)	10 questions (2.5%) 7 minutes	30%	Approx. 80 min.
	Paragraph Completion (Without Root Words)	10 questions (2.5%) 8 minutes		
	Informal Writing	1 prompt (5%) 10 minutes		
	Formal Writing (Integrated Skills)	1 prompt (20%) 55 minutes		
Part B: Speaking	Informal Speaking (Simulated Conversation)	5-6 response prompts (10%) 20 seconds to respond to each	20%	Approx. 20 min.
	Formal Oral Presentation (Integrated Skills)	1 prompt (10%) 2 minutes to respond		

AP Spanish Language 2007 Exam Format copyright © 2007 The College Board. Reproduced with permission. All rights reserved. http://apcentral.collegeboard.com.

*Advanced Placement, Advanced Placement Program, and AP are registered trademarks of The College Board, which was not involved in the production of and does not endorse, this book.

An Introduction to Pre-AP* Strategies for Spanish

The College Board's Equity and Access Statement[1] seeks to make Advanced Placement* programs available to students everywhere. A goal of the Statement is for the enrollment in any given school's AP* program to reflect the demographics of the entire school population. This is best achieved in a Spanish AP* program by targeting two critical objectives. First, the district's Spanish program must be aligned between levels to include integrated AP* skill building over the duration of the program. Second, teachers should identify a broad range of potential AP* students early in their academic careers and provide them with opportunities to enhance their proficiency.

The preparation for the AP* program ought to begin as soon as students embark upon the first level of formal language study, which can be as early as the middle school. Often, the designated AP* Spanish teacher is the only person in the department who is familiar with the rigorous demands of the AP* Exam. Other teachers, especially those who teach the very beginning levels of Spanish, may not realize the important role that they play in the process. For this reason, we have developed the REALIDADES Pre-AP* Resource Book with all secondary Spanish teachers in mind. Furthermore, since the AP* Spanish Language Exam is a measure of students' overall proficiency, strategies that are used to prepare students for the exam are also helpful in building proficiency at all levels.

In my experience, teachers and students are often intimidated by the concept of Advanced Placement*. Some assume that the challenge will be too difficult for even the most dedicated or gifted students. In order to dispel the notion that the exam is too difficult, the Pre-AP* program focuses on strategies that will not only help students prepare for the exam, but that will also help them build proficiency at every level.

As a Pre-AP* strategies program evolves from beginning levels on up, teachers will enjoy a sharing of ideas and reflective practice as part of a greater AP* teaching community. Students will benefit from their teachers' combined efforts to collaborate and establish effective strategies that are reinforced at each level. Because the AP* Spanish Language Exam is proficiency-based, adopting the Pre-AP* preparation continuum is appropriate in any Spanish program where proficiency is the goal.

Pre-AP* is not intended to be a separate course for gifted students only. Instead, the Pre-AP* concept is intended to represent instructional strategies designed to help all students achieve success. As you use the REALIDADES series, you will see how it aims for overall proficiency, and how it is an ideal resource for teachers who want to build their students' skills while keeping AP* goals in mind. The REALIDADES Pre-AP* Resource Book aims to:

- acquaint all levels of teachers with the sorts of tasks required on the AP* Spanish Language Examination.

- demonstrate very simple and direct ways that teachers can incorporate strategies and activities from all three levels of the REALIDADES series into their instruction, in order to prepare students for the AP* Spanish Language Exam.

Based on college comparability studies, the AP* Spanish Language Course and Exam are equivalent to a fifth- or sixth-semester college Spanish course. As of May 2007, the AP* Spanish Language Exam aligns itself more closely with twentieth-century instruction and assessment practices and with the Standards for Foreign Language Learning in the 21st Century[2]. As a departure from its long-term format of testing the four skills in isolation (listening, reading, writing, speaking), the 2007 revisions to the exam format reflect an integration of skills that is more reflective of real-life language use. The exam prompts are

---

[1] http://apcentral.collegeboard.com/article/0,3045,150-157-0-2200,00.html

[2] American Council on the Teaching of Foreign Languages. (1999). Standards for foreign language learning in the 21st century. Lawrence, KS: Allen Press, Inc.

*Advanced Placement, Advanced Placement Program, and AP are registered trademarks of The College Board, which was not involved in the production of and does not endorse, this book.

increasingly from authentic sources (radio broadcasts and interviews, magazine and newspaper articles, etc.). In 2007 and beyond, students are expected to:

- Answer multiple-choice questions in Spanish based on an auditory selection from an authentic source, possibly supported by a visual aid.
- Answer multiple-choice questions in Spanish related to authentic reading selections. The questions are often of a higher-order thinking skills type, requiring inference, interpretation, and synthesis. The questions reach beyond mere factual recall of the passage.
- Complete an authentic passage, filling in the blanks with the correct form in Spanish of a given root word.
- Complete an authentic passage, filling in the blanks with a grammatically and lexically correct word in Spanish. No root word is given.
- Engage in informal writing (e.g., writing a personal note, message, etc.).
- Write a formal essay based on a given topic statement. Students must read passages and listen to an audio prompt before writing, and are required to synthesize and refer to each of the prompts appropriately within the essay.
- Engage in informal speaking (e.g., leave a message on a friend's answering machine, etc.). Students' answers are recorded on an audiotape or CD.
- Synthesize a printed text and an audio prompt on a given topic, then prepare and deliver a formal, two-minute speech on that topic. Students' answers are recorded on an audiotape or CD.

The newly revised AP* Spanish Language Exam format is intended to serve as an instrument for providing the evidence needed to support claims about what a student knows and can do in Spanish at the fifth-or sixth-semester level in college. The claims state that a student who receives a score of 3, 4, or 5 on the AP* Exam is capable of: communicating accurately and fluently in the interpersonal, interpretive, and presentational modes; understanding and being understood by a variety of speakers and in different settings; and acquiring information from authentic sources, remaining aware of cultural perspectives.

What students need to know and be able to do for both the AP* Spanish Language and AP* Spanish Literature Exams goes well beyond mere language acquisition. Teachers will want to provide language-use opportunities in Spanish that require their students to engage in higher-order thinking skills, reaching to the upper levels of Bloom's Taxonomy. Not only must students have the ability to comprehend the information presented to them in Spanish, but they also need the ability to synthesize and analyze what they have learned. The output tasks on the revised 2007 AP* Spanish Language Exam are designed to reflect those higher levels of capability.

By examining the skills needed to successfully complete the AP* Exam, departments can use backwards planning to determine how much time is required to prepare students to be ready for the challenge. Many schools offer the AP* Spanish Language Exam as the fifth year of the program. Others are able to accomplish this in the fourth year. Since each school is unique, teachers and administrators must determine the amount of time that they have to prepare students. Regardless of the skills that are designated as goals for a particular level of Spanish, it remains essential that teachers ensure that the students have an in-depth understanding of the concepts covered. Developing students' long-term retention of materials is key. It can be frustrating for both you and your students when a concept was covered in a previous level, but was never quite learned. Thus, the manner in which the material is taught is just as important as the amount of material covered. If the right strategies are taught, the students will grasp and retain key information with ease. By making sure that students are equipped from the beginning with strong learning skills, you can help them maximize their learning and ensure their proficiency.

*Advanced Placement, Advanced Placement Program, and AP are registered trademarks of The College Board, which was not involved in the production of and does not endorse, this book.

Though proficiency is the primary goal of the *REALIDADES* program, written and spoken accuracy is also important to a student who is learning Spanish. However, the direct instruction of grammar often fuels methodological debates. While it should not become the focal point or the goal of instruction, brief explanations can speed acquisition and lead to more accurate usage.[3] Since syntactic control is a key component of the AP* Spanish scoring guidelines, providing students with concise grammatical patterns and formulas can serve as valuable tools.[4] As you help students achieve greater accuracy, however, it is essential that you keep in mind that the first objective of instruction should be communication.

Students must be aware of the expectations that you have of them. They should also understand what is expected of them on the AP* exam. An excellent way to clarify expectations is to review scoring guidelines from previous exams with students. For your convenience, the *REALIDADES* Pre-AP* Resource Book includes a variety of suggested rubrics that have been simplified, yet remain similar to the rubrics that students will encounter on the AP* Exam. Review these rubrics with students and make sure that they understand what is expected of them. Ask them to identify their strengths and weaknesses on the rubrics, and help them focus on improvement. By acquainting students with the "rules of the game" early on, you can help your students to be winners.

Pre-AP* Strategies for Spanish is about building students' proficiency by providing them with the tools to comprehend and produce the target language. When students have effective strategies and clear expectations, they can all be successful. When students achieve success, they gain confidence and further motivation. Your instruction and the resources available in the *REALIDADES* series can combine to achieve student success on the AP* exam and help your students become confident and proficient Spanish speakers outside of the classroom.

MARCIA WILBUR

---

[3] Ellis, R. (1997). *Second Language Acquisition*. Oxford: Oxford University Press.

[4] Bransford, J. D., Brown, A. L., Cocking, R. R., & Educational Resources Information Center (U.S.). (1999). *How People Learn: Brain, Mind, Experience and School*. Washington, D.C.: National Academy Press.

*Advanced Placement, Advanced Placement Program, and AP are registered trademarks of The College Board, which was not involved in the production of and does not endorse, this book.

Listening

In order to prepare students at the Pre-AP* level for listening success, you must prepare them to be skillful listeners. Teaching strategies such as sound-symbol recognition and listening for the gist of a passage or a dialogue at the earlier levels will provide a strong foundation for overall comprehension. As students become more skilled, encourage them to listen for details and extract meaning from longer passages. Listening strategies such as these will prepare your students to be strong AP* students.

Preparing Students for Listening to Dialogues

Teaching Tips

Make the input comprehensible

Use as much Spanish as possible in the classroom at the earliest levels. It is important that the level of language used be salient to the learner. Non-comprehensible input does not have positive effects on students' listening abilities. You can make the language more meaningful by simplifying it as appropriate for the level of study. Gestures, pictures, and props also help to convey meaning. Students have access to comprehensible input in the *A primera vista* section of each chapter. The *Escuchar* activities found on the second page of each *A primera vista* section can help you to assess students' comprehension of the new language. You also will find many useful suggestions on how to deliver language effectively by using the input scripts in the *Teacher's Resource Book*. In addition, the transparencies in the *Vocabulary and Grammar Transparencies* and clip art in the *Teacher's Resource Book* can be used as resources around which you can design supplemental listening activities. *TPR Stories* also provides suggestions for delivering language input that students can comprehend.

Recycle Listening Activities

It is important that students do not shut down when given a listening task. You may want to "recycle" listening activities from year to year. Occasionally allow students who are using *REALIDADES 3* to listen to activities from *REALIDADES 1* and *2* that talk about the same topics as your current chapter. You may want to do these reviews as a quick warm-up activity at the beginning of class. Students will gain more confidence listening when they have the opportunity to succeed.

Try to simulate the exam activities when possible

It is important that students be familiar with the exam format as well as with the content. Multiple-choice questions are commonly found throughout the AP* Exam. Use activities from *REALIDADES* such as the questions in the *¿Eres tú, María? Video Workbook* or in the *Writing, Audio & Video Workbook* to help students practice answering multiple-choice questions. You can supplement activities found in *REALIDADES* textbooks and workbooks with quick comprehension checks that are in a multiple-choice format. Develop two or three questions to put on an overhead projector and have students copy the answers in their notebooks. Review the answers and have students describe their strategies for getting certain answers. Help students to use the process of elimination and educated guessing when doing such activities. You may want to simply give some multiple-choice questions in order to further the listening activity.

Sample Activities

Dialogue input from classmates

Encourage active listening to dialogues. Dialogues presented to the class are an integral part of early levels of language learning. While one pair or group of students is in front of the class presenting their dialogue, have all other students write a question that they could pose to the speakers when they finish. Then choose volunteers to ask their questions. This activity holds the audience accountable for listening participation and also allows for continued communication after the dialogue is complete.

True / False comprehension

Ask students to write true / false sentences about the content of a dialogue presented. Then, have volunteers read their true / false

sentences to the class, who will respond accordingly.

Listening and Speaking

Have pairs of students record their own dialogues about a topic in your current *REALIDADES* chapter. (See the section on Speaking, p. 40 for suggestions on how to record.) Then, ask those students to listen to their dialogues again and create 5 multiple-choice questions to accompany what they say. Collect tapes and dialogues, and redistribute them to other pairs. Have each pair of students listen to the dialogues and answer the questions.

Graphic organizers

Using the example below, have students prepare a T-chart on a blank piece of paper. Have the whole class decide on the most important topics that students should be listening for in a given dialogue, and ask them to list those topics in the first column. Then, have students take notes on what each group is saying about each topic in the appropriate spot in the second column. You might want to ask students to extend their charts if more than one pair of students is presenting a dialogue.

Temas importantes	Lo que dicen_____ *(nombres de los participantes)*

Identify the situation

On index cards (so they can be reused) or on slips of paper, write a description in Spanish of a situation that is appropriate to the chapter topic. Make as many cards as necessary so that there can be one situation for each pair of students in the class. The *REALIDADES* Situation Cards, as well as other speaking prompts in the series, are good sources for ideas. Have each pair of students randomly draw one scenario from the cards. Allow the pairs enough time to prepare a dialogue appropriate to their situation. Provide a handout or prepare an overhead that lists a one-line description of each situation on the cards. Have students present the dialogues to the class without explaining the situation beforehand. As the students listen to each dialogue, have them correctly match the situation on the sheet with the dialogue they hear.

Sample Activity

Sample situations: *REALIDADES* 2– Capítulo 3B

1. Explícale a un nuevo estudiante cómo llegar a tu casa desde la escuela.
2. Visitas una ciudad que no conoces. Pregúntale a un(a) policía dónde estás y cómo llegar a la casa de tu tía quien vive en la Calle del Cristo.
3. Estás en el coche con un(a) amigo(a) nervioso(a) quien acaba de recibir su permiso de manejar. Ayúdale con las señales de tráfico mientras te lleva a casa después de la escuela.
4. Tu hermano(a) no quiere ayudarte a limpiar la cocina después de la cena. Dile cómo puede ayudarte.
5. Eres un(a) estudiante que está aprendiendo a manejar. Estás poniendo nervioso(a) a tu instructor(a) porque estás mirando a la gente y no estás mirando a la calle.
6. Explícale a tu papá o mamá por qué saliste mal en tu examen de manejar.

Teléfono

This activity can be done at all levels. Write sentences that are appropriate to the current unit of study on slips of paper. Divide the class into teams of four or five. Each team sits in a row, facing away from the board, one

behind the next. Distribute the same sentence to the last person in each row. On cue, the person farthest from the board turns to face the board and speaks the sentence to the person seated directly in front of him or her. That person says the sentence to the next person in the row, etc. The person seated closest to the board must correctly write the sentence on the board in the space assigned to that team. (Students should be encouraged to whisper so as not to help the other teams.) The person who started the *teléfono* is responsible for noticing any errors in the sentence written on the board and must pass the necessary corrections up the telephone wire! The first team to correctly write the sentence on the board scores a point. After each sentence, have students rotate and give the new person a different sentence. The team with the most points after five rounds wins the game.

Teaching Tips

Point out the importance of listening to (not just viewing) videos

Encourage active listening when using videos. Videos are important for communicating cultural values and developing listening skills. Normally, students tend to focus on the visual, not the auditory, aspect of a video. To emphasize the importance of listening, bring in a video (ideally one that students have not seen yet) in which two people are simply seated at a table, having a conversation. Play the segment with the sound down. Ask students what the scene is about. After students have tried to guess, play the video again, pointing out the value of understanding what is seen *and* heard.

Maintain variety when using videos

Showing video segments in class is an excellent way to supplement your lesson and to build listening skills. However, a video may do more harm than good, depending on its length. It's important to remember that a student's attention span is generally about half as long as his/her age. In other words, a fourteen year old has an attention span of about seven minutes. In order for instruction to be effective, you must remember to change what the student *does* every seven to ten minutes. The change

should be more significant than merely changing from activity 4 to activity 5 in the textbook. It is best to change the sensory modality that the student is using. For this reason, care should be taken when considering the use of a lengthier video. Students are not likely to be actively engaged in the viewing (or listening) for a long period of time. Show video clips and follow them up with short discussions or quick written comprehension checks. Longer videos might be more effectively implemented if spread out over several days.

Pre-listening suggestions

When using videos from the *REALIDADES* series, be sure to review ideas, listening strategies, and photos that accompany the *Videohistorias* or *Videomisterios* in the student texts. As students review the information, encourage them to talk about things that they might be listening for as they watch the video. Refer also to the notes in the Teacher's Edition that can help you maximize students' comprehension of the video. The comprehension activities in the student text and the *Writing, Audio & Video Workbook* provide you with ways to check what students understand.

Sample Activities

Pre-listening predictions

Show the video the first time with the sound off. Have students talk about what is happening and what the people might be saying. Then play the video and see how their predictions match what they hear.

The second time around

When using the *Videohistoria* videos, play the second segment (which has no words on the screen) a few days after seeing the first segment. Pause the video periodically and ask students informal questions about what is being said. They will be amazed at how their comprehension has developed and how they no longer depend upon the written words to understand the story.

Video true / false

Ask students to write three true and three false statements about the main events in the video. Encourage them to avoid statements

that could be answered by only seeing the video. In other words, have them write statements about what is being *said* in the video. Have students read the statements to a classmate after showing them the video again. The classmate will answer according to what he or she understood from the video.

Video plot summary

On an overhead transparency, create a random list of quotes from characters in the video. Make sure that the quotations you choose are relevant to the plot. After showing students the video, have them number the quotes in the order that they were said. Students can do this activity alone or with a partner. This activity serves as a reading comprehension exercise also.

Can't see the TV!

Turn the television around (or ask students to turn their chairs to face away from it). Allow students to listen to the video segment. Pause the video periodically and ask students to speculate about what is happening. Turn the television back around and have students determine how accurate they were by watching the video. If you choose to do this activity with the *Videohistoria* videos, you might want to make photocopies of the eight panels that that are found in the *A primera vista* section in the textbook. As students listen without watching the television, have them point to the panel that corresponds with what they hear.

Video cloze activity

Type a short portion of the script of a *Videomisterio* episode and create a cloze activity. Leave blanks for certain key words that students must listen for and write.

Teaching Tips

Using dictation exercises

Dictation practices and quizzes are helpful during the early levels of Spanish instruction to ensure that students are making correct sound-symbol correlations. In the *REALIDADES* series, you will notice activities entitled *Escucha y escribe*. These are meaningful dictations that help students to practice writing the vocabulary and grammar structures for the given unit of study.

When doing dictation activities, be sure to read the script three times. First, read the selection naturally. Have students listen, but not write. During the second reading, students should write. Read the passage in short segments, linking the words within a segment, but pausing in between segments so that students have time to write. Encourage students to leave a blank space if they miss a word, but remind them not to interrupt the dictation in progress to ask for a repetition. For the third reading, read naturally, but just a bit more slowly than the first time so that students can proofread their work and fill in any missing words. Remind students to check for spelling and correct accentuation. To assess dictations, make each correct word worth a point. Give students half credit if the word has only one incorrect letter or an incorrect accent mark.

Sample Activities

Textbook selections

Choose a reasonable amount (about two pages) of text from your current *REALIDADES* chapter. The day before the dictation, ask students to read the pages carefully as a homework assignment. Remind them to pay special attention to any word that might cause spelling challenges. Encourage them to read the text aloud at home as a preparation strategy. Recommending that students write out difficult words can also be helpful. In class the next day, read only a portion of the assigned pages (not the entire selection) as the dictation. One paragraph generally should be enough. Have students write what they hear. It is helpful for students to check their own work. After they finish writing, point out the paragraph you read in the book, and have students use a different colored pencil or pen to correct their answers.

Student-created dictations

Have students work in pairs and have each student write a six-line dialogue. Then, have them take turns reading their dialogues to their partners. Encourage them to follow the dictation pattern of reading the text three times. While the one partner reads, the other partner should write down what is being

said. After the third reading, students should check for errors. Students can then switch roles and repeat the activity.

Dictation as a final evaluation

As part of a chapter evaluation, you might consider creating sentences using vocabulary and structures from the current *REALIDADES* chapter, and dictating them one at a time. Or, you can create small paragraphs or use scripts from audio activities listed in the *REALIDADES Teacher Resource Book* for dictations. It is helpful to review scoring guidelines with students before beginning the evaluation.

Turn songs into cloze passages

The *REALIDADES* series is accompanied by a varied selection of songs in Spanish on the *Canciones CD*. The lyrics can be found beginning on p. 189 of the *Level 1 Writing, Audio & Video Workbook*. Create a cloze activity by distributing a handout of the lyrics with key words left out. You may choose to leave blanks for certain types of words such as adjectives, nouns, and pronouns, to reinforce a particular structure being discussed in class. Allow students two or three opportunities to listen to the song and to correctly fill in as many of the missing words as possible. After students have completed the activity, put a list of all of the correct words on an overhead transparency, and play the song again, so that students can recognize any words that they may have missed.

> ### Strategy for Students
> Remind students that when doing listening and drawing activities, they should focus on the listening. Many students are too busy trying to be artists to be effective listeners. Have them listen once to the entire passage, and draw a rough sketch. Then, on the second time around, they can begin to add details. By the third reading, students should have detailed drawings that they can share with classmates for future activities or discussions.

Listen and draw

Look for two illustrations that can be reproduced in your current *REALIDADES* chapter. Choose from any *REALIDADES* text, workbook, or ancillary. Be sure to select drawings

for which students will generally possess the vocabulary needed to describe the picture. The drawings need to be simple enough for students to easily describe them, yet complex enough to create rich descriptions. (See sample drawings on p. 25 of the *REALIDADES Level 1 Teacher's Resource Book, Para Empezar–Tema 4* and p. 131 of the *REALIDADES Level 2 Writing, Audio & Video Workbook*.) Be sure each student has a blank piece of paper and a pencil. Have students work in pairs. One student describes the chosen drawing to his or her partner while the other student tries to recreate the drawing based on the description he or she hears. Discourage students who are describing the drawing from showing their partners the drawing or helping them in any way. Once the new drawing is complete, ask students to compare their efforts to the original. Have students switch roles, using the second drawing.

Preparing Students for Listening to Narrations

Teaching Tips

Using *REALIDADES* resources for narration activities

On the AP* Exam, students listen to short narrations which are followed by multiple-choice questions. Students also hear two longer narrations, each being approximately five minutes in duration. The questions for the longer narrations are also printed in the test booklet along with the possible multiple-choice answers to those questions.

You can help students be better prepared to listen to these narrations on the AP* Exam by using the resources available to you in the *REALIDADES* series. For example, at the end of each chapter of *REALIDADES 3* there is a *¿Qué me cuentas?* page which has a listening section. This listening section is a part of the chapter review, which prepares students for the chapter test and, ultimately, for the AP* Language test. These activities mirror the listening portions of the AP* Exam. Additionally, the activities in the Prentice Hall *Reading and Writing for Success* workbook are easily adaptable at the intermediate level as practice for narrative listening tasks on the AP* Spanish

Language Exam. You may wish to read the passages to your students. To give them a more authentic practice activity, have a native speaker record a passage (or record it yourself) before you do the activity. Provide questions that accompany each passage. Let students scan the questions before they respond, and then read the passage or play the recording. When students are finished listening to the narration and answering the questions, give them a printed copy of the segment and have them listen again as they read along. See the *Reading and Writing for Success* book for samples of this activity.

Sample Student Activities

Dictogloss activity

The Dictogloss activity is highly effective in helping to prepare students to be able to extract meaning from longer listening selections. In this activity, the focus is on what students *do* understand. Students should not be expected to comprehend each and every nuance of the selected piece. With practice, students will become adept at performing this type of task. This activity can and should be practiced at all levels of study. Follow these five steps for optimal results.

1. Choose any reading passage from your current chapter of *REALIDADES*. The length may vary depending on the students' level of study. One half to one page is sufficient in length. It is not necessary to use an entire reading.

2. Have students close their books as you read the selected passage aloud, at a natural rate of speech. Ask them to listen and concentrate on trying to extract the most essential points.

3. Read the passage aloud to students a second time at the same rate of speech and ask them to jot down, in Spanish, the main ideas and most important details of the reading. Students should not try to capture every word as in a dictation exercise.

4. Ask students to combine their efforts with a partner and write a one-paragraph summary of what they heard.

5. Once students have finished, you can choose any of the activities below as an effective follow-up:

   a. Have two or three sets of partners share their summaries aloud for the class. Have other students share any details that they did not hear during the presentations.

   b. Ask each pair to share one main idea from their summary. List the main ideas on the board or overhead. Continue to ask pairs until all of the main ideas of the reading have been listed.

   c. Ask each pair to use their summaries to prepare two questions about the reading. Collect the questions and ask some of them to the class. Encourage students to be creative when giving answers that cannot be taken directly from the passage.

   d. Prepare a short list of questions to ask students about the main ideas of the story. You may want to ask students in a whole-class setting, or walk around to each pair as students finish their summaries. Have students use their writing to support their answers.

   e. You may want to continue reading the entire text containing the passage that you are working on, thus using the Dictogloss as a pre-reading activity. After students summarize and share details of the passage, allow them to open their texts and read the selected passage aloud with a partner. By already participating in an in-depth discussion about a portion of the reading, students will be more familiar with it as they read for meaning.

Strategy for Students

Students must be prepared to answer multiple-choice questions that accompany the listening section of the AP* Exam. When preparing them, encourage students to scan the questions that accompany a listening activity before they listen. By reading the questions, they know what to listen for. When students have multiple-choice questions that accompany a listening activity, ask them to use common sense to eliminate any illogical answers right away.

Creating questions

Choose two different segments of one reading from a *REALIDADES* student textbook to record or read aloud to the class. Divide the class in half and give each group a different reading. Have them create multiple-choice questions for the segment they were given. Then, collect the questions and redistribute them to the opposite group of students. Ask students to take a few moments to read the questions that they received. Next, read aloud or play a tape of each segment (one at a time). The students with the multiple-choice questions listen for the correct answers, while the students who wrote the questions follow along with the passage as it is being read.

Listening and memory

The *REALIDADES Writing, Audio & Video Workbook* has many activities that require students to correlate the events from a story or a series of descriptions to a drawing. (For examples, see p. 102 of the *Level 2 Writing, Audio & Video Workbook* and p. 94 of the *Level 3 Writing, Audio & Video Workbook*.) To develop students' capacity for listening to longer selections, you might consider reading all of the prompts related to the pictures for the activity while students have their workbooks closed. After reading the script, direct students to open their workbooks and complete as many of the identifications as possible from memory and/or any notes that they might have taken. If students have difficulties, repeat the script a second time and allow them to have their workbooks open as they listen.

Listening for details

A second step that requires students to listen for additional details can be added to some of the activities in the *Writing, Audio & Video Workbook*. Have students do the activity as indicated in the *Writing, Audio & Video Workbook*. Then, replay the audio CD and ask students to write details that support the answers they gave. This scaffolding approach to listening allows students to focus on the main idea first, and then the supporting details.

Preparing for AP* Listening with *REALIDADES* Components

The following charts provide examples of where to find materials in *REALIDADES* components that correlate to Pre-AP* activities.

SE = Student Edition
TE = Teacher's Edition
AP = Assessment Program
PW = Practice Workbook
TRB = Teacher's Resource Book
WAVW = Writing, Audio & Video Workbook

Preparing to Listen to Dialogues

Activity	Level A	Level B	Level 1	Level 2	Level 3
Situation cards	SE p. 145, *Preparación* PW p. 62 WAVW p. 37 WAVW p. 49 TRB p. 118 AP p. 50-D	SE p. 315, Act. 3 PW p. 151 TRB p. 84 AP p. 211-D	SE p. 343, *Preparación* SE p. 361, Act. 21 PW p. 81 PW p. 144 WAVW p. 37 WAVW p. 136 TRB Vol. 1 p. 170 TRB Vol. 2 p. 128 AP p. 102-D AP p. 129-D	SE p. 192, Act. 10 SE p. 317, *Preparación* PW p. 42 PW p. 68 WAVW p. 105, Act. 12 WAVW p. 84, Act. 10 TRB Vol. 1 p. 145 TRB Vol. 2 p. 74 AP p. 22-D AP p. 79-D	SE p. 180, Act. 28 SE p. 459, Act. 35 PW p. 71 PW p. 129 WAVW p. 60 WAVW p. 129 TRB p. 125 TRB p. 74 AP p. 33-D AP p. 56-D
Active video "watching"	TE p. 182, *Presentación* WAVW p. 18	SE p. 121 WAVW p. 74	SE p. 243 WAVW p. 161	SE p. 207	WAVW p. 132
Multiple-choice comprehension questions	WAVW p. 82, Act. 8	WAVW p. 12, Act. 2	WAVW p. 74, Act. 9	SE p. 131, Act. 2 SE p. 207 WAVW p. 151, Act. 9	SE p. 280 SE p. 326 WAVW p. 52, Act. 4
Dictation quiz	SE p. 230, *Lectura* TRB p. 189 #07 AP p. 49, *Leer*	SE p. 240, *Lectura* PW p.127* *fill blanks TRB p. 212 #09	SE p. 138, *Lectura* PW p. 150 TRB Vol. 1 p. 63 #14 AP p. 88, *Leer*	SE p. 92, *Cultura en vivo* PW p. 163 TRB Vol. 2 p. 63 #01 AP p. 35, *Leer*	SE p. 304, Act 8 PW p. 101 TRB p. 196 #17 AP p. 123, *Leer*
Describe & draw	SE p. 185, Act. 7 PW p. 46 WAVW p. 47 #2 AP p. 181	SE p. 193, Act. 9 WAVW p. 30, Act. 11 AP p. 181	SE p. 302, *Manos a la obra* PW p. 145 WAVW p. 56, Act. 10 AP p. 165	SE p. 249, Act. 13 PW p. 86 WAVW p. 121, Act. 9 WAVW p. 142 AP p. 13	SE p. 78 Act. 18 WAVW p. 74, Act. 12

Preparing to Listen to Narrations

Activity	Level A	Level B	Level 1	Level 2	Level 3
Dictogloss	SE p. 260, *Lectura*	SE p. 146, *Lectura*	SE p. 440, *Lectura*	p. 176, *Perspectivas*	SE p. 238, *Lectura*
Listening & remembering longer selections	WAVW p. 76, Act. 11 WAVW p. 77, Act. 7	AP p. 127-A	WAVW p. 93, Act. 8 AP p. 156-A	WAVW p. 169, Act. 5 AP p. 119-A	WAVW p. 66, Act. 4 AP p. 32-A

Reading

Teaching students to read in Spanish presents a unique challenge. For many students, reading is a difficult exercise in decoding and translating. It is important to teach students to read for overall meaning from the very beginning, and to avoid trying to translate every word. Do not develop or use activities that require them to extract every minute detail from the reading. Instead, point out to them that a global understanding is sufficient at first. As their reading fluency develops, they become better prepared to take on a passage for a deeper understanding. Once they are equipped with the right strategies to master texts at their reading level, they will want to read for enjoyment or information. Practice will result in fluency, which will help students advance their reading level. For success on the reading comprehension section of the AP* Exam, students must be able to know the content and vocabulary, but they must also have strong strategies to apply to material that may be above their reading level. Therefore, your two main goals as a teacher should be to instill useful strategies in students' reading practices and to promote fluency to make reading Spanish less intimidating for them.

The Role of Pre-reading

Teaching Tips

Pre-reading at all levels

Regardless of the reading level of the assigned text or the students' abilities, it is always important to prepare them for what they will be reading. Use visuals around a text and the title of the passage to provide indications to students about the content of the passage.

Also, remind students to notice what type of text they are going to be working with, and encourage them to handle it appropriately. For example, students would not approach a short story with the same reading skills as they would an informational text. In one, they are focusing on a developing plot and characters, while in the other they are looking to gain factual information. Students may have already been taught about various texts in their Language Arts classes, and may already be aware of how to treat each type of text. Remind them to use these practices in Spanish, too.

A third important factor in gauging how much students will comprehend from a given text is their background knowledge. When presenting students with a text (fiction or non-fiction), try to access the information that they already know. If you find that they are limited in background knowledge for a particular text, be sure to provide them with comprehensible information that they can use to better understand the text.

Finally, it is recommended that you carefully examine a reading selection prior to presenting it to the class. This way, you can choose to focus on a selected set of vocabulary and/or structures that are present in the reading. Make sure that students are familiar with the vocabulary and grammar in the reading. By using the vocabulary from the chosen text in other activities prior to doing the reading, students will feel less intimidated. The same is true for syntax. If a reading is particularly heavy with a certain type of structure, extract some samples of the structure from the reading and use them to practice the structure before doing the actual reading.

Activities

Student Strategy

Encourage students to scan the last paragraph or sentence of a passage before they begin reading. By doing this, students can form expectations for the content of the text, which will help them focus more on the content when they do go back and read it.

Two possibilities

Have students read the last sentence or paragraph of any text you may assign to them. Based on what they read in that segment, have students conjecture two possible details about the body of the text. Ask them to write these guesses down on a piece of paper to

share with a partner. As students share their work, have them determine which two possibilities are the most probable. It will be helpful for reading comprehension if students not only make predictions, but also discuss them with someone else. When students read the text, have them check their predictions for accuracy.

Dictation and the Dictogloss activity

Before reading, have students write out a dictation of a segment of the text. (See p.12 of the Listening section for a complete description of this activity.) This will help to familiarize them with the content and type of text you are using. Or, have students do a Dictogloss activity, which is a listening activity that provides a thorough introduction to the gist of a longer passage. (See p. 14 of the Listening section for a complete description of this activity.) If students understand the basic gist of the passage before beginning, they will have an easier time when it comes to reading.

Teaching Beginning Reading

Teaching Tips

Promoting thoughtful responses

Often, students are assigned to read a passage in their textbook and answer the associated questions. They become quite adept at copying a corresponding phrase from the reading without ever truly reading the selection itself or understanding it. Even at the most basic levels, it is essential that they try to read for understanding, and not just write the answers. Vary activities that accompany a text in a way that promotes open responses and discussions about what students thought of the content of the reading. Supplement the activities in the *REALIDADES* reading sections with some of the suggested activities to help build reading comprehension and, consequently, reading enjoyment. Students will fare much better on the AP* Exam if they read for meaning and not just for answers.

Graphic Organizers

Graphic organizers are one way for students to obtain information and show comprehension of a text. The type of organizer you use depends on the type of text students are being asked to read. For example, when reading short pieces of fiction, you may wish to have students use a flowchart to show main events of the story. The *REALIDADES Vocabulary and Grammar Transparencies* include reproducible graphic organizers. There are also many graphic organizers available on the Internet. Explain how to use the organizer before beginning the reading, and then have students fill in information after they have read the passage, or during a second read.

Strategy sharing

Don't forget to point out all of the strategy boxes that accompany each reading in the *REALIDADES* series. It is also helpful to ask students to share their own strategies for obtaining information from a text. Have students explain how they got a particular answer, or ask them to back their opinions up with passages from the text.

Reading aloud

Encourage beginning readers to read aloud at home. Often, the sound of a word will trigger comprehension, and this provides good speaking practice. However, try to avoid having students read aloud in a round-robin fashion in class. Students will only focus on their segment of the text and will not gain meaning from the entire passage. Of course, it is often the case where students are eager to read aloud in class. In this case, instead of calling on students to read, you should model the pronunciation of the passage first, and then have volunteers repeat what you say. In this way, students will be modeling your correct pronunciation and intonation as well as reinforcing the content of the text by re-reading.

Cognates

Remind students that cognates can be helpful in understanding the meaning of a word that has not yet been formally introduced to them. However, advise them to be aware that false cognates, such as *asistir* and *realizar*, can throw off their understanding. When they are not sure if a word is truly a cognate, suggest that they try to read the entire sentence and determine its meaning through the context.

Activities

Paired Reading

Choose a variety of texts from the *REALIDADES* series, as well as from outside sources. Assign the readings to pairs of students. Separate the students in your classroom so that they will be able to read the passages aloud in a low voice without disturbing other pairs. Give students three minutes to discuss what they read and list the main ideas. Then, have two sets of partners join together to share the information that they read.

True / false

Have each student or pair of students write one true sentence and one false sentence about the reading. Tell students that the sentences should be in their own words, rather than taken directly from the text. Have students share their sentences aloud with classmates, or you may prefer to compile a list of their statements on an overhead projector to review with students. Have students turn false statements into true statements using information from the reading.

Plot summary

This activity is best completed with a narrative. Have each student or pair of students write one sentence on the board that summarizes the main events of a reading. Monitor students' choices to ensure that no events are repeated. When students are finished writing their statements on the board, label each sentence with a letter. Students must put the sentences in the order that best reflects the events from the reading.

> #### Student Strategy
> Have students read, read again, and then re-read! Reading a passage the first time gives the general sense or gist of what it is about. The second time, students should use decoding skills for the difficult vocabulary and structures. A third time allows students to synthesize the passage and complete any comprehension activities.

Random answers

After students have completing a reading, allow them to choose from questions that cor-

respond to the text, instead of requiring them to answer all of the questions. It's okay if students tend to focus on the easier questions in the early levels. It builds confidence when they focus on what they *do* understand. As students become more confident, you may decide to ask your advanced students to choose from the more difficult questions. When students finish answering the questions, ask volunteers to read their answers, without revealing the corresponding question. Have the class listen to the answer and determine the correct question. As a variation, you may want to create and read the answers yourself.

Cloze passages

Type a summary of a reading from your current *REALIDADES* chapter, leaving out key phrases, information, or vocabulary. Then, create a series of multiple-choice answers (similar to what students will see on the AP* Exam). (See the sample activity below.) Distribute these activities to students as a practice test. When discussing the answers, have students explain their responses. Note: When creating your own multiple-choice question and answer sets, it is essential that all of the possible answers are written in correct Spanish, and that the wrong choices are only incorrect because of content and context. Students should *never* see incorrect Spanish (spelling or grammar errors) on an exam or activity.

Sample Activity

Choose the answer that best completes the passage:

Me llamo Pablo Nicolás Urdangarín de Borbón. Mi __(1)__ es el 6 de diciembre. Nosotros __(2)__ muchas fiestas en mi familia. En la foto __(3)__ un día muy especial para mí. Es el día de mi bautizo. Yo tengo un __(4)__ mayor que se llama Juan Valentín. También yo tengo dos primos; Felipe, que tiene dos __(5)__, y una prima, Victoria. Victoria tiene sólo tres meses más que yo. Felipe y Victoria son los hijos de mis __(6)__, la infanta Elena y su __(7)__, Jaime. Están a la derecha en la foto. A la izquierda están mi tío—el príncipe Felipe—y mis padres. Mi hermano está en los __(8)__ de mi padre, Iñaki. Yo __(9)__ en los brazos de mi __(10)__, la infanta Cristina. Mis

abuelos, el rey Juan Carlos y la reina Sofía, tienen 62 años. Ellos son los reyes de España. Me encanta tener una familia __(11)__.

1. a) decoración
   b) cumpleaños
   c) globo

2. a) rompemos
   b) sacamos
   c) tenemos

3. a) celebramos
   b) abrimos
   c) jugamos

4. a) abuela
   b) tía
   c) hermano

5. a) cabezas
   b) flores
   c) años

6. a) tíos
   b) abuelos
   c) padres

7. a) esposo
   b) abuela
   c) hermanastra

8. a) pies
   b) pelos
   c) brazos

9. a) estás
   b) están
   c) estoy

10. a) madre
    b) hermano
    c) esposo

11. a) americana
    b) grande
    c) reservado

Teaching Intermediate and Advanced Reading

Teaching Tips

Building skilled readers

At the intermediate and advanced stages, students should have a fair amount of fluency. The goal at this point is to continually advance students' reading levels. Raise the bar for students, and promote independent reading with open discussions. (However, do not forget to reinforce strategies that students have been using as beginning readers.) Have students discuss their reflections and opinions as they read passages. To increase student interest in reading, be sure to provide a wide variety of reading materials. You may wish to develop a classroom library of short story collections, novels, Internet articles, and magazines in Spanish. Make sure you have plenty of authentic texts (those written for a native speaker) in your classroom. Use these varied resources to create your own reading comprehension activities. Student comprehension is attained with greater ease when the topic that they are reading about is of high interest to them.

Reading as vocabulary building

As a culmination to reading selections in intermediate and advanced courses, have students keep a "vocabulary journal" of new words that have been learned through readings. This could simply be a small pocket notebook that they keep in their backpacks. The vocabulary they note could be representative of a particular topic of interest or a list of high frequency vocabulary that the students have not yet mastered. By making their own lists, students are associating meaning to words, and by revisiting the list from time to time and creating meaningful usage situations with the list, students can enrich their working vocabularies.

Additional reading strategies

It is important that students be able to use their reading strategies to make sense of a passage, even if it is above their reading level. Intermediate and advanced readers may be interested in reading authentic texts that are too difficult for them. However, they can still get the gist of the passage by applying effective reading methods. In addition to the strategies already mentioned, remind students to use strategies that they have learned from reading in their own language. For example, point out to students the importance of context to determine meaning. A second strategy is having students identify the part of speech of a word that they do not recognize. Often, they have an easier time determining the meaning when they know the function of the word. A third option is to have them remove prefixes and endings from unknown words to get at a word root which may help to reveal its meaning. By teaching and reinforcing these strategies, you are helping students to be more independent readers and to develop greater comprehension of challenging texts.

Using *REALIDADES* resources to prepare for the AP* Exam

The *REALIDADES* series offers a wide variety of resources to help you advance your students' reading capabilities and prepare them for the AP* Exam. Use the readings from the book and create activities that simulate the AP* Exam. For example, you may want to create multiple-choice questions to accompany a

reading in the *Lectura* section of the student textbooks. Be sure to include some questions that require the students to make inferences about the reading. In addition to the readings in the book, the *Reading and Writing for Success* ancillary has a selection of intermediate-level readings accompanied by multiple-choice questions.

Along with multiple-choice questions, you may want to look for activities that require passage completion. There are many such activities in the *REALIDADES* student text. (See student edition of Level 2 p. 219, Act. 10 for an example.)

An additional option for reading comprehension activities is to use the listening scripts for each chapter of the *REALIDADES* series. You can reproduce these scripts and the listening activities that accompany them, and turn them into reading comprehension exercises. Promote fluency by having the students read along as you play the recording.

Activities

Show what you know

Give students a reading that is likely to be above their reading level. Be sure each student has highlighters of two different colors. Have them work with a partner. Ask students to scan the text and highlight each and every word in the passage that they *do* understand in one color. Then, using decoding skills, have students use a different color to highlight all of the words that they are able to understand using good decoding skills (such as saying the word aloud, breaking it down into roots and affixes, or using the context of the text). Then, ask both students to read the passage aloud in small sections. Have them pause intermittently to discuss what the selection means. After they have read it together the first time, ask them to write down the main ideas. Then, have a group discussion on the reading and on the process that the students used.

Make your own quiz

You will need at least two different texts to do this activity. Give students copies of the different reading selections as homework. Have them read the passage and create six multiple-

choice questions. Ask them to turn in a separate answer key so that you can check their work. The next day, collect the texts and questions and redistribute them to other students. Have students complete the quizzes. Then, allow students time to discuss their results with the author of their quiz. Have volunteers share some sample questions and answers, as well as strategies that they used to take the quiz.

Sample activity to accompany *REALIDADES* reading

Have students choose the best answer in a sample multiple-choice activity that you create using the *Lecturas* in the *REALIDADES* student editions. Review the answers in class, making sure that students detail their strategy for finding each answer. The following activity assesses students' comprehension of *La mariposa monarca* found in *REALIDADES 3* student edition, pp. 422–424.

1. ¿Cuál es una de las diferencias principales entre la mariposa monarca y las otras mariposas?
   a. Es un importante polinizador.
   b. Es más bello.
   c. Llega a vivir nueve meses.
   d. Tres cuartas partes de los animales que viven en la Tierra son insectos.
2. ¿Qué causa que la mariposa monarca sea desagradable a los otros animales?
   a. su dieta
   b. su resistencia a los cambios de clima
   c. Es venenosa.
   d. su polinización
3. ¿Por qué le gusta a la mariposa monarca la zona entre Michoacán y el Estado de México?
   a. Hay una gran variedad de plantas.
   b. Es una zona tropical.
   c. Es boscosa con valles.
   d. Hay mucho oxígeno y protección del viento polar.
4. ¿Cuál elemento <u>no</u> amenaza la vida de la mariposa monarca?
   a. las asclepias
   b. el clima extremadamente frío
   c. los depredadores
   d. los ataques por otros bichos

5. ¿Cuántas mariposas monarca suelen sobrevivir el invierno en México?
   a. entre los 100 y 400 millones
   b. casi 65%
   c. casi 35%
   d. aproximadamente 50%
6. Las mariposas monarca se reproducen
   a. donde hay aire polar y cambios de clima.
   b. durante tormentas de nieve en el Canadá.
   c. en el invierno en los refugios de México.
   d. a mediados de abril durante el viaje de regreso.
7. ¿Por qué no sufrieron daños las mariposas monarca durante el incendio de 2001?
   a. El fuego afectó hectáreas localizadas a 500 metros de altitud sobre el nivel del mar.
   b. Un grupo de turistas lo apagaron.
   c. La población de mariposas recuperó su nivel de años anteriores.
   d. Ya habían salido para el Canadá.

Using student work

With their permission, use students' own writing samples as reading material for the class. Have students sit in a circle of 4 people, with their own corrected writing pieces in hand. Students pass the writing to the right and read the piece they have received. They continue passing and reading until they have received their own work back. This exercise serves as a confidence-builder. If students do not want to share their writing, give them a copy of a different text to pass through the circle. After everyone has read all of the selections, encourage students to discuss the work in small groups.

Student Strategy

When answering multiple-choice questions about a reading, remind students to skim through the passage once to gain a general sense of the passage. Next, encourage them to read the questions, but not the answers. Suggest that they re-read the passage for the answer and have them write it on a separate paper. Finally, have them compare the answer they got to the multiple-choice options, and select the option that most closely matches the written answer.

Student experts

When reading a longer piece, assign each pair of students a specific section. All students should read the entire piece, but only be held responsible for the portions to which they are assigned. For their respective section, pairs of students should:

- Write, in their own words, a brief summary of the main points or actions.
- Decode any unfamiliar vocabulary and be ready to share their strategies with the class.
- Create questions with multiple-choice answers to be shared with the class.

Once students have finished their preparations, have the class retell the story by going around the room and asking each pair, in order, to share their summary. Collect all of the multiple-choice questions and compile them into a longer activity that students can complete in class or as a homework assignment.

Preparing for AP* Reading Comprehension with *REALIDADES* Components

The following chart provides examples of where to find *REALIDADES* components that correlate to Pre-AP* activities.

SE = Student Edition
TE = Teacher's Edition
AP = Assessment Program
PW = Practice Workbook
TRB = Teacher's Resource Book
WAVW = Writing, Audio & Video Workbook

Building Reading Comprehension

Activity	Level A	Level B	Level 1	Level 2	Level 3
Plot Summary	SE pp. 260–61	SE pp. 240–241	SE pp. 312–13	SE pp. 256–67	SE pp. 376–77
Random Answers	SE p. 199 SE p. 219	SE p. 55 SE p. 177	SE p. 239 SE p. 417	SE p. 203 SE p. 337 SE p. 419	SE p. 362, Act.24 SE p. 406, Act.22
Pre-Reading	SE pp. 168–69 TE p. 230	SE p. 176, Strategy SE pp. 208-9 TE p. 116	SE pp. 440–441 TE p. 364	SE p. 118–19 TE p. 364	SE pp. 358–59 SE p. 284, *Al leer*
Cloze Passages	SE p. 138 SE p. 160, Act. 17 SE p. 219, Act. 13 PW p. 62 AP p. 46	SE pp. 300–1 SE p. 46, Act. 21 SE p. 112, Act. 29 PW p. 172 AP p. 140	SE pp. 364–365 SE p. 284, Act. 22 SE p. 332, Act. 17 PW p. 99 AP p. 155–C	SE p. 146 SE p. 57, Act. 16 SE p. 110, Act. 13 SE p. 197, Act. 17 PW p. 104 AP p. 77	SE pp. 370–71 SE p. 19, Act. 7 SE p. 30, Act. 14 SE p. 42, Act. 36 SE p. 382 SE p. 474 PW p. 100 AP p. 41
Using Listening Scripts	TRB p. 213 #13, & WAVW p. 83	TRB p. 158 #07 & WAVW p. 56, Act. 5	TRB Vol. 1, p. 191 & WAVW p. 74, Act. 9	TRB Vol. 1, p. 222 & WAVW pp. 78–9, Acts. 2 & 3	TRB p. 361 #06 & WAVW p. 121, Act. 2 TRB p. 114 #20 & SE p. 142, Act.1
Strategy Sharing	SE p. 260	SE p. 240	SE p. 440	SE p. 310	SE p. 330
Graphic Organizers	SE p. 261	SE p. 241	SE p. 391	SE p. 121	SE p. 379
Student Experts		SE pp. 240–241	SE pp. 312–13	SE pp. 442–43	SE pp. 330–32
Multiple-choice Reading Comprehension	SE p. 77	SE p. 317, Act. 8	SE p. 454, Act. 4	SE p. 469	SE p. 382, Act. 1
Additional Reading Strategies	SE, *Exploración del lenguaje*	SE, *Exploración del lenguaje*	SE, *Exploración del lenguaje*	SE, *Exploración del lenguaje*	SE, *Ampliación del lenguaje* SE p. 284, *Estrategia*

Preparing to Write in Spanish

The AP* Spanish Language Exam requires that students write with both formal and informal styles. For the informal writing piece, students have 10 minutes to write a note, postcard, e-mail message, or other similar informal text based on a given prompt. In the formal writing piece, students are expected to synthesize two printed articles and one auditory source to create a well-organized essay of approximately 200 words. A prompt is given and students must reference all three sources (text and auditory) in the response.

Journal Writing

Teaching Tips

Keeping a journal

Journal writing can be a very effective writing task. Even beginning students can make weekly journal entries using newly acquired words and phrases. Using a journal, students can express their thoughts and feelings in a private, non-intimidating way. Students will inevitably improve their writing skills with regular practice, especially when they choose topics that interest them.

When and where to write

Journaling can be done as homework. However, it can also be done in class. Students can write as a warm-up, at a learning station during an independent writing period, or after they finish an assignment that others are still working on. Have beginning students write directly into a section of their notebook that has been reserved for this purpose. You may choose to keep small notebooks in crates (separated by class) in the classroom for more advanced students who will most likely write longer entries. These students should also be held accountable for weekly journal entries done outside of class.

Electronic journals

If possible, have students e-mail you their journal entries. This way, you will be free from managing large stacks or bins of journals. Set up an electronic folder on your computer desktop for students' journal entries. If you decide that this is a better option for your class, be sure to also provide students with ample opportunities to write assignments by hand, as that is what they will have to do for the AP* Exam.

Journal topics

Every chapter of *REALIDADES* is packed with ideas for writing. By making use of these topics, you will reinforce the use of the current lesson's vocabulary. You may want to use the appendix for other ideas. Or, have students create a list of topics that interest them on the first page of their journal. Whenever they are at a loss for what to write about, have them refer to their lists and choose a topic.

> ### Student Strategy
> **Subject + verb + rest of sentence**
> Encourage beginning students to follow this very straightforward structure as they begin to write. Once students gain control over the basic "subject + verb + rest of sentence" format, they can then begin to add more advanced grammatical structures.

Correcting student journals

As a teacher, your greatest challenge is finding time to do everything that is necessary for students to learn effectively. Often, teachers avoid having students create journals because it seems like an intense amount of extra work. However, if you serve as the audience for your students, instead of the editor, you'll find that journals can be fun to read and often only create a minimal amount of work. It is important to remember that you should *not* correct the students' journals, unless you expect them to publish a certain entry. If they are not publishing or re-writing the piece, they will most likely ignore your corrections. Furthermore, you run the risk of discouraging them from writing by sending them the message that they should focus on form over content. Remember that the journals are students' personal reflections, and you should focus on the content of what they are saying. Consider the following options to help you adopt the use of journals in your classroom:

- Quickly skim each journal entry and place a sticker or a rubber stamp on the page to show students that you are looking at their work. This can take less than 10 minutes per class.

- Write a comment back to students about the content of their entry and encourage them to write back to you if you posed a question.

- If you notice common errors in several students' journals, bring those to the whole class' attention without naming the students who committed them.

- If you see a student making the same mistake repeatedly, write a response to that student using the difficult word or structure correctly. You will be correcting their trouble spot subtly by providing an accurate model.

- Use a colored highlighter to highlight phrases in the journal that were extremely well done. Students will compare how much highlighting they have received and celebrate their successes.

- If you *must* make corrections, it is best to choose the worst error you see and correct it, but no more. Drawing students' attention to just one error per week can add up to gradual improvements in their writing without intimidating them. Tell students that you are not correcting every error in this environment, but that their best efforts are expected. Remind them, however, that you will be checking for correct work in other writing assignments, and that they will be scored on the precision of their writing on the AP* Exam. Keeping a journal is a safe way for them to practice their skills.

- Hold a short conference with students who have persistent problems writing in their journals.

- Check journals once a week, and make sure to hold students accountable for a certain number of entries. Develop a schedule that students can follow to work independently. Remind students to be on time. Likewise, it's important that you return the journals to students as soon as possible.

Grading journals

If journal writing is done in class, you may wish to include it as part of the class participation grade. Journals done at home can count as completed assignments. Journals should never be graded for a letter grade as one might grade a formal essay. However, it is often difficult to get students to do written work without receiving a grade. To keep students motivated, assign a number from 1 to 4 to each of their entries (1 being little effort, 4 being strong effort). Write the numbers in your grade book to keep track of their independent writing efforts each week. Add these points up and develop an independent writing grade to factor into students' overall grade. You may wish to develop an independent writing rubric or find one on the Internet so that students are aware of your expectations. This way, students will be graded on their writing effort, not the final product. The purpose of journal writing is to provide a forum for practice. Writing should only be graded if students have the opportunity to review and edit their work.

Activities

Spanish only!

Remind students that they should never approach a composition using English vocabulary when the Spanish vocabulary is unknown. If they can't express their ideas due to a lack of vocabulary or structures, they should consider what other ideas related to the essay topic that they can express with the tools at their disposal. Likewise, encourage them to avoid writing an assignment in English and then translating it, which leads to reliance on a dictionary and an often-incomprehensible product. Have students limit themselves to only two or three words from the dictionary when writing.

Comic strip

Have students make a comic strip of a completed journal entry. Ask them to re-read their entries, choose one, and draw a four-panel strip depicting the events or words of the passage. Remind them to choose small excerpts to use in the speech bubbles for each panel.

This activity encourages students to review their own work and practice visualizing their writing. It is an excellent step to complete before revising a journal entry for publication.

Audio entries

Have students use a hand-held recorder to record one of their journal entries (see Speaking section of this book, p. 40 for instructions on how to record). As they read aloud and hear what they wrote, students may begin to notice things in their writing that doesn't "sound right." Consequently, they will begin to make their own corrections and monitor their writing more closely.

The Writing Process

Teach students the steps to the writing process. Point out that they should apply the following steps when writing in Spanish. Remind them that they may already use these steps when they write in English.

- pre-write / brainstorm
- draft
- revise
- edit
- publish

Pre-Writing and Brainstorming

Teaching Tips

Organizers

Use the diagrams and charts in the beginning of the transparencies for each level of *REALIDADES* to help students collect and organize their ideas before they draft a passage. Choose a chart that is appropriate for the assigned task. For example, you may want to distribute Venn diagrams if students are preparing to write a compare and contrast essay. Other examples include a "fishbone" diagram, which helps students to add details to a main idea, and a flowchart that helps them to sequence events. These organizers can serve as brainstorming sheets to prepare students to write. See the organizers in the *Practice Workbook* for additional options. For example, the organizer on p. 174 of the *A/B Practice Workbook* could be a pre-

writing activity for writing a piece about using electronics in our everyday lives.

Activities

Partner practice

Make several copies of the organizers found in the *REALIDADES* overhead transparencies and distribute them to the class. In pairs, have students complete the organizer as they share their ideas on the assigned topic. Have partners brainstorm their ideas as a class and write their suggestions on the appropriate transparency.

Student Strategy

Organize to write

Once students have finished brainstorming ideas on the topic, they can number their ideas in the order that they will appear in the essay. By following the ideas in numerical order, the draft will unfold in a logical manner. Remind students that they might not use every single idea that they created in the pre-writing activity, and that it is even helpful to eliminate some of the details that do not directly relate to the main idea. Students must also remember to plan for how they will include the references to the information received in the text and audio prompts when writing the formal essay.

Individual practice

After students have become familiar with how to use a graphic organizer to brainstorm their ideas on a topic, have them complete the organizer on their own. Then, have students convene in small groups to discuss their ideas. Encourage them to "borrow" ideas from classmates that will improve their own essays, and have them note those ideas in their organizers.

Drafting

Teaching Tips

Preparing a draft on the computer

If possible, have students write and store their formal essays on a computer. The essays should be double-spaced and typed for easy

reading and editing. Having the drafts on the computer makes it easier for students to rework their writing after peer and teacher editing.

Taking the draft step by step

Trying to write a lengthy essay in Spanish can be intimidating to students. Have them break the draft into parts: the introduction, the body, and the conclusion. Show them how to handle each part individually before having them organize their entire essay.

I. Introduction

For the purpose of the AP* essay, the introduction should serve two purposes: introduce the topic in the writers' own words, and state the plan for the remainder of the essay. The intro should serve as a sort of "road map" of where the essay will go. Remind students that they do not need to state all of their ideas in the introduction.

II. The body

As they draft each paragraph, remind students that it is essential that they focus on the content. Point out that they should not spend time on perfecting their grammar or spelling. Concentrating too much on the form may impede the message that students are trying to send. Remind them that editing will take place later in the writing process.

III. The conclusion

Point out to students that the conclusion must do more than merely restate what has already been stated in the body of the essay. The purpose of the conclusion is to close the essay. Possible ways of doing this include stating an opinion, creating a solution, making a recommendation, or providing a reflection on the topic.

Encourage use of connecting words

Have students practice using a minimum number of appropriate connecting words in each essay.

Common Connecting Words:

y / e	pero
o / u	sino
entonces	sin embargo
por eso	a lo menos
luego	porque
pues	a causa de
después	aunque
al principio	finalmente

Essay writing in Spanish

It is important that you recognize that some students may not be familiar with the essay as a genre. Students probably are more accustomed to writing personal narratives. Therefore, if you are having students draft essays, be sure that they understand some key aspects of the genre, such as the inclusion of the introduction, body, and conclusion. Also, remind them that essays are not generally written in the first person. Students often struggle with how to express an impersonal "you" in the essay. Before they begin to write the first draft, spend a moment reminding them how to use some common structures in Spanish essays, such as: *se* (impersonal), *ellos* (impersonal), *uno* as the impersonal subject of a reflexive verb, and *la gente* as opposed to *las personas*.

Activities

Writing an introduction

To get students accustomed to writing introductions, have them practice in pairs. Give pairs of students a body of text that doesn't have an introduction. Then, have students develop an introduction on transparencies to share with the rest of the class. Ask classmates to critique the introductions based on these criteria:

- Does the introduction state the theme of the essay?
- Does the introduction outline the plan for the essay?
- Does the author say too much in the introductory paragraph?

Writing a conclusion

You may wish to try a similar pair-work activity to get students on track with writing conclusions. As students share their work on transparencies, encourage others to use these criteria to determine if the conclusion is appropriate for the passage.

- Does the conclusion summarize the contents of the essay?
- Does the conclusion contain the authors' reflections about the topic?
- Does the conclusion "look ahead" to possible solutions or recommendations about the topic of the essay?

Revisions

Teaching Tips

Checklists

Give students a checklist that reflects your writing scoring guide or rubric. The checklist should be simple, but tailored to a specific activity. For example, sample checklist items for a memoir could include:

___ Did the student include an introduction, body, and conclusion?

___ Did the student successfully reflect on a personal experience?

___ Did the student consistently use the past tense?

Filling out a checklist like this helps you to provide students with quick feedback, and helps them to identify the areas that they need to improve.

Peer revisions

It is helpful for students to share their work with one another. Often, students feel comfortable taking and giving feedback with their peers. Allow time in class for students to sit together and read each other's essays and discuss their content. Students should consider the organization and comprehensibility of the piece and make any necessary suggestions. During the revision phase, urge students to ignore any possible grammatical errors in the writing that they are reading. This may be a welcome relief to them! The focus during this time is on meaning and content.

Activity

Self and peer revision

Have students re-read their own work, using a colored highlighter to mark areas in which they think they need to improve. Then, have them work together with a partner to discuss suggestions for the highlighted areas. Once students have feedback, ask them to write the changes into the essay and share it once more with their partner. After everybody has revised their works and received input from their partners, have a whole-class discussion about helpful strategies that surfaced during the discussions.

Student Strategy

Recommending changes

When students are peer editing, have them discuss any possible changes with the author, instead of writing them on the paper. This allows the author to ask for clarification and provide comments on the input. This discourse is much more effective in improving writing skills than written communication between the writer and the reader.

Editing and Publishing

Teaching Tips

Remind students that control of basic structures, such as orthography and agreement, is important when writing the essay for the AP* Spanish Exam. The following suggestions will help you to prepare students to edit their own work and write more accurately. Once students have an edited piece, have them carefully make changes to their work for publishing.

Peer editing

Peer editing is an excellent way to help students learn how to edit their own work and to be more conscious of common errors. The most fundamental types of errors that students need to overcome at the beginning and intermediate levels are regarding agreement. Basically, students need to watch for subject-verb agreement, as well as article and adjective agreement with nouns. Spelling problems can also require some attention. To

teach students to manage these types of errors better, consider the following:

- Again, require that errors be discussed with a partner. Do not allow students to simply write on each other's papers.

- Encourage students to give themselves visual clues to help them identify the parts of speech in a sentence. Once they recognize the part of speech of an individual word, they will have an easier time understanding its role in the sentence, and how that role might affect other words based on grammar rules that students have learned.

Group revision

A great way to model essay revision is by using an essay from a student of a previous year or by gaining permission to use the work of one of your own students. Reproduce the typed essay (without the name) on a transparency and on sheets to distribute to students. Then, model a revision of the first two or three sentences of the essay, explaining your reasons for making changes as you go. Have a few student volunteers work on revising the next few sentences, and then have students finish the revision on their own. Afterwards, discuss the results as a class, focusing on strategies that students used to revise the work. Point out that they should look for content, flow, and organization as well as spelling and grammatical errors. Practicing and modeling in class will lead to more thorough student editors.

Activities

Timed practice

In order to acquaint students with the experience of writing with a limited amount of time, provide them with a writing prompt. (See p. 131 of the Level 3 *Writing, Audio & Video Workbook* for an example.) Ask them to complete the task in 20–25 minutes. Remind them to use the writing process. Encourage them to take the time to scan their passages for agreement errors and other simple mistakes.

Parts of speech

Have students practice editing for agreement by identifying all of the parts of speech in a sentence. They might do this with different colored highlighters (pink for nouns, yellow for verbs, etc.) or with adhesive notes labeled with each part of speech. As a TPR activity, have students identify parts of speech by using the right index finger to touch the noun or the verb. Ask them to use the left index finger to touch the subject, adjective, or other related word. If the two do not agree, a change must be recommended. If the subject of the verb is understood, as is often the case in Spanish, students can just place the left index finger on their heads and *imagine* the subject. Once they have identified each part of speech, have them check for agreement. Remind them of the different types of agreement by writing common relationships on the board.

Evaluating Students' Compositions

Teaching Tips

Making corrections

Only after students have completed peer revisions, editing, and have re-written the original draft, should you begin to correct their work. Do NOT assign a formal grade to any essay that has not had the benefit of revision, editing, and rewriting of the original draft. Having double-spaced essays makes correcting easier.

Correcting can take a variety of forms:

- Make the corrections directly on the students' essays. This is most helpful when students need to rework an entire phrase or require assistance with a complex structure.

- Establish a routine set of symbols to indicate the type of error to the students. For example: a circle for an agreement error, a box for an incorrectly conjugated verb, an underline for an incorrect vocabulary word choice, and so on. You may want to check with the Language Arts teachers at your school to see if students are already familiar with a set of correction symbols.

- Use highlighters of different colors. Errors of one type get the same color (i.e., agreement mistakes in blue, conjugation problems in green, etc.). When students receive their corrected essays, they can easily tell which type of error is the most problematic for them, based on which color they see most. You can also highlight students' papers on the computer if they send the works to you electronically.

- With electronically-submitted essays, you can use the "Insert Comment" function if available. Simply go to *insert*, and click on *comment*. Your comment will be inserted with your initials and a highlighted background.

Writing rubrics

By helping to familiarize students with the contents of the AP* Exam essay-grading rubrics in early levels of study, they can focus on mastering each element as they work to become better writers. Consider the following generic writing rubric and be sure to consult the *REALIDADES Assessment Program* for many task-specific writing rubrics.

Composition Rubrics

Score	4	3	2	1
Structures	Excellent control of structures, almost no errors	Good control of structures with a few minor errors, or errors in complex structures	Weak control of structures with frequent errors in simple structures	Little to no control of structures with frequent, serious errors
Vocabulary	Rich, precise vocabulary and use of idiomatic expressions	Vocabulary is adequate for addressing the topic	Limited vocabulary with some interference from English	Poor vocabulary use with frequent interference from English
Organization and Content	Very clear introduction and conclusion with well-developed ideas overall	Basic organization and idea development	Not completely organized, some ideas fragmented	No clear organization, ideas are poorly developed

Self-evaluation

In order to better acquaint students with the writing rubrics that are used for formal evaluation, allow them the opportunity to apply the rubrics to a practice piece of writing. Students could discuss in pairs or small groups how they would apply the rubrics to each other's work.

Producing the final product

After you have returned students' corrected and graded essays, there is great value in having them rewrite the essay once again. If not, all of your work is easily ignored. By rewriting, students learn from their revisions. You may wish to require a rewrite for an additional grade or an improved original grade. Or, offer incentives to students who are willing to rewrite an essay until it is perfect. This can take two or three tries and often leads to a conference regarding difficult errors. One-on-one consultations bring great rewards in terms of student improvement. Writing fewer compositions with more rewrites will likely improve students' writing more than writing multiple compositions without attention to revision, editing, and rewriting. As students submit rewritten

essays, require that they attach the new version on top of the previous version(s) so that re-examination is made easier. As the essay nears perfection, you will need only to glance at the previous version to verify that the new corrections have been inserted.

Preparing for the Grammar Fill-ins

The AP* Spanish Language Exam requires that students complete a cloze passage with the correct form of a given word—an infinitive, adjective, article, etc. In a similar task, students are also expected to complete a cloze passage with a word in Spanish. The completion must be accomplished correctly, logically, grammatically. No root word is provided for the second type of passage completion.

Achieving Syntactic Control

Teaching Tips

The role of grammar

Having a grammatical framework can speed language acquisition at the secondary level as well as increase students' accuracy. Along with the grammar section on the AP* Exam, grammatical accuracy is taken into consideration in the speaking and writing portions of the exam. Providing students with brief linguistic explanations can be beneficial. Grammar should never replace communicative efforts in language teaching; however, it should be considered a significant component to the development of fluency.

Conjugation mastery

Students retain information when they have an opportunity to apply it. As students learn new verb tenses, it is important that they have the chance to continue practicing the tenses that they have already mastered. In this way, students will be able to have success speaking and writing using correct forms. Give frequent, quick verb quizzes in the early-intermediate and intermediate levels to help students use each tense that has been introduced.

- Change the quiz to reflect which tenses the students have learned and omit those that they have not yet learned. As students

add new tenses, the length of the verb quiz can grow to reflect their learning.

- Give verb quizzes two or three times a week at the beginning of a class period during the second semester of the course. By then, students are probably trying to manage several tenses.

- Provide space in the quiz box for students to demonstrate the English equivalent of the tense you are focusing on in a particular lesson.

- You may want to assign a list of verbs to be studied as well as the desired tenses the night before the quiz, so that students can be well prepared.

- At the beginning, quiz regular -ar, -er, and -ir verbs. Next, work on verbs with stem changes and spelling changes. Finally, work through the verb appendix in *REALIDADES*, quizzing on the high frequency irregular verbs.

Correcting verb quizzes

You may wish to have students correct their own quizzes with colored pens by reviewing the answers on an overhead. This way, students are aware of their own errors. This can be time consuming to complete in class, until students are familiar with the system. Collect students' corrected work and hold them accountable for both the completion of the test as well as their own corrections. If you do not want to correct the quizzes in class, it is still helpful to require students to correct all errors, even small accent errors. Return the graded quizzes and have students correct their work in a different color, directly on the quiz. Students can find correct answers by consulting with a peer or by using the *REALIDADES* verb appendix. Have students keep their quizzes in a folder. Check the folders periodically to monitor improvement and assess what areas you need to focus on in future lessons.

Accents

Since items on the grammar fill-in section of the AP* Exam are completely rejected if the accentuation is incorrect, it is vital during the Pre-AP* levels that you hold students accountable for correct accentuation. Consider offering half-credit for words with

incorrect accents during the earliest levels, and become stricter in levels three and above.

Activities

Board game

Students can practice verb tenses with a board game. Make a game board by drawing a series of small squares on a piece of paper. Inside of each square, write a verb tense that is familiar to students. You will need spaces for start and finish, and you may want to add other spaces to the game, such as *Pierde tu turno* and *Avance dos espacios*. Then, make a stack of twenty cards for each game board. On each card, write the present tense form of a verb that has been studied. You may want to have students do this to save time and give them further practice. To play, have students get into groups of two or three. The first student should take a card and move to the first space on the board. He or she should change the verb on the card into the tense on the board. (See blank game board template, p. 44.) A correct answer allows the student to advance to the next space and have another turn. Students can use the appendix of their *REALIDADES* textbook to check for correct answers after the answer has been given. A student's turn lasts until an incorrect answer is given, at which point play goes to the next student. The first person to complete the game board wins.

Preparing for Cloze Passage Completion

Teaching Tips

On the AP* Exam, students will be asked to complete cloze passages in which they will need to determine factors such as verb tense, mood, and agreement to get a correct answer. Use some of the suggestions below to help students prepare for these activities.

Chapter review

In *REALIDADES 3*, the *Preparación para el examen* section of each chapter contains a *Gramática* portion with a multiple-choice review of structures. You can easily convert the *Gramática* into a cloze passage exercise by providing students with only the infinitive instead of four possible choices.

Using the *Actividades* for practice

Many of the *REALIDADES* "*Escribir*" activities found in the student editions provide excellent cloze passage practice, even at the very beginning levels. (See *Actividad 14*, p. 133, Level 1; *Actividad 17*, p. 331, Level 2; *Actividad 30*, p. 132, Level 3 for sample activities.)

Adapting passages from *REALIDADES*

In order to create cloze passage completions that closely resemble those on the AP* Exam and remain close to the students' level of ability, adapt short reading passages from the text. Consider the following example taken from the Level 3 student edition, *Actividad 24*, p. 362:

Mi nombre es Neomí y _____ (nacer) en la ciudad de Santo Domingo, en la República Dominicana. Soy _____ (resultar) de una mezcla de razas y culturas. De mi padre _____ (recibir) mi herencia _____ (africano). Los antepasados de mi madre _____ (ser) españoles e indígenas. Desde niña, la cultura dominicana _____ (tener) más influencia en mi vida. Ahora yo _____ (vivir) en los Estados Unidos y me _____ (encantar) ir a la República Dominicana, donde hay _____ (mucho) riqueza cultural y donde lo paso muy bien con mi familia y _____ (mi) amigos. Sin embargo, cuando yo _____ (estar) en la República Dominicana, quiero _____ (volver) a los Estados Unidos porque _____ (identificarse) con este país.

Vivo en Nueva York, una ciudad donde se encuentran y se _____ (mezclar) muchas culturas: la cultura dominicana, la _____ (estadounidense), la africana, entre otras. Para mí, en Nueva York es fácil aprender sobre mi herencia cultural. Voy a una iglesia dominicana, escucho cantantes dominicanos y _____ (oír) español en la radio. También, voy a festivales de música y presentaciones de arte _____ (africano). Las culturas que _____ (formar) mi herencia _____ (influir) mucho en la vida de toda la ciudad. _____ (sentirse) muy orgullosa de mi herencia.

Activities

Student Strategy

It just looks right

When students are unsure how to correctly fill in an answer in a cloze passage, encourage them to narrow down their possibilities to two or three options. Then, suggest that they rewrite the entire sentence over for each possibility. Seeing an incorrect answer in a phrase will help students to recognize answers that just "looks right."

Student-created cloze passages

Have students take a piece of their own writing that they are willing to share with a partner and re-write it in the form of a cloze passage. Have them remove ten words. Encourage them to remove verbs and adjectives that require agreement with the rest of the sentence. Then, have students exchange their papers and complete each other's cloze passages. The author of the cloze passages should then provide the other student with the original copy of the passage so that the work may be checked.

Preparing for AP* Writing with *REALIDADES* Components

The following charts provide examples of where to find *REALIDADES* components that correlate to Pre-AP* activities.

SE = Student Edition
TE = Teacher's Edition
AP = Assessment Program
PW = Practice Workbook
TRAN = Vocabulary and Grammar Transparencies
TRB = Teacher's Resource Book
WAVW = Writing, Audio & Video Workbook

Preparing to write an essay in Spanish

Activity	Level A	Level B	Level 1	Level 2	Level 3
Prompts for: • **Journal writing** • **Timed practice**	SE p. 111 SE p. 129, Act. 15 SE p. 165, Act. 25 SE p. 188, Act. 14 PW p. 44 WAVW p. 59 WAVW p. 78 AP p. 22 TRB p. 170	SE p. 20, Act. 19 SE p. 25, Act. 24 SE p. 94 PW p. 107 PW p. 151 WAVW p. 30 WAVW p. 101 AP p. 197-C TRB p. 194	SE p. 58, Act. 1 SE p. 418 SE p. 437, Act. 16 SE p. 454, Act. 4 PW p. 95 WAVW p. 69 WAVW p. 182 AP p. 76-C TRB Vol. 1 p. 220	SE p. 112, Act. 17 SE p. 164, Act. 9 SE p. 200, Act. 23 SE p. 313 PW p. 146 WAVW p. 90 WAVW p. 97 AP p. 120-C TRB Vol. 2 p. 212	SE p. 9, Act. 15 SE p. 125, Act. 20 SE p. 170, Act. 15 SE p. 216, Act. 16 PW p. 80 WAVW p. 85, Act. B WAVW p. 103 AP p. 124-C
Organizers	SE pp. 104–5 TRANS pp. 2–10 WAVW p. 55 TRB p. 219	SE p. 87 TRANS pp. 2–10 WAVW p. 48 WAVW p. 87 AP p. 160 TRB p. 85	SE p. 393 TRANS pp. 2–10 AP p. 160 WAVW p. 70 TRB Vol. 2 p. 235	TRANS pp. 2–10 WAVW p. 123 TRB Vol. 1 p. 147	TRANS pp. 1–10 TRANS p. 12 WAVW p. 75
The writing process	SE p. 79 SE p. 141 TRB p. 3	SE p. 211 SE p. 275 TRB p. 69	SE p. 466 SE p. 265 TRB Vol. 2 p. 113	SE p. 65 SE p. 231 TRB Vol. 2 p. 227	SE p. 15 SE p. 144 SE p. 328

Preparing for the grammar fill-ins

Activity	Level A	Level B	Level 1	Level 2	Level 3
Cloze passage practice	SE p. 160, Act. 17 SE p. 219, Act. 13 PW p. 62 AP p. 46	SE p. 46, Act. 21 SE p. 112, Act. 29 PW p. 172 AP p. 140	SE p. 284, Act. 22 SE p. 332, Act. 17 PW p. 99 AP p. 155-C	SE p. 57, Act. 16 SE p. 110, Act. 13 SE p. 197, Act. 17 PW p. 104 AP p. 77	SE p. 19, Act. 7 SE p. 30, Act. 14 SE p. 42, Act. 36 SE p. 382 SE p. 474 PW p. 100 AP p. 41
Creating cloze passages	SE p. 108 SE p. 138 PW p. 64 AP p. 2	SE p. 6 SE p. 54 SE p. 84 PW p. 150	SE p. 368 SE p. 432, Act. 9 SE p. 440 PW p. 88 AP p. 170-B	SE p. 59, Act. 21 SE p. 91 SE pp. 102–3 PW p. 105 AP p. 119-B	SE p. 6, Act. 9 SE p. 35, Act. 25 PW p. 72 AP p. 145

Speaking

Since the AP* Spanish Language Exam is a proficiency–based exam, the types of preparation that might be included along the preparation continuum are not so very different from the strategies that might be included in any Spanish course where proficiency is the goal. This is especially true of speaking proficiency. On the AP* Exam, students are required to complete two separate speaking tasks: one formal presentation and one interactive speaking exercise. For the formal presentation, students are presented with one printed text and one recording to consider. They are given a prompt that suggests the general topic of the presentation. Students have two minutes to prepare their speech and two minutes to give the speech. Speech samples are expected to address the prompt and incorporate information provided in the text and audio prompts. During the interactive task, students must record their responses to an auditory stimulus, such as participating in a phone conversation. After a brief preparation time, students have 20 seconds to record each of their responses. The strategies in this section are designed to help students develop narrative skills, to train them to respond quickly so that they can be successful on the Speaking portion of the AP* Exam, and to help them with circumlocution skills. Helping students become accustomed to evaluating their speech performances with a rubric similar to the one used in grading the AP* Exam will serve to shape their efforts.

Preparing for the Formal Presentation

Teaching Tips

Brainstorming

After providing the class with a listening and a reading text on a similar topic, have the class brainstorm together what the outline of a speech on the topic might be. Having them brainstorm key vocabulary words on the topic can also be helpful.

Pair practice

Allow students to practice presentations in pairs. You may want to have the "stronger" student in the pair complete the presentation first, while the second student listens. Before the second student begins, the pair should discuss the strengths and weaknesses of the first presentation. In this way, the first student provides a successful model for the second student.

Time limits

In beginning level classes, allow students unlimited time to practice and complete presentations. As they progress to the intermediate level, begin to impose time limits on both preparation and execution of the presentations.

Avoid writing first

Discourage students from trying to write out complete scripts for their formal presentations, since they will not likely be able to write two minutes worth of speech. At most, they should develop an outline, including key vocabulary words, conjugated verb forms, and references to the background materials provided in the printed and audio sources.

Sample Activities

> **Strategy for Students**
>
> **Say what you know**
>
> Learning to work with the language that students know will help them avoid reverting to English when speaking. A useful rule for students to follow: If you can't say it, don't.

Beginning level variation: Have students work in pairs to write as many true/false sentences as possible about a printed text or an audio recording. Students can then choose two or three of their statements and ask the class to respond *cierto* or *falso*.

Strategy for Students
Circumlocution

A critical skill for AP* students, especially in oral production, is the ability to circumlocute, or to express an idea without knowing precise vocabulary words. Students may find that they cannot identify all objects within an illustration. Being able to get an idea across in the target language, without knowing the exact vocabulary word, is a valuable AP* skill. At the earliest levels, students can use *la cosa que…* or *la cosa* + (adjective).

Group crossword practice

A group crossword activity is an excellent way to foster the development of circumlocution skills. This activity is most useful after students become familiar with the chapter vocabulary. Prepare a crossword puzzle using vocabulary words currently being studied. Write the answer for each puzzle entry on a separate index card, then create a set of these cards for each group that you will have. Divide students into groups. Give each group a blank puzzle and a set of answers. Distribute the answers evenly among all the members of a group, or have students draw them from a pile. Students must explain their words to the rest of the group without using the words themselves. The other group members must determine the word being described and write it in the appropriate space on the puzzle. Allow students plenty of time to express themselves. This exercise should be done entirely in the target language. The added benefit to this activity, in addition to building circumlocution skills, is practice with vocabulary words. You will find crossword puzzles already created in the *REALIDADES Writing, Audio & Video Workbook*. You may also find it helpful to use one of the many crossword puzzle generators available on the Internet. You will find a sample group crossword puzzle activity at the end of the Speaking section on pp. 42–43.

Variation: Depending on how familiar your students are with the vocabulary, you may wish to allow them to have their word list available during the activity. This activity is best suited for intermediate level students, since beginning students lack the resources to conduct this activity entirely in Spanish.

Strategy for Students
Connecting words

Provide students with basic connecting words such as: *pues, entonces, después, por eso, sin embargo*, and *a causa de* to help them connect their ideas. You can find further connecting words in the *¿Qué me cuentas?* features in *REALIDADES 3*.

Preparing for Timed Interactive Responses

Teaching Tips

Practice in pairs

Have students practice often in pairs. Provide one student with the printed stimuli to read and have the opposite student provide the responses. Students should switch roles and repeat the exercise.

Recycle questions

By continuing to recycle questions from previous chapters and levels, you can help enhance your students' long-term retention. Students will also gain confidence as they learn to respond with ease to familiar material.

¿Y tú qué dices?

Use the *¿Y tú qué dices?* activities found throughout the *REALIDADES* student books and the Situation Cards found in the *Teacher Resource Book* as sources for additional questions.

Participation points

Give daily oral participation points based on students' ability to respond, as well as their participation in the activities that are described in the Sample Activities section. You may also want to include their participation in pair and group work.

Sample Activities

Preguntas rápidas

Create a bank of *preguntas rápidas* that reflect questions found in normal, everyday conversations. Take these open-ended questions from textbook activities found throughout *REALIDADES*, like the *Y tú ¿qué dices?* activities. Or you may use the bank of *preguntas rápidas* found on pp. 166–168 of the *REALIDADES* Pre-AP* Resource Book. Write each question on a separate index card (some teachers write them on other objects like tongue depressors) and store them in a filing box or jar for regular use in class. Continue to add to the bank with each new chapter covered. Be sure to limit the questions to vocabulary and topics that are appropriate to your students' level of Spanish. Use them as warm-up activities, end-of-class activities, for team competitions, or simply for a break in the middle of class.

Quick response game

Create game boards that incorporate quick responses to *preguntas rápidas*. This will allow students to practice responding to everyday questions in a fun and challenging activity. Have students use the game board on p. 44 as a template. You can set the game up like this:

1. Create a list of the *preguntas rápidas* or use the bank of *preguntas rápidas* found on pp. 166–168 and number them. Approximately 35–50 questions can be used in a game at a time.

2. Create a game board by putting numbers in most spaces and some other game terms such as *pierdes tu turno, avanza dos pasos,* and *tira los dados otra vez* in the remaining spaces. Each box can contain two numbers, one above the other. The first time through the game, students should refer to the top number. The second time through, they should refer to the bottom number.

3. Form groups of 3 or 4 students. Each group needs one game board and one set of numbered questions. One student rolls a die and moves to the appropriate space. If the space has numbers, another student in the group reads the question indicated by the number. The first student has 20 seconds (or more if necessary) to answer the question as completely as possible. The group judges if it was an adequate response. If it was not, the student returns to the space where he or she was before beginning the turn.

4. Play continues two times through the game board. The winner is the first player to reach *El fin*.

One minute of questions *(For Levels 1 and 2)*

Prepare a handout with 20 questions pertinent to the current lesson. Use vocabulary and structures from the lesson and vary the subject of the question so that not all questions are about "you and I." (See the following list of *preguntas rápidas*.) Here is how the activity works:

Sample Activity

Preguntas rápidas: REALIDADES 2, Tema 4

1. ¿Cómo eras de niño(a)?
2. ¿Dónde vivía tu familia hace diez años?
3. De niño(a), ¿cuáles eran tus juguetes favoritos?
4. Por lo general, ¿qué te molesta más?
5. ¿Qué te regalaron tus padres para tu último cumpleaños?
6. ¿Cuáles programas de tele veías de pequeño(a)?
7. ¿Obedecías a tus padres siempre, a menudo o a veces?

8. ¿Qué clases te interesaban más en la escuela primaria?
9. ¿Les permitían correr en la escuela primaria?
10. ¿Te portabas bien en la casa de los vecinos?
11. De niño(a), ¿les prestabas tus juguetes a los demás?
12. ¿Cómo celebraba tu familia los cumpleaños?
13. ¿En qué días hay fuegos artificiales?
14. ¿Los miembros de tu familia se abrazan?
15. ¿Te despides de tus padres cuando sales para la escuela?
16. ¿Cuándo naciste?
17. ¿Dónde se reúnen tú y tus amigos?
18. ¿Llorabas a menudo de niño(a)?
19. ¿Les cuentas chistes a tus amigos durante la clase de español?
20. ¿Cuántos alumnos había en tu clase el año pasado?

Preparation

- As a homework assignment or together in class, have students make flashcards with the questions on one side and the correct response on the other side. Check that the answers are correct so students can use the cards effectively.
- Allow students several days to prepare for the evaluation. Give them time to practice the questions in class with a partner. You may also choose to allow students to work in teams to ask the questions on the list to the opposite team in an attempt to stump their opponents.

Activity

- This activity is very effective when done a few days prior to the unit test. Each student sits with you for one minute and answers as many questions as possible.
- When asking the questions, you should use a stopwatch or other timing device.
- Allow students to answer as many questions as possible. Tell them if they answer more than eight questions in a minute, they will receive extra credit or any other type of reward that you may use. Their performances will amaze you.

- If students have trouble understanding you, remind them to ask you to say the questions more slowly. Since repeating questions takes up more time, it's a good idea to encourage students to answer as quickly as possible.
- Students should be allowed to skip a question. The clock keeps ticking, so skipping too many questions isn't a good idea.
- You may choose to allow beginning students to have a second chance to repeat the assessment (on their own time after school) if they are unhappy with their performance.

Evaluation

- Eight questions is the minimum necessary for a perfect score.
- Questions are scored as follows:

  3 *points* for a correct answer
  2 *points* for an answer with one error
  1 *point* for a response that answers the question, but has major flaws
  0 *points* for an inappropriate or unrelated response or a skipped question

- For easy scoring, use a set of questions on index cards and as the student answers, divide the cards into four separate piles: one for 3-point answers, one for 2-point answers, and so on. Count the total when the student finishes. The scores can be incorporated into students' chapter test grades, or separate speaking assessment grades could be given. Remember to shuffle the questions after each student performs so that questions are asked randomly.
- Because this assessment takes only one minute per student, it is fairly easy to speak with all of the students in your class during one period. Have a reading, writing, or quiet review activity to engage students while individuals come forward for assessment.
- Create a set of questions for each unit and reuse them from year to year. You may consider recycling the questions as part of the semester exam.

Strategy for Students

Use your imagination

Students should practice using their imaginations. Sometimes students get trapped trying to say what they *want* instead of what they *know*. Remind them that their answers don't have to be true, they just have to be correct. Fiction is fine! It is important that students show the language skills they have and not flounder as they reach for language that they have not yet acquired.

20-second timed questions *(For Level 3)*

By Level 3, teachers can use questions from many different sources. The format of the questions should elicit direct responses requiring spontaneous replies similar to those questions students will find on the AP* Spanish Language Exam. You should begin using an AP*-type format by repeating each question twice and timing the answer for 20 seconds. Let students know that they should never fail to answer a question. Even if they are not sure of the answer, they should try to answer it by picking out something from the question and speaking about it.

Recording and Evaluating

Recording Students' Speech Samples

Recordings can be captured in a variety of ways:

- on individual cassette recorders
- in a language lab
- on voice-mail
- on a computer, using digital sound files

One of the least expensive ways for your students to have their speech samples recorded is with handheld cassette recorders. If you are able to obtain several handheld recorders, your students could work in groups and take turns using the recorders. While one member of the group is recording, the other members could work quietly on an alternate activity. You may want to set the recorders apart from the groups and have students take turns going to the recording stations so that other students do not distract the speakers. This is also a good way to allow all students enough time to make their recordings. If there are groups of five students and the recordings last two minutes each, the entire group can be finished in 10 minutes.

Intermediate and advanced students could be asked to make weekly two-minute recordings, completed outside of class as a homework assignment. Tape recorders could be available in the school's media center or, if students have their own recorders, they could complete the assignment at home. Students should record their samples end-to-end rather than recording over a previous sample. This will allow them to monitor their own progress throughout the year. You may choose to assign a homework completion credit for many of the recordings and formally evaluate the recordings as time allows. Students could also exchange tapes with a classmate for peer feedback.

Recordings can be captured in a variety of ways.

1. On individual cassette recorders:
   a. Students can capture practice sessions of the picture sequence narration on their own cassette at home, in the school's media center, or on a machine in the classroom. They can give you the cassette with their name on it. Encourage students to record the same narration two or three times. All recordings should be cued up to the appropriate place on the tape to hear the current recording. By recording each entry end-to-end instead of erasing each one and recording over it, you and your students can monitor the progress made.
   b. Students can record, one at a time, one after another, on the same tape using a recorder in the classroom. Students can hear their own work and other students' work. You and the students can provide constructive feedback and suggestions for improvement as you listen to the recordings in class.
   c. To practice directed responses on an individual recorder, two machines are needed. One machine plays the "master tape" with the questions and the timed

pauses (which can be more than 20 seconds for Pre-AP* students). On a second machine, students record their responses, one student after another. Only the master tape is rewound after each student recording session.

2. In a language lab:
This is truly the most effective way to simulate proper AP* recordings. Each student records a speech sample under your direction or by listening to a master recording. Students can record onto a cassette tape, which they then give to you. Or, if the lab is digital, the sound files can all be burned on to one CD, making your load lighter by not having to carry bags or boxes of cassettes.

3. On voice-mail:
Shorter recordings (six to seven sentences describing a given picture as a homework assignment) can be accomplished by recording it at a voicemail number that you have at your school. If possible, you can even set up different voicemail boxes for each class.

4. On a computer, using digital sound files:
While there are programs available to compress and store sound files varying from setting to setting, the basic concept is to use the sound recording device on the computer and capture a recording. Hand–held computer microphones made for this purpose can be helpful. Once recorded, students can save their sound files in a designated folder on a school server for you to access. Students can also save their sound files on a local machine and e-mail them to you as an attachment.

Evaluating Students' Speech Samples

Pair and group work practices can be very effective; however, by creating opportunities for students to record their speech samples, you will be able to provide easier and more thorough evaluations. Feedback is an invaluable step in helping your students improve their speaking skills. Once the recordings are done, you can either grade the samples yourself, or have your students grade them. Either way, an evaluation rubric is essential to insure consistency and fairness. Be sure students understand what is expected of them to successfully complete the task. Before recording, students should be given time to study the rubric and should understand how it applies to their task. This can be accomplished by playing a few sample recordings for the class, followed by a discussion about how each sample would be scored. Once trained, students can generally give each other appropriate feedback and become better prepared to meet your expectations. Student-evaluated samples should not be graded, but rather should serve as practice. You may choose to evaluate your students' speech samples yourself for a formal evaluation from time to time. Students could also save their recordings and choose their best sample to be submitted for a grade.

The rubric on p. 45 represents standards similar to those used to evaluate students' speech samples during the grading of the AP* Spanish Language Exam. Familiarizing students with AP* expectations from their first year of Spanish will help guide their efforts. The rubric can be used with *any* speech sample, regardless of the task. For example, beginning students might apply this rubric to a prompt given in English such as, "Describe the members of your family." Or, it might be used in conjunction with the evaluation of picture sequence narrations.

Group Crossword Puzzle Clue Cards
REALIDADES 3, Capítulo 7

Horizontal 4. medir	Horizontal 7. cubrir	Horizontal 11. Luna	Horizontal 12. observatorio	Horizontal 14. escritura
Horizontal 15. mito	Horizontal 17. diseño	Horizontal 18. universo	Horizontal 19. sagrado	Horizontal 20. creencia
Vertical 1. excavar	Vertical 2. pesar	Vertical 3. arqueólogo	Vertical 5. Tierra	Vertical 6. ruinas
Vertical 8. redondo	Vertical 9. pirámide	Vertical 10. conejo	Vertical 13. inexplicable	Vertical 16. sombra

Realidades

Group Crossword Puzzle Activity
REALIDADES 3, Capítulo 7

Work in groups to complete this crossword puzzle. Take turns describing the words on the cards that you have been given without mentioning the words themselves. The other members of your group will try to fill in the crossword puzzle with the appropriate words based on your clues.

Realidades

Nombre _____   Clase _____

Fecha _____

Quick Response Game Board

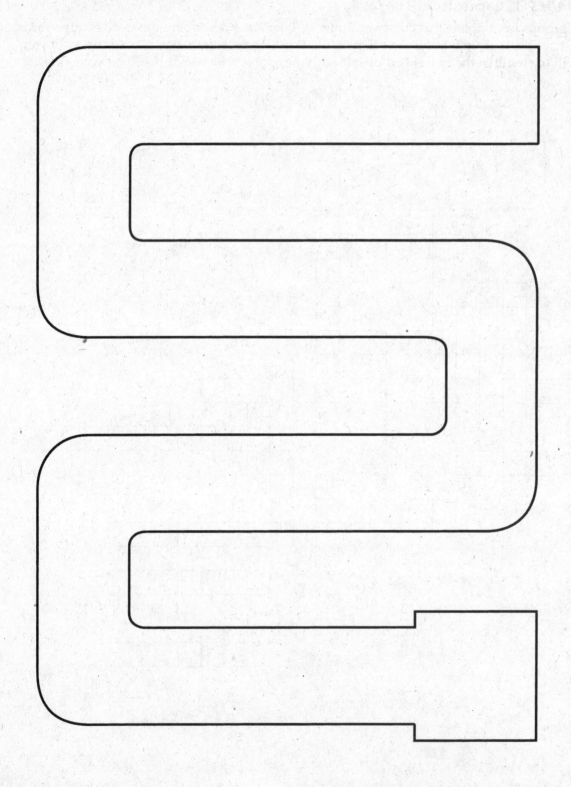

Realidades

Score	4	3	2	1
Content	Thoroughly and completely addresses the topic or task	Adequately completes the topic or task	Addresses the topic in a very basic, limited manner	Irrelevant to the topic or with a very limited amount of speech provided
Structures	Excellent control of structures	Good control of structures with a few minor errors	Weak control of structures with frequent errors	Little to no control of structures with frequent, serious errors
Vocabulary	Rich, precise vocabulary and use of idiomatic expressions	Vocabulary is adequate for addressing the topic	Limited vocabulary with some interference from English	Poor vocabulary use with frequent interference from English
Fluency**	Considerable ease; pronunciation is virtually free of of serious errors	Task completed with ease; good pronunciation	Some hesitation; possible pronunciation errors	Halting and hesitation; frequent serious pronunciation errors that interfere with communication

**For the purpose of the AP* Examination, "fluency" is considered the ease and natural flow of speech, free of hesitation, halting, and groping for words. It encompasses how all of the parts of speech fit smoothly together. It does *not* imply the rate or speed of the speech sample.

Note: The *REALIDADES Assessment Program* contains several sets of rubrics to be applied to specific assessment tasks. Acquainting students with the use of rubrics sets the bar for their performance and helps them to understand the grading criteria.

Preparing for AP* Speaking with *REALIDADES* Components

The following charts provide examples of where to find *REALIDADES* components that correlate to Pre-AP* activities.

SE = Student Edition
AP = Assessment Program
PW = Practice Workbook
TRAN = Vocabulary and Grammar Transparencies
WAVW = Writing, Audio & Video Workbook

Preparing to make a formal oral presentation

Activity	Level A	Level B	Level 1	Level 2	Level 3
Using sources to create a presentation*	SE p. 141 SE p. 201	SE p. 119 SE p. 243	SE p. 291 SE p. 393	SE p. 313 SE p. 421	SE p. 97 SE p. 327 SE p. 373 SE p. 419
Group Crossword Puzzle		PW p. 137	PW p. 146	PW p. 149 PW p. 169	

*Suggest reading and/or listening sources that can help to inform students' presentations.

Preparing to interact informally

Activity	Level A	Level B	Level 1	Level 2	Level 3
Developing question banks for *Preguntas rápidas* and other activities	SE p. 19, Act. 3 SE p. 97, Act. 12 PW p. 52 WAVW p. 15 WAVW p. 27 AP p. 70	SE p. 111, Act. 28 SE p. 229, Act. 15 WAVW p. 29 WAVW p. 49 AP p. 106 AP p. 204	SE p. 161, Act. 20 SE p. 205, Act. 12 PW p. 81 WAVW p. 156 AP p. 205	SE p. 52, Act. 9 SE p. 197, Act. 18 PW p. 32 WAVW p. 144 AP p. 220 AP p. 102	SE p. 129, Act. 25 SE p. 396, Act. 9 PW p. 67 WAVW p. 49, Act. 17 WAVW p. 60 AP p. 69
Informal exhanges	SE p. 171 SE p. 233 PW p. 73 WAVW p. 37	SE p. 179 WAWV p. 49	SE p. 141 SE p. 191 SE p. 339 PW p. 73 WAVW p. 37 WAVW p. 136	SE p. 259 PW p. 185 WAVW p. 144	WAVW p. 27 WAVW p. 60 WAVW p. 62, Act 14

Pre-AP* Vocabulary Building

One of the most fundamental elements for AP* success is quick access to a rich variety of vocabulary resources. A wide range of vocabulary is essential for successful performance on listening and reading comprehension sections of the AP* Exam. Vocabulary is also a necessary tool for self-expression on the essay and speaking portions of the AP* Exam. The key to building lexical success is thorough learning that leads to long-term retention. By teaching students a variety of study skills, incorporating daily activities that focus on vocabulary acquisition, and testing vocabulary in ways that require higher order thinking skills, you can enhance students' in-depth vocabulary retention.

Effective Methods for Studying Vocabulary

Teaching Tips

Since students all have different learning styles, it is critical that you present a variety of strategies to help them to learn vocabulary effectively. Study skills should be directly taught in the first year of Spanish, and should be reinforced regularly throughout that year and at subsequent levels of study. Introduce the strategies discussed here (along with those that you know and find effective) directly to the students, and remind them of how to apply each one as they see new vocabulary in each chapter.

The very act of making the flashcards, tapes, or sheets causes students to interact with the vocabulary and allows them to begin to retain it. Have students try a variety of strategies at the beginning. For example, have them use one type of study strategy during the first chapter, a different type for the second chapter, and yet another type of strategy while working on the third chapter. After students have tried a variety of approaches, allow them to choose which method works best for them.

Flashcards

Have students cut 3"x 5" index cards into thirds for the ideal size. Give students a rubber band to put around each lesson's cards or have students store them in a small resealable plastic bag. A hole can be punched in the bag so that the cards can be carried in students' notebooks. Have students store the cards from every lesson throughout the semester in a common place and encourage them to use the cards for an organized final exam review.

Have students make a new set of flashcards immediately after you present the information in the *A primera vista* section of each *REALIDADES* chapter. Have students clearly print the Spanish vocabulary word or phrase on one side and write its English equivalent on the reverse side. It may be helpful if they create a color scheme to help them remember a word's part of speech (verbs / green, adjectives / purple, etc.). Also, students may find it helpful to write feminine nouns in one color and masculine nouns in another.

As an alternative, students can use PowerPoint to develop electronic flashcards. The first click makes the Spanish or English word appear, and after a delay, the translation can come onto the screen. Be sure that they make screens that work from Spanish to English as well as from English to Spanish. Have them duplicate the entire file so that one set of vocabulary words can be easily stored for exam review. Suggest that they have a second set from which they can continually delete words as they memorize them. Students can also use clip art in place of English when creating electronic flashcards.

Suggest that students spend five minutes a day studying the flashcards. They can do this alone or with another person. Even if that other person does not speak Spanish, students can practice spelling the word to them after the other person says its English meaning. Point out to them that even though they may not be studying the cards for very long each day, they are becoming much more familiar with the vocabulary every time they use their flashcards. Have them study each side, so that they practice the Spanish to English as well as the English to Spanish. As they get to know certain

words by heart, have them take those cards out of the pile so that they may focus on the more difficult words. In this way, students will eliminate the extra work of reviewing all words and will be able to focus on those that they require more practice to learn. Have them put all of the words back into the pile a day or two before a test for a final review.

Flashcards can be an extremely effective classroom management tool. If students finish a task before the rest of the class, have them use the class time to study their flashcards. They will get their study time in and you will have more time to focus on helping students finish a task instead of monitoring those who have already finished.

Audio vocabulary drills

Have students study vocabulary by listening to it being read repeatedly. At the beginning of a chapter, have them record the vocabulary in a clear voice. (See the Speaking section of this book, p. 40 for recording instructions.) Suggest that they say the Spanish word first, pause for a few seconds, and then say the corresponding word in English. Encourage students to listen to the recordings on the bus, at home while they do chores, or when they are in the car. While auditory studying will provide extra vocabulary comprehension and retention, it does not give students the necessary spelling practice they need with new vocabulary. Therefore, it is wise to suggest that they combine this method with a visual form of studying.

Studying vocabulary from a prepared list

It may be helpful for students to simply copy the words on a two-column chart and study them as a list. To make the chart, have them fold a lined piece of paper in half and print the vocabulary from the chapter in the two columns. Have them write one Spanish word per line going down the left side of the paper, and the corresponding English word going down the right side of the paper. (This can also be done electronically.) Make sure that students write the words close to the center-fold of the page, instead of on the left-hand side of each column. (See the sample on p. 49 for a clear picture of how to arrange the words on the page.) Students may want to use different colored pens or text fonts to distinguish gender, part of speech, or other vocabulary features.

To use the list, have students cover the folded paper with another paper or a book. Suggest that they look at only one word at a time, say the word, and then say its meaning. They should check for accuracy after each word. Encourage them to study from Spanish to English and vice-versa. Have them highlight the more difficult words that they need to spend more time on. It may be helpful for students to keep all of their vocabulary lists in a binder so that they can easily access them during other activities and use them to study for midterm or final exams.

Sample Vocabulary Study List
REALIDADES 1, Chapter 6A

la alfombra	rug
el armario	closet
la cama	bed
la cómoda	dresser
las cortinas	curtains
el cuadro	painting
el despertador	alarm clock
el dormitorio	bedroom
el espejo	mirror
el estante	shelf, bookshelf
la lámpara	lamp
la mesita	night table
la pared	wall
el disco compacto	compact disc
el equipo de sonido	sound (stereo) system
el lector DVD	DVD player
el televisor	television set
el video	videocassette
la videocasetera	VCR
¿De qué color...?	What color . . . .?
los colores	colors
amarillo, -a	yellow
anaranjado, -a	orange
azul	blue
blanco, -a	white
gris	gray
marrón	brown
morado, -a	purple
negro, -a	black
rojo, -a	red
rosado, -a	pink
verde	green
bonito, -a	pretty
feo, -a	ugly
grande	large
importante	important
mismo, -a	same
pequeño, -a	small
propio, -a	own
a la derecha (de)	to the right (of)
a la izquierda (de)	to the left (of)
mejor(es) que	better than
el, la mejor	the best
los, las mejores	the best
menos...que	less, fewer . . . than
peor(es) que	worse than
el, la peor	the worst
los, las peores	the worst
la cosa	thing
para mí	in my opinion, for me
para ti	in your opinion, for you
la posesión	possession

Activities

Quiz Show

Have students work in groups of four and use their flashcards to host a quiz show. Three students are contestants and one is the host. The host will use his or her flashcards to quiz the other three students for two rounds. Each correct answer gets those students a point. A new host is chosen every two rounds. After all eight rounds, the student with the most points wins the game.

Student Strategy

Study aloud

Remind students that they shouldn't just think the words as they study. Instead, they should say them out loud. This helps them to get auditory reinforcement of their learning.

Self-quiz

Have students place their flashcards in a stack, English side up. Then, have them write the correct corresponding word for each card on a separate piece of paper. Have them check for accuracy and correctly rewrite any words they missed.

Beat the clock

If students have made audio recordings of the vocabulary, have them use the recordings for a game in class. Give pairs of students a cassette or CD player to play one of the recordings. Have them play the recording and take turns trying to say the meaning of the word on the tape during the pause. Students who identify the meaning before it is given on the recording are given a point. The student with the most points at the end of the vocabulary list wins.

Classroom Vocabulary Practice

Vocabulary is one area where students can have fun and be actively engaged in their learning. Hands-on vocabulary activities that are incorporated into the daily lesson make class fun and foster long-term vocabulary retention.

Teaching Tips

Games

Try to play vocabulary games with your students at least once per chapter. Students learn more easily in the low-stress environment that games provide. As long as students are engaged in the activity, it tends to benefit them as much as, if not more than, controlled academic activities. Prizes are a great motivator for students, too. Whether they are in the sixth grade or seniors in high school, students are always eager to win and receive a prize or extra credit point.

Make it a race

Consider making any vocabulary activity (such as a crossword puzzle from the *Writing, Audio & Video Workbook* or a vocabulary cloze passage using a word bank from the *Practice Workbook*) as a race. Allow students to work in pairs and reward the first two or three pairs who finish correctly. Once the winners have been determined, quickly bring the activity to a close by having the winners share the correct answers with the rest of the class. Since all of the sections of the AP* Exam are timed, teaching students to work quickly and under the pressure of time is very beneficial.

Cut-apart cards

For each chapter, prepare a handout on which you have 25 squares, with one vocabulary word written in Spanish on each square. When possible, you may want to include pictures of vocabulary words instead. (See the *REALIDADES Teacher's Resource Book* for

chapter-specific clip art.) You could also have students print the Spanish words in each of the 25 squares. Give each student a handout and a pair of scissors. Have them cut the squares apart and put their initials on each card, so that they can distinguish their own from a partner's. The students should keep the cards in a small plastic bag to use for each of the activities below. Keep a separate shoebox for each chapter to store the students' cut-apart cards in your classroom.

Activities Using Cut-Apart Cards

Rápido

Have students work in pairs and place one set of cards face down on the desk. To play, have one student flip the top card over. The first student to say the meaning of what is on the card keeps the card. If neither student knows the word on the card, they look it up in their chapter vocabulary list and then place it back on the bottom of the pile. Students play until the pile is gone. The person with the most cards is the winner.

Pescar

Have students place two sets of cards face down in a scrambled pile. Each student takes three cards. The goal is to find a match for each card. To play, one student asks his or her partner if they have a certain card. For example: *¿Tienes "alfombra"?* The partner either hands over the card and says, *Aquí la tienes*, or says, *No. Ve a pescar*. If students get a match, they go again. Students play until the pile is gone. If a student runs out of cards, he or she takes another from the pile. The winner is the student that has the most matched pairs when the time is up.

Memoria

Have students work in pairs to play this memory game. Pairs should mix their cards and put them face down in rows on the desk. One at a time, students turn over one card from the desks, trying to make a match. Have students say the word out loud as they turn the picture over. If a match is made, an extra turn is granted. Students can play under a time limit or until all pairs have been matched. The student with the most matches wins. However, students must be able to identify the meaning of each matched pair in order for the pair to count!

Bingo

Ask students to place their own cards face up on their desks in five rows of five. Then, call out words from the vocabulary list. Students turn cards over, face down, when a word on their desk has been called out. A complete row of face down cards is a "bingo."

Definiciones

When students have finished using the cards for other activities, challenge them to a definition race. Use a stopwatch to time students in a race for who can write the meanings of the words on the back of each card the fastest. For pictures, students should write the word in Spanish. For words in Spanish, students should write the English meaning. Give each student their time, and have them log their times in their notebooks. Challenge them to improve their times after each chapter. The cards can also be used as flashcards for study.

Additional Vocabulary Activities

The Elimination Game

Using a permanent marker, write a list of current vocabulary on an overhead. Be sure to have at least one word for each student in the class. If your class has fewer students than there are words on the vocabulary list, it is wise to choose the words that require extra practice. As a warm-up to the game, have students work in pairs to quickly say what each word means. Next, each student secretly writes any two Spanish words from the list on a tiny slip of paper. When play begins, students hold their papers in their hands and stand next to their desks. Go around to the individual students, and call out one of the words on the overhead and the English meaning of that word. When a word is said, cross it off of the list. Once both of the words on a student's papers have been called, that student must sit down; he or she has been eliminated. Continue around the room. Even students that have been eliminated are allowed their turn to call out a word still remaining on the list. If a student doesn't know any of the remaining words on the list, the play passes to the next student, who then chooses a word from the list. The winner is the last student still standing with a word that hasn't been called.

As a follow-up, circle the four most difficult words to remember. Ask students to work in pairs and use each of the four words in a complete sentence. Have pairs share their sentences with the class.

Draw and Guess

Have students work with a partner. All pairs should be lined up in a straight row facing each other. Give each pair of students scrap paper to draw on. Stand on one side of the room and hold up a vocabulary word in Spanish from the current *REALIDADES* chapter. Be sure to write in big, bold letters. Those students facing you must draw the picture of the word for their partner. Those students with their backs to you must guess what their partner has drawn. The first person to guess the word wins the point for their pair. Have students stand and say the word loudly so that you are sure who was first to respond correctly. After the first round, move to the opposite side of the room and hold up a new word. Play continues with the opposite person drawing and the partner guessing. The pair with the most points wins.

Matamoscas

Enlarge the clip art images from the *Teacher's Resource Book* and tape them to the chalkboard. Divide the class into two teams. One member from each team approaches the screen holding a fly swatter. Call out a word in Spanish that represents one of the pictures being displayed. The student who swats the corresponding picture first scores a point for the team. Tell students to leave the swatter in place so that you can tell which picture was swatted. Once a student wins two points in a row, a new team member moves forward to swat. The team with the most points after you have called out all of the vocabulary words wins. As an alternative, you can write the words in Spanish on the board and play as above, calling out the word in English.

Testing Vocabulary

Teaching Tips

When to test vocabulary

Consider giving a short vocabulary quiz two or three days prior to each chapter test. This allows students to focus on vocabulary first. Then for the chapter test, they can focus more on structures and on the bigger picture of putting the chapter elements together. Creating a vocabulary test that encompasses all of the vocabulary covered during half of the year and another one just prior to the final exam is an excellent way to reinforce long-term recall of vocabulary.

How to test vocabulary

It is beneficial for students if you move beyond any sort of simple vocabulary assessments, such as writing the word which corresponds to a picture, giving the Spanish definitions for a list of words in English, or matching Spanish words with given definitions in English. Testing in a way that causes students to *use* vocabulary, synthesize meaning, and move beyond mere recall will enhance their retention. A vocabulary quiz should be an opportunity to *use* vocabulary, rather than a memorization drill. A chapter vocabulary quiz might include some or all of the following:

- Banks of words that are used to complete sentences or paragraphs (see examples on p. 40 of the *REALIDADES 2 Practice Workbook* or pp. 171–173 of the *REALIDADES 3 Assessment Program*)

- Multiple-choice sentence completions (see p. 136 of the *REALIDADES 3 Assessment Program* or the *Computer Test Bank* multiple-choice segments)

- True and False sentences that contain vocabulary from the current chapters

- A short list of vocabulary words in Spanish that students are asked to use in a sentence or paragraph (When testing in this fashion, it is important that you make students understand that their sentence must *clearly* demonstrate the meaning of the word for credit.)

- Groups of four or five words in Spanish with one word that does not logically belong to the group because of its meaning (not because of its gender or part of speech)

- Matching activities for synonyms or antonyms in Spanish

Grading techniques will vary depending on what types of quiz you decide to give. Be sure to consider students' use of the word as well as the accuracy with which they write it.

PRENTICE HALL
Realidades

Levels A/B/1
Resource Support

Introduction: Pre-AP* Student and Teacher Activity Sheets

The activities in this section are intended as simulations of the types of tasks and skills that students are asked to engage in on the AP* Spanish Language Exam. The level of difficulty has been adjusted to meet students' AP* abilities and obtained skills along their journey through *Realidades* 1, 2, and 3. Some of the activities will cause students to stretch themselves, but this sort of rigor will serve to prepare students for the challenge of AP*. The activities themselves can be used as such—classroom exercises. Or, they can be used as additions to a chapter assessment. If they are used as assessments, it is recommended that students have had practice accomplishing a similar exercise in class, first.

Using rubrics, or as they are called by the AP* Program, scoring guidelines, is an essential component to familiarizing students with the caliber of work that is expected of them. Time used in class to allow students to critique each others' work in groups using scoring guidelines is time well spent. Once students are familiar with this sort of evaluation, the teacher can assign and collect a task for formal grading, using the same types of scoring guidelines.

For Level 1, the timed nature of the activities is left very open, building gradually to suggested time and length of the final student products. At first, the goal should be to familiarize students with the types of tasks they will need to be able to do. As students' skills mature and improve, it will be essential to require that the tasks be performed within a given amount of time and that the tasks produced conform to a specified length.

Finally, the many exercises across the *Realidades* suite of activities and components, when used together, will be vital for the preparation of successful future AP* students. AP* is about moving beyond the memorization of lists of vocabulary and verbs and into language use situations. It is about what students know and can do with the Spanish that they have learned.

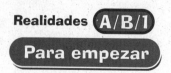

Realidades A/B/1

Para empezar

Pre-AP* Resource Chart

	Student Edition/Teacher's Edition		Ancillaries
	Page #	**Activity**	
Vocabulary	p. 8	Supplemental Pre-AP* Activity	*Go Online:* Self-test
Listening	p. 8	Supplemental Pre-AP* Activity	*MindPoint Quiz Show* *Pre-AP* Resource Book:* p. 57
Reading			*Teacher's Resource Book:* Situation cards, p. 16 *Pre-AP* Resource Book:* p. 57
Speaking			*Pre-AP* Resource Book:* p. 57
Writing	p. 14	Differentiated Instruction: Advanced Learners/Pre-AP*	*Pre-AP* Resource Book:* p. 57
	p. 18	Differentiated Instruction: Advanced Learners/Pre-AP*	

Student Activity 1
Paragraph Completion

Directions: Read the following passage, completing the blanks with a word in Spanish that is logical and grammatically correct. You must spell and accent the word correctly.

Buenos (1) _____. Me (2) _____ Joaquín. La (3) _____ de mi

cumpleaños es el (4) _____ de (5) _____. (6) _____ estudiante en

la escuela secundaria. Como hoy es (7) _____, tengo clase de matemáticas. Mi clase

es a las ocho y (8) _____. El (9) _____ de la clase se llama el Señor

Martínez. ¿Y tú? ¿(10) _____ clases tienes? ¿Seis o siete?

Student Activity 2
Informal Speaking

Directions: Practice the following with a classmate. Imagine that you just won a radio call-in contest. Give the spelling of your name and your telephone number to the radio station employee so that someone may contact you to arrange for you to pick up your prize.

Student Activity 3
Informal Speaking

Practice this exercise aloud with a classmate, switching roles so that each may have a turn being Student A and Student B, respectively.

Directions: Imagine that it is the first day of class and your teacher has asked you to get to know one other person in the room. A classmate will ask you several questions. Respond to his or her questions:

STUDENT A: Buenas tardes. Me llamo _____. Y tú, ¿cómo te llamas?

STUDENT B: _____

STUDENT A: ¿Cómo estás hoy?

STUDENT B: _____

STUDENT A: ¿Cuál es la fecha de tu cumpleaños?

STUDENT B: _____

STUDENT A: Repite, por favor.

STUDENT B: _____

STUDENT A: Muy bien. ¿Qué hora es?

STUDENT B: _____

STUDENT A: Pues, adiós.

STUDENT B: _____

	Student Edition/Teacher's Edition		Ancillaries
	Page #	Activity	
Vocabulary	p. 29	Supplemental Pre-AP* Activity	*Assessment Program:* Prueba 1A-2, pp. 15–16 *Go Online:* Self-test
Listening	p. 35	Supplemental Pre-AP* Activity	*Video Program* Chapter 1A *Video Teacher's Guide* Chapter 1A *Writing, Audio & Video Workbook:* Act. 6, p. 11 *Pre-AP* Resource Book:* pp. 60–61
Reading	p. 35 p. 38	Supplemental Pre-AP* Activity Act. 19	*MindPoint Quiz Show* *TPR Stories,* El día horrible de Juan Pablo, p. 22 *Realidades* para hispanohablantes: ¡Adelante!, Lectura 1, p. 22 *Realidades* para hispanohablantes: Lectura 2, p. 24 *Pre-AP* Resource Book:* pp. 60–61

Speaking	p. 29
	p. 43
		Supplemental Pre-AP* Activity
		Presentación oral
			Assessment Program: Examen de 1A, Hablar, p. 22
			Teacher's Resource Book, Para empezar–Tema 4:
			  Communicative Activity 1A-1, pp. 38–39
			Teacher's Resource Book, Para empezar–Tema 4:
			  Situation cards, p. 42
			Realidades para hispanohablantes: Presentación
			  oral, p. 27
			TPR Stories: Personalized Mini-situations,
			  pp. 18–21
			Pre-AP* Resource Book: pp. 60–61

Writing	p. 35 p. 36 p. 38 p. 41	Supplemental Pre-AP* Activity Differentiated Instruction: Advanced Learners/Pre-AP* Act. 19 Supplemental Pre-AP* Activity	*Go Online:* Internet Link Activity *Realidades* para hispanohablantes: Act. O, p. 25 *Assessment Program:* Examen 1A, Escribir, p. 22 *Writing, Audio & Video Workbook:* Act. 13, p.17 *Reading and Writing for Success:* Test 1, pp. 1–3 *ExamView:* Pre-AP* Question Bank *Pre-AP* Resource Book:* pp. 60–61

	Student Edition/Teacher's Edition		Ancillaries
	Page #	Activity	
Vocabulary	p. 57	Supplemental Pre-AP* Activity	*Realidades* para hispanohablantes: Act. B, p. 19 *Assessment Program:* Prueba 1B-2, p. 28–29 *Go Online:* Self-test
Listening	p. 57	Supplemental Pre-AP* Activity	*Writing, Audio & Video Workbook:* Act. 9, p. 24 *Video Program* Chapter 1B *Video Teacher's Guide* Chapter 1B *Pre-AP* Resource Book:* pp. 60–61
Reading			*Realidades* para hispanohablantes: Lectura 1, p. 42 *Realidades* para hispanohablantes: Lectura 2, p. 44 *Reading and Writing for Success:* Test 19, pp. 57–59 *Go Online:* Internet Link Activity *MindPoint Quiz Show* *TPR Stories:* ¡Marilú no es simpática!, p. 27 *Pre-AP* Resource Book:* pp. 60–61
Speaking	p. 57 p. 60	Supplemental Pre-AP* Activity Differentiated Instruction: Advanced Learners/Pre-AP*	*Assessment Program:* Examen 1B, Hablar, p. 36 *Teacher's Resource Book, Para empezar–Tema 4:* Communicative Activity 1B-1, pp. 64–65 *Teacher's Resource Book, Para empezar–Tema 4:* Situation cards, p. 68 *TPR Stories:* Personalized Mini-situations, pp. 24–26 *Pre-AP* Resource Book:* pp. 60–61
Writing	p. 53 p. 60 p. 63 p. 65 p. 67	Supplemental Pre-AP* Activity Differentiated Instruction: Advanced Learners/Pre-AP* Act. 21 Supplemental Pre-AP* Activity Presentación escrita	*Writing, Audio & Video Workbook:* Act. 13, p. 28 *Reading and Writing for Success:* Test 2, pp. 4–6 *Realidades* para hispanohablantes: Presentación escrita, p. 47 *Assessment Program:* Examen 1B, Escribir, p. 36 *Go Online:* Internet Link Activity *ExamView:* Pre-AP* Question Bank *Pre-AP* Resource Book:* pp. 60–61

Teacher Activity 1
Listening Comprehension

Before the students watch the *Realidades* Video for *Capítulo* 1A, play the video with the TV screen covered. Use the audio portion to engage students in the Dictogloss activity on p. 14. Once the students have completed the steps to the Dictogloss activity, uncover the TV screen, watch the video, then have them complete the video activities on pp. 8-9 of the *Realidades* Writing, Audio & Video Workbook.

Teacher Activity 2
Reading Comprehension

As an alternative, photocopy the *Realidades* Video Script for *Capítulo* 1A, *A primera vista: Y tú, ¿cómo eres?* Distribute the copies to students. In pairs, have students read the script aloud with a classmate and subsequently complete the video activities on pp. 8-9 of the *Realidades* Writing, Audio & Video Workbook. For follow-up and closure, allow students to watch the *Realidades* Video.

Teacher Activity 3
Special Focus: Scoring Guidelines and Writing Tasks

Have students complete the *Amigo por correspondencia* assignment found on p. 67 of the *Realidades* Student Textbook. Collect the assignment and select four or five student samples. Type those samples for photocopying so that the work will be anonymous. Distribute copies of the sample student work to the class. Distribute copies of the scoring guidelines found on p. 45. Since this is a writing task, the *Fluency* category on the bottom row can be ignored at this time. Have students read the first sample aloud with a partner. As a class, discuss where on the range of scoring guidelines the particular piece falls. Repeat this activity with subsequent samples. Making students familiar with how to apply scoring guidelines will help them engage more effectively in group evaluations to take place later during the course.

Student Activity 1
Presentational Speaking

Listen to the "match up" recording that accompanies the *Examen* 1A, pp. T60-T61 in the *Realidades* Assessment Program. Decide which one of the five people, based on their voicemail messages, you would most like to be friends with. Be sure to cite reasons for your choices based on what you heard as well as on your own likes and dislikes. You will have three minutes to prepare your answer and one minute to present your response to a classmate.

Student Activity 2
Informal Speaking

Work with a partner to write complete-sentence answers to the following questions. Be sure to verify the correctness of your answers. Then, use the questions (and answers) to play *Preguntas rápidas* (see p. 38) or to prepare for *One minute of questions* (For Levels 1 and 2) (see p. 38).

1. ¿Cómo te llamas? _____
2. ¿Cómo eres? _____
3. Según tus amigos, ¿cómo eres? _____
4. ¿Eres más serio(a) o más gracioso(a)? _____
5. ¿Qué te gusta hacer? _____
6. ¿Qué no te gusta hacer? _____
7. ¿Te gusta pasar tiempo con tu familia? _____
8. ¿Cuál deporte te gusta practicar? _____
9. ¿Te gusta cantar o dibujar? _____
10. ¿Te gusta trabajar mucho? _____
11. ¿Cómo es tu profesor(a) favorito(a)? _____
12. ¿Como es tu mejor amigo(a)? _____
13. ¿Cómo se llama tu amigo(a)? _____
14. ¿Cómo es un buen estudiante? _____
15. ¿Cuál color te gusta más? _____
16. ¿Te gusta hablar por teléfono con amigos? _____
17. ¿Te gusta ir a la escuela? _____
18. ¿Eres trabajador(a) en la clase? _____
19. ¿Quién es deportista? _____
20. ¿Quíen es peresozo(a)? _____

	Student Edition/Teacher's Edition		Ancillaries
	Page #	**Activity**	
Vocabulary	p. 77	Supplemental Pre-AP* Activity	*Assessment Program:* Prueba 2A-2, p. 43–44 *Go Online:* Self-test *Realidades para hispanohablantes:* Act. 2A-1, p. 21
Listening			*Writing, Audio & Video Workbook:* Act. 9, p. 34 *Video Program* Chapter 2A *Video Teacher's Guide* Chapter 2A *Pre-AP* Resource Book:* pp. 64–65
Reading	p. 81 p. 91	Supplemental Pre-AP* Activity Supplemental Pre-AP* Activity	*Realidades* para hispanohablantes: Lectura 1, p. 62 *Realidades* para hispanohablantes: Lectura 2, p. 64 *MindPoint Quiz Show* *TPR Stories:* Pepe el desordenado, p. 33 *Pre-AP* Resource Book:* pp. 64–65

Speaking	p. 77
	 p. 81
	 p. 93
		Supplemental Pre-AP* Activity
		 Supplemental Pre-AP* Activity
		 Presentación oral
			TPR Stories: Personalized Mini-situations,
			   pp. 30–32
			 Assessment Program: Examen 2A, Hablar, p. 50
			 Teacher's Resource Book, Para empezar–Tema 4:
			   Communicative Activity 2A-1, pp. 90–91
			 Teacher's Resource Book, Para empezar–Tema 4:
			   Situation cards, p. 94
			 Realidades para hispanohablantes: Presentación
			   oral, p. 67
			 Pre-AP* Resource Book: p. 64

Writing	p. 74 p. 81 p. 87	Differentiated Instruction: Advanced Learners/Pre-AP* Supplemental Pre-AP* Activity Act. 19	*Writing, Audio & Video Workbook:* Act.13, p. 38 *Realidades* para hispanohablantes: Act. M, p. 65 *Reading and Writing for Success:* Test 3, pp. 7–9 *Go Online:* Internet Link Activity *ExamView:* Pre-AP* Question Bank *Assessment Program:* Examen 2A, Escribir, p. 49 *Pre-AP* Resource Book:* pp. 64–65

	Student Edition/Teacher's Edition		Ancillaries
	Page #	**Activity**	
Vocabulary	p. 103	Supplemental Pre-AP* Activity	*Go Online:* Self-test
Listening	p. 103 p. 115	Supplemental Pre-AP* Activity Supplemental Pre-AP* Activity	*Writing, Audio & Video Workbook:* Act. 6, p. 42 *Video Program* Chapter 2B *Video Teacher's Guide* Chapter 2B *Pre-AP* Resource Book:* pp. 64–65
Reading	p. 115	Supplemental Pre-AP* Activity	*Reading and Writing for Success:* Test 4, pp. 10–12 *Realidades* para hispanohablantes: Lectura 1, p. 82 *Realidades* para hispanohablantes: Lectura 2, p. 84 *TPR Stories:* La clase de fobias, p. 35 *MindPoint Quiz Show* *Pre-AP* Resource Book:* pp. 64–65

Speaking	p. 105
	p. 107
		Supplemental Pre-AP* Activity
		Supplemental Pre-AP* Activity
			Assessment Program: Examen de 2B, Hablar, p. 63
			Teacher's Resource Book, Para empezar–Tema 4:
			  Communicative Activity 2B-2, pp. 116–117
			Teacher's Resource Book, Para empezar–Tema 4:
			  Situation cards, p. 118
			Pre-AP* Resource Book: p. 64

Writing	p. 103 p. 105 p. 112 p. 117	Supplemental Pre-AP* Activity Supplemental Pre-AP* Activity Act. 20 Presentación escrita	*Assessment Program:* Examen de 2B, Escribir, p. 63 *Writing, Audio & Video Workbook:* Act. 13, p. 48 *Reading and Writing for Success:* Test 4, pp. 10–12 *Realidades* para hispanohablantes: Act. P, p. 83 *Realidades* para hispanohablantes: Act. R, p. 85 *Realidades* para hispanohablantes: Presentación escrita, p. 87 *Go Online:* Internet Link Activity *ExamView:* Pre-AP* Question Bank *Pre-AP* Resource Book:* pp. 64–65

Teacher Activity 1
Formal Oral Presentation

1. Have students listen to Audio Activity 9 on p. 34 in the *Realidades* Writing, Audio & Video Workbook.

2. Next, have students prepare a one-minute talk about which of the four students they would most like to host as an exchange student, giving reasons to justify their choice and comparing their own likes and dislikes with the potential guest.

3. The amount of preparation time can vary, but should not be longer than three or four minutes.

4. Students are then allowed one minute to record their presentations, or they may make their presentations to a group of three or four students.

5. In groups of three or four, students should listen to each recording (or hear each presentation) and discuss the content and quality using the scoring guidelines on p. 45.

Teacher Activity 2
Reading Comprehension

After students have completed Student Activity 3 on the following page, make three photocopies of each student's written work. Place students in groups of four. Distribute copies of the scoring guidelines found on p. 45. (Since this is a writing task, the *Fluency* category on the bottom row can be ignored at this time.) Distribute the copies of the students' work within each group. Have each student read his or her writing aloud to the group, one piece at a time, and discuss the content and quality of each writing piece using the scoring guidelines. Each group may select one sample to share with the whole class.

Student Activity 1
Listening Comprehension

Select the correct answer for each of the multiple-choice questions below after listening to Audio Activity 7 on p. 32 in the *Realidades* Writing, Audio & Video Workbook.

1. ¿Cuándo tiene Diana la clase de español?
   a. la primera hora
   b. la segunda hora
   c. la quinta hora

2. ¿Cuál clase es difícil para Diana?
   a. la de español
   b. la de arte
   c. la de matemáticas

3. ¿Por qué estudian mucho Diana y Emilio?
   a. Son divertidos.
   b. Son trabajadores.
   c. Son atléticos.

Student Activity 2
Paragraph Completion

Directions: Read the following passage, completing the blanks with the correct form of the word in parenthesis that is grammatically correct. You must spell and accent the word correctly.

Me llamo Teresa. (1) _____ (tener) un problema (2) _____ (serio) con mis

clases. Yo (3) _____ (estar) con la Señora Chávez para mi clase de inglés la (4)

_____ (tercero) hora. Es una profesora bien (5) _____ (estricto). Mi amiga

Luz (6) _____ (estar) detrás de mí. A menudo nosotras (7) _____ (hablar)

durante la clase. La profesora no (8) _____ (estar) (9) _____ (contento) con

nosotras. Sin embargo, Luz y yo (10) _____ (trabajar) mucho y (11) _____

(estudiar) las lecciones que la profesora (12) _____ (enseñar).

Student Activity 3
Informal Writing

Write an e-mail to a cousin in another state or town describing your favorite class. The message should include:

- The name of the subject
- Which period the class meets and at what time
- A description of the teacher
- Why it is your favorite class
- What items are needed for the class

	Student Edition/Teacher's Edition		Ancillaries
	Page #	**Activity**	
Vocabulary	p. 127	Supplemental Pre-AP* Activity	*Go Online:* Self-test
Listening	p. 128	Differentiated Instruction: Advanced Learners/Pre-AP*	*Writing, Audio & Video Workbook:* Act. 6, p. 52 *Video Program* Chapter 3A *Video Teacher's Guide* Chapter 3A
	p. 138	Supplemental Pre-AP* Activity	*Pre-AP* Resource Book:* pp. 68–69
Reading	p. 137	Act. 20	*MindPoint Quiz Show* *Realidades* para hispanohablantes: Lectura 1, p. 102 *Realidades* para hispanohablantes: Lectura 2, p. 104 *TPR Stories:* La buena comida de todos los días, p. 42 *Pre-AP* Resource Book:* pp. 68–69
Speaking	p. 127	Supplemental Pre-AP* Activity	*Realidades* para hispanohablantes: Presentación oral, p. 107
	p. 128	Differentiated Instruction: Advanced Learners/Pre-AP*	*Assessment Program:* Examen de 3A, Parte II, Hablar, p. 77
	p. 137	Act. 20	*Teacher's Resource Book, Para empezar–Tema 4:* Communicative Activity 3A-2, pp. 142–143
	p. 141	Presentación oral	*Teacher's Resource Book, Para empezar–Tema 4:* Situation cards, p. 144 *TPR Stories:* Personalized Mini-situations, pp. 38–41 *Pre-AP* Resource Book:* pp. 68–69
Writing	p. 132	Supplemental Pre-AP* Activity	*Realidades* para hispanohablantes: Act. P, p. 103
	p. 137	Act. 20	*Assessment Program:* Examen de 3A, Parte II, Escribir, p. 76 *Writing, Audio & Video Workbook:* Act. 13, p. 59 *Reading and Writing for Success:* Test 5, pp. 13–15 *Go Online:* Internet Link Activity *ExamView:* Pre-AP* Question Bank *Pre-AP* Resource Book:* pp. 68–69

Realidades A/B/1

Capítulo 3B

Pre-AP* Resource Chart

	Student Edition/Teacher's Edition		Ancillaries
	Page #	**Activity**	
Vocabulary	p. 153	Supplemental Pre-AP* Activity	*Go Online:* Self-test
Listening	p. 151	Supplemental Pre-AP* Activity	*Video Program* Chapter 3B
	p. 153	Supplemental Pre-AP* Activity	*Video Teacher's Guide* Chapter 3B
	p. 162	Supplemental Pre-AP* Activity	*Writing, Audio & Video Workbook:* Act. 9, p. 65
			Pre-AP* Resource Book: pp. 68–69
Reading	p. 161	Act. 19	*Realidades* para hispanohablantes: Lectura 1, p. 122
	p. 162	Supplemental Pre-AP* Activity	*Realidades* para hispanohablantes: Lectura 2, p. 124
			Reading and Writing for Success: Test 6, pp. 16–18
			MindPoint Quiz Show
			TPR Stories: El camarero horrible, p. 47
			Pre-AP* Resource Book: pp. 68–69
Speaking	p. 151	Supplemental Pre-AP* Activity	*TPR Stories:* Personalized Mini-situations, pp. 44–46
	p. 153	Supplemental Pre-AP* Activity	*Teacher's Resource Book, Para empezar–Tema 4:* Communicative Activity 3B-1, pp. 166–167
			Teacher's Resource Book, Para empezar–Tema 4: Situation cards, p. 170
			Assessment Program: Examen de capítulo 3B, Parte II, Hablar, p. 89
			Pre-AP* Resource Book: pp. 68–69
Writing	p. 151	Supplemental Pre-AP* Activity	*Writing, Audio & Video Workbook:* Act. 13, p. 69
	p. 153	Supplemental Pre-AP* Activity	*Realidades* para hispanohablantes: Act. R, p. 125
	p. 161	Act. 19	*Realidades* para hispanohablantes: Presentación escrita, p. 127
	p. 162	Supplemental Pre-AP* Activity	*Reading and Writing for Success:* Test 6, pp. 16–18
	p. 165	Presentación escrita	*Go Online:* Internet Link Activity
			ExamView: Pre-AP* Question Bank
			Assessment Program: Examen de capítulo 3B, Parte C. Escribir, p. 89
			Pre-AP* Resource Book: pp. 68–69

Teacher Activity 1
Paragraph Completion (without Root Word)

Make a transparency of the postcard from *Actividad* 14, p. 133 of the *Realidades* Student Textbook, leaving out all verb choices. Have students complete the exercise with the correct form of a verb that makes sense in the context of the message. Model the activity as a whole class, completing the first one or two responses all together. Students may work with a partner or alone to finish the activity.

Teacher Activity 2
Formal Writing

Provide students with the printed listening script for *Examen del capítulo*, 3B (See p. T63 of the *Realidades* Assessment Program.) Students should write two paragraphs describing what they believe to be a healthy lifestyle, including diet and activities, using the students in the reading (listening script) as examples to support their opinions. Then make three photocopies of each student's written work. Place students in groups of four. Distribute copies of the scoring guidelines found on p. 45. (Since this is a writing task, the *Fluency* category on the bottom row can be ignored at this time.) Distribute the copies of the students' work within each group. Have each student read his or her writing aloud to the group, one piece at a time, and discuss the content and quality of each writing piece using the scoring guidelines. Each group may select one sample to share with the whole class.

Teacher Activity 3
Paragraph Completion

Make a transparency of the following passage. Have students, as a class or in pairs, complete the blanks with the correct form of the word in parenthesis that is grammatically correct. They must spell and accent the word correctly. Ask students to explain to the group how they made decisions to arrive at the correct answer.

Yo (1) _____ (trabajar) mucho para mantenerme la salud. Primero,

(2) _____ (hacer) ejercicios, (3) _____ (levantar) pesas y (4) _____

(caminar) todos los días. (5) _____ (preferir) comer frutas (6) _____(fresco)

cada día. No como (7) _____ (mucho) pasteles ni helado. Cuando tengo mucha sed,

el agua (8) _____ (frío) es mi bebida (9) _____ (favorito). A mis padres les

(10) _____ (encantar) los espaguetis con salchichas (11) _____ (italiano).

Pero a mí, no me (12) _____ (gustar) nada los espaguetis.

Realidades A/B/1

Tema 3

Student Activity 1
Informal Speaking

Work with a partner to write complete-sentence answers to the following questions. Be sure to verify the correctness of your answers. Then, use the questions (and answers) to play *Preguntas rápidas* (see p. 38) or to prepare for *One minute of questions* (For Levels 1 and 2) (see p. 38).

1. ¿Cómo es tu dieta?

2. ¿Qué frutas te gustan más?

3. Describe tu sándwich favorito.

4. ¿Prefieres el desayuno o el almuerzo? ¿Por qué?

5. ¿Qué almuerzas los sábados?

6. ¿Cuál bebida tomas con la pizza?

7. ¿Cuál postre le gusta más a tu mejor amigo?

8. ¿Qué hay de almorzar en la cafetería de tu escuela?

9. ¿A tus amigos les gusta comer verduras?

10. ¿Qué tipo de sopa prefieres?

11. ¿En cuál restaurante te gusta comer? ¿Por qué?

12. ¿Compartes tu postre favorito con un amigo?

13. ¿Qué tipos de ejercicio haces?

14. ¿Qué haces para mantener la salud?

15. ¿Crees que es importante comer bien?

16. ¿Tomas vitaminas cada día?

Pre-AP* Resource Chart

	Student Edition/Teacher's Edition		Ancillaries
	Page #	**Activity**	
Vocabulary	p. 173	Supplemental Pre-AP* Activity	*Go Online:* Self-test *Assessment Program:* Prueba 4A-2, pp. 95–96
Listening	p. 173	Supplemental Pre-AP* Activity	*Video Program* Chapter 4A *Video Teacher's Guide* Chapter 4A *Writing, Audio & Video Workbook:* Act. 6, p. 73 *Pre-AP* Resource Book:* pp. 72–73
Reading			*MindPoint Quiz Show* *Realidades* para hispanohablantes: Lectura 1, p. 142 *Realidades* para hispanohablantes: Lectura 2, p. 144 *TPR Stories:* ¡Vamos a la playa!, p. 54 *Pre-AP* Resource Book:* pp. 72–73

Speaking	p. 173
	p. 183
	p. 186
	p. 191
		Supplemental Pre-AP* Activity
		Supplemental Pre-AP* Activity
		Act. 18
		Presentación oral
			TPR Stories: Personalized Mini-situations,
			  pp. 50–53
			Realidades para hispanohablantes: Presentación
			  oral, p. 147
			Teacher's Resource Book, Para empezar–Tema 4:
			  Communicative Activity 4A-1, pp. 194–195
			Teacher's Resource Book, Para empezar–Tema 4:
			  Situation cards, p. 198
			Assessment Program: Parte II, Hablar, p. 102
			Pre-AP* Resource Book: pp. 72–73

Writing	p. 176 p. 183 p. 186 p. 188	Differentiated Instruction: Advanced Learners/Pre-AP* Supplemental pre-AP* Activity Act. 18 Supplemental Pre-AP* Activity	*Writing, Audio & Video Workbook:* Act. 13, p. 77 *Realidades* para hispanohablantes: Act. Ñ, p. 143 *Reading and Writing for Success:* Test 7, pp. 19–21 *Go Online:* Internet Link Activity *ExamView:* Pre-AP* Question Bank *Assessment Program:* Parte II, Escribir, p. 102 *Pre-AP* Resource Book:* pp. 72–73

	Student Edition/Teacher's Edition		Ancillaries
	Page #	**Activity**	
Vocabulary	p. 201	Supplemental Pre-AP* Activity	*Go Online:* Self-test *Assessment Program:* Prueba 4B-2, pp. 107–108
Listening	p. 201 p. 212	Supplemental Pre-AP* Activity Supplemental Pre-AP* Activity	*Video Program* Chapter 4B *Video Teacher's Guide* Chapter 4B *Writing, Audio & Video Workbook:* Act. 9, p. 83 *Pre-AP* Resource Book:* pp. 72–73
Reading	p. 209	Act. 20	*Reading and Writing for Success:* Test 8, pp. 22–24 *MindPoint Quiz Show* *TPR Stories:* A Jorge le gusta besar, pp. 60–61 *Realidades* para hispanohablantes: Lectura 1, p. 162 *Realidades* para hispanohablantes: Lectura 2, p. 164 *Pre-AP* Resource Book:* pp. 72–73
Speaking	p. 201 p. 203 p. 209	Supplemental Pre-AP* Activity Supplemental Pre-AP* Activity Act. 20	*TPR Stories:* Personalized Mini-situations, pp. 56–59 *Teacher's Resource Book, Para empezar–Tema 4:* Communicative Activity 4B-1, pp. 216–217 *Teacher's Resource Book, Para empezar–Tema 4:* Situation cards, p. 220 *Assessment Program:* Parte II, Hablar, p. 113 *Pre-AP* Resource Book:* p. 73
Writing	p. 206 p. 209 p. 212 p. 215	Differentiated Instruction: Advanced Learners/Pre-AP* Act. 20 Supplemental Pre-AP* Activity Presentación escrita	*Writing, Audio & Video Workbook:* Act. 13, p. 87 *Realidades* para hispanohablantes: Act. N, p. 163 *Realidades* para hispanohablantes: Presentación escrita, p. 167 *Reading and Writing for Success:* Test 8, pp. 22–24 *Go Online:* Internet Link Activity *ExamView:* Pre-AP* Question Bank *Assessment Program:* Parte II, Escribir, p. 113 *Pre-AP* Resource Book:* pp. 72–73

Teacher Activity 1
Listening Comprehension

Before watching the *Realidades* video for *Capítulo* 4B, play the video with the TV screen covered. Use the audio portion to engage students in the Dictogloss activity on p. 14. Once students have completed the steps to the Dictogloss activity, uncover the TV screen, watch the video, then have students complete the video activities on pp. 79-80 of the *Realidades* Writing, Audio & Video Workbook.

Teacher Activity 2
Listening Comprehension

Listen to the audio recording for *Examen Cumulativo* I, Listening Exercise B, then answer the following questions. (See the *Realidades* Assessment Program, p. T65.) Variation: By providing students with a printed copy of the related audio script, Student Activity 3 on the next page can become a **reading comprehension** activity, as another option.

1. ¿Quiénes hablan?
    a. Victoria y una amiga
    b. Victoria y su hermana
    c. Victoria y su mamá

2. ¿Por qué va Victoria al centro commercial?
    a. Un amigo celebra su cumpleaños.
    b. Tiene que ir a la iglesia.
    c. Le gustaría ir a la piscina.

3. ¿Por cuánto tiempo va a la iglesia?
    a. dos horas
    b. seis horas
    c. unos minutos

Teacher Activity 3
Paragraph Completion

Make a transparency of the following passages. Have students complete the blanks with a word in Spanish that is logical and grammatically correct. They must spell and accent the word correctly.

A. En este momento, estoy en (1) _____ clase de historia con mi amigo

(2) _____ simpático. Él es (3) _____ Panamá. A él (4) _____

encanta hablar (5) _____ la historia. (6) _____ viernes vamos

(7) _____ gimnasio (8) _____ levantar pesas. Después de

(9) _____ al gimnasio, quiero ir (10) _____ casa porque voy a

(11) _____ bien cansado.

B. Mi amiga Elena trabaja (1) _____ un restaurante chino (2) _____

sábados. Trabaja a (3) _____ cuatro y media de la tarde. (4) _____ fin de

semana Elena (5) _____ trabaja (6) _____ está enferma. Tengo

(7) _____ visitar a Elena (8) _____ prepararle sopa de pollo.

Student Activity 1
Informal Speaking

Work with a partner to write complete-sentence answers to the following questions. Be sure to verify the correctness of your answers. Then, use the questions (and answers) to play *Preguntas rápidas* (see p. 38) or to prepare for *One minute of questions* (For Levels 1 and 2) (see p. 38).

1. ¿Cuándo estás cansado(a)?

   _____

2. ¿Adónde vas los domingos?

   _____

3. ¿A qué deporte juegas?

   _____

4. ¿Qué quieres comer después de ver una película?

   _____

5. ¿De dónde eres?

   _____

6. ¿Con quién vas al parque?

   _____

7. ¿Cuántas carpetas tienes?

   _____

8. ¿Por qué tienes que estudiar mucho?

   _____

9. ¿Sabes jugar al vóleibol?

   _____

10. ¿Te gustaría ir de pesca conmigo?

   _____

11. ¿Qué haces en tu tiempo libre?

   _____

12. ¿Qué vas a hacer mañana por la tarde?

   _____

13. ¿Cuándo empiezan las vacaciones?

   _____

14. ¿A qué hora vas a la escuela?

   _____

15. ¿Cuántas personas hay en tu clase de español?

   _____

16. ¿Cuál clase te gusta más? ¿Por qué?

   _____

	Student Edition/Teacher's Edition		Ancillaries
	Page #	Activity	
Vocabulary	p. 225	Supplemental Pre-AP* Activity	*Go Online:* Self-test
Listening	p. 238	Supplemental Pre-AP* Activity	*Video Program* Chapter 5A *Video Teacher's Guide* Chapter 5A *Writing, Audio & Video Workbook:* Act. 9, p. 94 *Pre-AP* Resource Book:* p. 76
Reading			*MindPoint Quiz Show* *TPR Stories:* La fiesta de sorpresa, p. 67 *Realidades* para hispanohablantes: Lectura 1, p. 182 *Realidades* para hispanohablantes: Lectura 2, p. 184 *Pre-AP* Resource Book:* pp. 76–77
Speaking	p. 233 p. 237 p. 241	Supplemental Pre-AP* Activity Act. 25 Presentación oral	*TPR Stories:* Personalized Mini-situations, pp. 64–66 *Realidades* para hispanohablantes: Presentación oral, p. 187 *Teacher's Resource Book, Temas 5–9:* Situation cards, p. 16 *Assessment Program:* Parte II, Hablar, p. 129 *Pre-AP* Resource Book:* p. 76
Writing	p. 225 p. 232 p. 237	Supplemental Pre-AP* Activity Differentiated Instruction: Advanced Learners/Pre-AP* Act. 25	*Writing, Audio & Video Workbook:* Act. 13, p. 98 *Reading and Writing for Success:* Test 9, pp. 25–28 *Realidades* para hispanohablantes: Act. L, p. 183 *Realidades* para hispanohablantes: Act. O, p. 185 *Go Online:* Internet Link Activity *ExamView:* Pre-AP* Question Bank *Assessment Program:* Parte II, Escribir, p. 128 *Pre-AP* Resource Book:* pp. 76–77

	Student Edition/Teacher's Edition		Ancillaries
	Page #	Activity	
Vocabulary	p. 251	Supplemental Pre-AP* Activity	*Go Online:* Self-test
Listening	p. 251 p. 260 p. 278	Supplemental Pre-AP* Activity Supplemental Pre-AP* Activity Supplemental Pre-AP* Activity	*Video Program* Chapter 5B *Video Teacher's Guide* Chapter 5B *Writing, Audio & Video Workbook:* Act. 8, p. 103 *Pre-AP* Resource Book:* p. 76
Reading			*Reading and Writing for Success:* Test 10, pp. 29–31 *MindPoint Quiz Show* *TPR Stories:* El jugo de aguacate, p. 75 *Realidades* para hispanohablantes: Lectura 1, p. 202 *Realidades* para hispanohablantes: Lectura 2, p. 204 *Pre-AP* Resource Book:* pp. 76–77
Speaking	p. 261 p. 262	Act. 20 Supplemental Pre-AP* Activity	*TPR Stories:* Personalized Mini-situations, pp. 71–74 *Lecturas* para hispanohablantes: Conversando con un campeón de surfing, pp. 52–54 *Teacher's Resource Book, Temas 5–9:* Situation cards, p. 42 *Assessment Program:* Parte II, Hablar, p. 142 *Pre-AP* Resource Book:* p. 76
Writing	p. 256 p. 260 p. 261 p. 262	Differentiated Instruction: Advanced Learners/Pre-AP* Supplemental Pre-AP* Activity Act. 20 Supplemental Pre-AP* Activity	*Writing, Audio & Video Workbook:* Act. 10, p. 105 *Realidades* para hispanohablantes: Act. N, p. 203 *Realidades* para hispanohablantes: Act. O, p. 205 *Realidades* para hispanohablantes: Presentación escrita, p. 207 *Reading and Writing for Success:* Test 10, pp. 29–31 *Go Online:* Internet Link Activity *ExamView:* Pre-AP* Question Bank *Assessment Program:* Parte II, Escribir, p. 142 *Pre-AP* Resource Book:* pp. 76–77

Teacher Activity 1
Informal Speaking—Simulated Conversation

1. Based on the *Hablar* activity p. 269 in the *Realidades* Student Textbook, allow students to read the given scenario, and then prepare (by writing down key words), how they would fill in the following conversation. Teachers may wish to ask the class to brainstorm together about some possible responses to the waiter's questions, but ultimately, the preparation should be accomplished individually. The amount of preparation time can vary, but should not be longer than three or four minutes.

Conversation:

CAMARERO: Buenas noches. ¿A qué hora tiene Ud. reservación?

ESTUDIANTE: (20-30 second response)

CAMARERO: ¿Hay otros que cenan con Ud. esta noche?

ESTUDIANTE: (20-30 second response)

CAMARERO: ¿Cómo es su tío?

ESTUDIANTE: (20-30 second response)

CAMARERO: ¿Y su tía?

ESTUDIANTE: (20-30 second response)

CAMARERO: Bueno, le aviso cuando lleguen.

2. Students are then allowed to record their conversations. (See Recording and Evaluating on p. 40.) The teacher can be the voice of the waiter, allowing no more than 30 seconds for each response from the students.

3. In groups of three or four, students should listen to each recording and discuss the content and quality using the scoring guidelines on p. 45.

Teacher Activity 2
Informal Writing

Complete the *Escribir* activity on p. 245 of the *Realidades* Student Textbook. The teacher should make three photocopies of each student's written work. Place students in groups of four. Distribute copies of the scoring guidelines found on p. 45. (Since this is a writing task, the *Fluency* category on the bottom row can be ignored at this time.) Distribute the copies of the students' work within each group. Have each student read his or her writing aloud to the group, one piece at a time, and discuss the content and quality of each writing piece using the scoring guidelines. Each group may select one sample to share with the whole class.

Student Activity 1
Paragraph Completion

Directions: Read the following passage, completing the blanks with the form of the word in parenthesis that is grammatically correct. You must spell and accent the word correctly.

Para (1) _____ (mi) cumpleaños, siempre (2) _____ (ir) con mi familia a mi restaurante (3) _____ (favorito). A papá le encanta (4) _____ (pedir) arroz con pollo. Mamá (5) _____ (pedir) camarones. Este año, como (6) _____ (cumplir) los dieciséis años, vamos a (7) _____ (celebrar) en casa. Los invitados (8) _____ (venir) a las siete. Deseo (9) _____ (mucho) regalos— especialmente una bicicleta (10) _____ (nuevo).

Student Activity 2
Paragraph Completion

Directions: Read the following passage, completing the blanks with a word in Spanish that is logical and grammatically correct. You must spell and accent the word correctly.

Querida Emilia,

Gracias (1) _____ escribirme. ¿Cuándo (2) _____ a visitarme aquí en Houston? Sabes (3) _____ mi otro primo Alberto (4) _____ con mi familia este semestre (5) _____ sus padres trabajan en Costa Rica. Alberto (6) _____ muy deportista. A Alberto, (7) _____ gusta jugar fútbol todas las tardes después (8) _____ las clases con (9) _____ amigos. Me encanta verlo jugar, y (10) _____ fotos de sus partidos para el periódico de la escuela. Y tú, ¿(11) _____ haces por la tarde?

Hasta pronto.

Tu prima,

Victória

	Student Edition/Teacher's Edition		Ancillaries
	Page #	**Activity**	
Vocabulary	p. 275	Supplemental Pre-AP* Activity	*Go Online:* Self-test
Listening	p. 275	Supplemental Pre-AP* Activity	*Video Program* Chapter 6A
	p. 278	Supplemental Pre-AP* Activity	*Video Teacher's Guide* Chapter 6A
			Pre-AP* Resource Book: pp. 80–81
Reading			*Reading and Writing for Success:* Test 24, pp. 72–74
			MindPoint Quiz Show
			TPR Stories: Buffy tiene sueño, p. 83
			Realidades para hispanohablantes: Lectura 1, p. 222
			Realidades para hispanohablantes: Lectura 2, p. 224
			Pre-AP* Resource Book: pp. 80–81
Speaking	p. 275	Supplemental Pre-AP* Activity	*TPR Stories:* Personalized Mini-situations, pp. 79–82
	p. 287	Act. 28	*Teacher's Resource Book, Temas 5–9:* Situation cards, p. 72
	p. 288	Supplemental Pre-AP* Activity	*Realidades* para hispanohablantes: Presentación oral, p. 227
	p. 291	Presentación oral	*Assessment Program:* Parte II, Hablar, p. 157
			Pre-AP* Resource Book: p. 80
Writing	p. 278	Supplemental Pre-AP* Activity	*Writing, Audio & Video Workbook:* Act. 13, p. 119
	p. 286	Differentiated Instruction: Advanced Learners/Pre-AP*	*Realidades* para hispanohablantes: Act. N, p. 223
			Reading and Writing for Success: Test 11, pp. 32–34
	p. 287	Act. 28	*Go Online:* Internet Link Activity
	p. 288	Supplemental Pre-AP* Activity	*ExamView:* Pre-AP* Question Bank
			Assessment Program: Parte II, Escribir, p. 157
			Pre-AP* Resource Book: pp. 80–81

	Student Edition/Teacher's Edition		Ancillaries
	Page #	**Activity**	
Vocabulary	p. 301	Supplemental Pre-AP* Activity	*Go Online:* Self-test
Listening	p. 301 p. 311	Supplemental Pre-AP* Activity Supplemental Pre-AP* Activity	*Video Program* Chapter 6B *Video Teacher's Guide* Chapter 6B *Writing, Audio & Video Workbook:* Act. 5, p. 123 *Writing, Audio & Video Workbook:* Act. 9, p. 125 *Pre-AP* Resource Book:* pp. 80–81
Reading			*Realidades* para hispanohablantes: Lectura 1, p. 242 *Realidades* para hispanohablantes: Lectura 2, p. 244 *Reading and Writing for Success:* Test 12, pp. 35–37 *MindPoint Quiz Show* *TPR Stories:* Bellasucia, p. 90 *Pre-AP* Resource Book:* pp. 80–81

Speaking	p. 301
	
	p. 304
	
	p. 309
	p. 312
		Supplemental Pre-AP* Activity
		Differentiated Instruction:
		  Advanced Learners/Pre-AP*
		Act. 20
		Supplemental Pre-AP* Activity
			TPR Stories: Personalized Mini-situations, pp. 86–89
			Teacher's Resource Book, Temas 5–9:
			  Communicative Activity 6B-1, pp. 94–95
			Teacher's Resource Book, Temas 5–9: Situation
			  cards, p. 98
			Assessment Program: Parte II, Hablar, p. 171
			Pre-AP* Resource Book: p. 80

Writing	p. 309
	p. 311
	p. 315
		Act. 20
		Supplemental Pre-AP* Activity
		Presentación escrita
			Writing, Audio & Video Workbook: Act. 13, p. 129
			Reading and Writing for Success: Test 12,
			  pp. 35–37
			Realidades para hispanohablantes: Act. N, p. 243
			Realidades para hispanohablantes: Presentación
			  escrita, p. 247
			Go Online: Internet Link Activity
			ExamView: Pre-AP* Question Bank
			Assessment Program: Parte II, Escribir p. 171
			Pre-AP* Resource Book: pp. 80–81

Teacher Activity 1
Listening Comprehension

The teacher should read aloud *El desastre en mi dormitorio* from p. 288 of the *Realidades* Student Textbook to engage students in the Dictogloss activity on p.14. Once students have completed the steps to the Dictogloss activity, have them read aloud to a partner the reply from Magdalena and follow-up with the *¿Comprendes?* and *Y tú, ¿qué dices?* activities found on p. 289 of the *Realidades* Student Textbook.

Teacher Activity 2
Evaluating with Rubrics

The teacher should make three photocopies of each student's written work for Student Activities 3 and 4 on the next page. Place students in groups of four. Distribute copies of the scoring guidelines found on p. 45. (Since this is a writing task, the *Fluency* category on the bottom row can be ignored at this time.) Distribute the copies of the students' work within each group. Have each student read his or her writing aloud to the group, one piece at a time, and discuss the content and quality of each writing piece using the scoring guidelines. Each group may select one sample to share with the whole class.

Teacher Activity 3
Paragraph Completion

Make a transparency of the following passage. Have students, in pairs, complete the blanks with a word in Spanish that is logical and grammatically correct. They must spell and accent the word correctly.

(De una mamá para su hija)

Marta, ¡(1) _____ la mesa y arregla tu cuarto antes de (2) _____ seis!

Y prepara la sopa de tomate. Está más rica (3) _____ la de verduras. Los

Martinez (4) _____ viajando desde Chicago para pasar el fin de semana con

nosotros. Yo (5) _____ trabajando todavía, pero pienso regresar pronto. No sé

(6) _____ el baño (7) _____ limpio o no. ¿Quieres (8) _____lo

para mí?

Hasta pronto.

Un beso,

Mamá

Student Activity 1
Listening Comprehension

After listening to the Video for *Capítulo* 6B (see *Realidades* Teacher's Resource Book, p. 64), have students select the most appropriate answer to the following:

1. ¿Por qué está mamá en el cuarto de Ignacio?
   a. Es la hora de la escuela.
   b. Necesita un disco compacto.
   c. Pone en orden el cuarto.

2. ¿Por qué está descontento Ignacio?
   a. Siempre duerme bien.
   b. Tiene muchas cosas encima de la cama.
   c. No sabe donde están sus cosas.

3. ¿Cuál es la mejor solución del problema, según mamá?
   a. Cerrar la puerta para no ver todas las cosas.
   b. Organizar el cuarto.
   c. Poner los libros y las revistas en el estante.

Student Activity 2
Informal Writing

Imagine that you have just moved to a different state. Write an e-mail to your best friend at your former school describing to him or her your new house. Be sure to describe the rooms, the furniture, the colors, etc. Then, compare your new house to your old house.

Student Activity 3
Formal Writing

Consider the two different houses on p. 168 of the *Realidades* Assessment Program and on p. 124 of the *Realidades* Writing, Audio & Video Workbook. Imagine that you are a real estate agent needing to write an article to compare the two houses and the advantages of each, in order to attract potential buyers. Write your article of at least 100 words with a thorough description of each house. Consider the selling points of each property.

	Student Edition/Teacher's Edition		Ancillaries
	Page #	**Activity**	
Vocabulary	p. 325	Supplemental Pre-AP* Activity	*Go Online:* Self-test *Assessment Program:* Prueba 7A-2, pp. 177–78
Listening			*Video Program* Chapter 7A *Video Teacher's Guide* Chapter 7A *Writing, Audio & Video Workbook:* Act. 7, p. 134 *Writing, Audio & Video Workbook:* Act. 9, p. 135 *Pre-AP* Resource Book:* p. 84
Reading			*MindPoint Quiz Show* *TPR Stories:* El viaje de Rosa, p. 99 *Realidades* para hispanohablantes: Lectura 1, p. 262 *Realidades* para hispanohablantes: Lectura 2, p. 264 *Pre-AP* Resource Book:* pp. 84–85

Speaking	p. 325
	 p. 330
	
	 p. 333
	 p. 336
	 p. 339
		Supplemental Pre-AP* Activity
		 Differentiated Instruction:
		   Advanced Learners/Pre-AP*
		 Act. 19
		 Supplemental Pre-AP* Activity
		 Presentación oral
			TPR Stories: Personalized Mini-situations, pp. 95–98
			 Teacher's Resource Book, Temas 5–9:
			   Communicative Activity 7A-2, pp. 126–127
			 Teacher's Resource Book, Temas 5–9: Situation
			   cards, p. 128
			 Realidades para hispanohablantes: Presentación
			   oral, p. 267
			 Assessment Program: Parte II, Hablar, p. 184
			 Pre-AP* Resource Book: pp. 84–85

Writing	p. 325 p. 330 p. 333 p. 336	Supplemental Pre-AP* Activity Differentiated Instruction: Advanced Learners/Pre-AP* Act. 19 Supplemental Pre-AP* Activity	*Writing, Audio & Video Workbook:* Act. 13, p. 139 *Reading and Writing for Success:* Test 13, pp. 38–40 *Go Online:* Internet Link Activity *ExamView:* Pre-AP* Question Bank *Assessment Program:* Parte II, Escribir, p. 183 *Pre-AP* Resource Book:* pp. 84–85

	Student Edition/Teacher's Edition		Ancillaries
	Page #	**Activity**	
Vocabulary	p. 349	Supplementary Pre-AP* Activity	*Go Online:* Self-test
Listening	p. 365	Supplementary Pre-AP* Activity	*Video Program* Chapter 7B *Video Teacher's Guide* Chapter 7B *Writing, Audio & Video Workbook:* Act. 9, p. 145 *Pre-AP* Resource Book:* p. 84
Reading			*Reading and Writing for Success:* Test 14, pp. 41–43 *MindPoint Quiz Show* *TPR Stories:* El regalo de Pepita, p. 105 *Realidades* para hispanohablantes: Lectura 1, p. 282 *Realidades* para hispanohablantes: Lectura 2, p. 284 *Pre-AP* Resource Book:* pp. 84–85
Speaking	p. 349 p. 353 p. 355	Supplementary Pre-AP* Activity Supplementary Pre-AP* Activity Act. 14	*TPR Stories:* Personalized Mini-situations, pp. 101–104 *Teacher's Resource Book, Temas 5–9:* Communicative Activity 7B-2, pp. 152–153 *Teacher's Resource Book, Temas 5–9:* Situation cards, p. 154 *Assessment Program:* Parte II, Hablar, p. 198 *Pre-AP* Resource Book:* pp. 84–85
Writing	p. 355 p. 358 p. 367	Act. 14 Differentiated Instruction: Advanced Learners/Pre-AP* Presentación escrita	*Writing, Audio & Video Workbook:* Act. 12, pp. 148–149 *Realidades* para hispanohablantes: Act. L, p. 283 *Realidades* para hispanohablantes: Act. N, p. 285 *Realidades* para hispanohablantes: Presentación escrita, p. 287 *Reading and Writing for Success:* Test 14, pp. 41–43 *Go Online:* Internet Link Activity *ExamView:* Pre-AP* Question Bank *Assessment Program:* Parte II, Escribir, p. 197 *Pre-AP* Resource Book:* pp. 84–85

Teacher Activity 1
Reading Comprehension

Provide students with the printed Video Script 7B on p. 147 of the **Realidades** Teacher's Resource Book. Have students read the script out loud with a partner, each taking one of the roles. After the reading, ask the partners to answer the questions on pp. 140-141 of the **Realidades** Writing, Audio & Video Workbook. Lastly, students should view the video.

Teacher Activity 2
Listening Comprehension

As an alternative to the above activity, play the **Realidades** Video to accompany *Tema* 7B with the TV screen covered. Students should have the **Realidades** Writing, Audio & Video workbook open to p. 140. The first time they listen, ask students to complete *Actividad* 2, p. 140 of the **Realidades** Writing, Audio & Video Workbook. Rewind the video and play it again, asking students to answer the questions in *Actividad* 3, p. 141 of the **Realidades** Writing, Audio & Video Workbook. After listening, they may confer with a partner to consider the correct answer choices. Finally, rewind the video and allow students to view the scene as a means to verify their responses to the two activities.

Teacher Activity 3
Informal Speaking—Simulated Conversation

Directions for Student Activity 1, p. 85

1. Teachers may wish to ask the class to brainstorm together about some possible responses, but ultimately, the preparation should be accomplished individually. The amount of preparation time can vary, but should not be longer than three or four minutes.

2. Students are then allowed to record their conversations. (See Recording and Evaluating on p. 40.) The teacher can be the voice of Mamá, allowing no more than 30 seconds for each response from the students.

3. In groups of three or four, students should listen to each recording and discuss the content and quality using the scoring guidelines on p. 45.

Student Activity 1
Informal Speaking—Simulated Conversation

Scenario: You are back-to-school shopping in a department store with your mom.

Read the conversation framework below, and then prepare (by writing down key words), how you would fill in the following conversation with rich and full responses to the questions. (The goal is to provide as much speech as possible in the time provided, rather than to settle on a basic but short response that is appropriate.)

Conversation:

MAMÁ: ¿Qué artículos de ropa necesitas más este año?

ESTUDIANTE: (20-30 second response)

MAMÁ: ¿No quieres buscar zapatos?

ESTUDIANTE: (20-30 second response)

MAMÁ: Pues, ¿qué te parece esta camisa?

ESTUDIANTE: (20-30 second response)

MAMÁ: ¿Cuánto cuesta cada artículo?

ESTUDIANTE: (20-30 second response)

MAMÁ: Bueno, pero prefiero buscar mejores precios.

Student Activity 2
Paragraph Completion

Directions: Read the following passage, completing the blanks with the form of the word in parenthesis that is grammatically correct. You must spell and accent the word correctly.

El año pasado, mis abuelos me (1) _____ (regalar) dinero para la Navidad. Con

(2) _____ (ese) dinero, (3) _____ (comprar) un par de zapatos

(4) _____ (negro). (5) _____ (pagar) veinte y cinco dólares por ellos.

El problema es que los zapatos me (6) _____ (quedar) mal y por eso, no me

(7) _____ (gustar). Creo que voy a (8) _____los (vender) en E-Bay, y con el

dinero que recibo, (9) _____ (poder) comprarme (10) _____ (otro) zapatos.

Desgraciadamente, (11) _____ (este) zapatos no me sirven para nada.

	Student Edition/Teacher's Edition		Ancillaries
	Page #	**Activity**	
Vocabulary	p. 377	Supplemental Pre-AP* Activity	*Go Online:* Self-test
Listening			*Video Program* Chapter 8A *Video Teacher's Guide* Chapter 8A *Writing, Audio & Video Workbook:* Act. 6, p. 153 *Writing, Audio & Video Workbook:* Act. 9, p. 155 *Pre-AP* Resource Book:* pp. 88–89
Reading			*MindPoint Quiz Show* *TPR Stories:* Los amigos, la cena y el campo, p. 113 *Realidades* para hispanohablantes: Lectura 1, p. 302 *Realidades* para hispanohablantes: Lectura 2, p. 304 *Pre-AP* Resource Book:* pp. 88–89

Speaking	p. 377
	p. 379
	p. 386
	p. 390
	p. 393
		Supplementary Pre-AP* Activity
		Supplementary Pre-AP* Activity
		Act. 18
		Supplementary Pre-AP* Activity
		Presentación oral
			TPR Stories: Personalized Mini-situations,
			  pp. 109–112
			Teacher's Resource Book, Temas 5–9: Situation
			  cards, p. 182
			Realidades para hispanohablantes: Presentación
			  oral, p. 307
			Assessment Program: Parte II, Hablar, p. 211
			Pre-AP* Resource Book: p. 88

Writing	p. 379
	p. 384
	
	p. 386
	p. 390
		Supplementary Pre-AP* Activity
		Differentiated Instruction:
		  Advanced Learners/Pre-AP*
		Act. 18
		Supplementary Pre-AP* Activity
			Writing, Audio & Video Workbook: Act. 12,
			  pp. 158–159
			Writing, Audio & Video Workbook: Act. 13, p. 159
			Reading and Writing for Success: Test 15, pp. 44–47
			Realidades para hispanohablantes: Act. L, p. 303
			Go Online: Internet Link Activity
			ExamView: Pre-AP* Question Bank
			Assessment Program: Parte II, Escribir, p. 211
			Pre-AP* Resource Book: pp. 88–89

	Student Edition/Teacher's Edition		Ancillaries
	Page #	Activity	
Vocabulary	p. 403	Supplementary Pre-AP* Activity	*Go Online:* Self-test
Listening	p. 416	Supplementary Pre-AP* Activity	*Video Program* Chapter 8B
			Video Teacher's Guide Chapter 8B
			Writing, Audio & Video Workbook: Act. 7, p. 164
			Pre-AP* Resource Book: pp. 88–89
Reading			*Reading and Writing for Success:* Test 16, pp. 48–50
			Teacher's Resource Book, Temas 5–9: Communicative Activity 8B-2, pp. 210–211
			Realidades para hispanohablantes: Lectura 1, p. 322
			Realidades para hispanohablantes: Lectura 2, p. 324
			MindPoint Quiz Show
			TPR Stories: Cómo ayudar el planeta, p. 120
			Pre-AP* Resource Book: pp. 88–89
Speaking	p. 403	Supplementary Pre-AP* Activity	*TPR Stories:* Personalized Mini-situations, pp. 116–119
	p. 409	Act. 11	*Teacher's Resource Book, Temas 5–9:* Communicative Activity 8B-2, pp. 204–205
	p. 414	Supplementary Pre-AP* Activity	*Teacher's Resource Book, Temas 5–9:* Situation cards, p. 206
	p. 416	Supplementary Pre-AP* Activity	*Assessment Program:* Parte II, Hablar, p. 225
			Pre-AP* Resource Book: p. 88
Writing	p. 403	Supplementary Pre-AP* Activity	*Writing, Audio & Video Workbook:* Act. 13, p. 169
	p. 408	Differentiated Instruction: Advanced Learners/Pre-AP*	*Realidades* para hispanohablantes: Presentación escrita, p. 327
	p. 409	Act. 11	*Reading and Writing for Success:* Test 15, pp. 48–50
	p. 416	Supplementary Pre-AP* Activity	*Go Online:* Internet Link Activity
	p. 419	Presentación escrita	*ExamView:* Pre-AP* Question Bank
			Assessment Program: Parte II, Escribir, p. 225
			Pre-AP* Resource Book: pp. 88–89

Teacher Activity 1
Evaluating with Rubrics

The teacher should make three photocopies of each student's written work for Student Activity 1 on the next page. Place students in groups of four. Distribute copies of the scoring guidelines found on p. 45. (Since this is a writing task, the *Fluency* category on the bottom row can be ignored at this time.) Distribute the copies of the students' work within each group. Have each student read his or her writing aloud to the group, one piece at a time, and discuss the content and quality of each writing piece using the scoring guidelines. Each group may select one sample to share with the whole class.

Teacher Activity 2
Formal Writing

1. Have students read *Hábitat para la Humanidad Internacional,* pp. 416-417 in the **Realidades** Student Textbook.

2. Have students watch the Video for *Capítulo* 8B. (See **Realidades** Teacher's Resource Book, p. 199.)

3. Ask students to write a composition of 100 words (minimum) in which they describe the benefits of different types of community service. They should cite the reading and the video using specific examples from each.

Student Activity 1
Informal Writing

Imagine that you just came home from working on a community volunteer project. E-mail a friend and tell him or her what you did, whom you helped, and why you got involved. Encourage him or her to engage in community service as well.

Student Activity 2
Reading Comprehension

Read *Las tortugas tinglar* on p. 415 of the *Realidades* Student Textbook. Then, respond to the following questions:

1. ¿Por qué es impresionante esta tortuga?
   a. Pone sus huevos entre febrero y julio.
   b. Vive en aguas frías cerca del Caribe.
   c. Es una de las tortugas más grandes del mundo.

2. ¿Por qué está en peligro de extinción la tortuga tinglar?
   a. Por falta de protección para los huevos.
   b. Por los voluntarios.
   c. Por los binoculares y las linternas.

3. ¿Cuánto tiempo pasan los huevos en el nido artificial?
   a. 28 horas
   b. dos meses
   c. el mes de febrero

Student Activity 3
Paragraph Completion

Directions: Read the following passage, completing the blanks with a word in Spanish that is logical and grammatically correct. You must spell and accent the word correctly.

El verano pasado, mi familia y yo (1) _____ a la playa cerca de Miami. Papá

(2) _____ mucho dinero por los billetes (3) _____ avión. Durante las

vacaciones, visitamos (4) _____ nuestros abuelos maternos quienes viven en la

Florida. Papí (5) _____ sesenta y tres años y mamí sesenta. (6) _____

jóvenes. Ellos trabajan como voluntarios (7) _____ la Cruz Roja (8) _____

día por semana. Mi hermano y yo los acompañamos al hospital de la comunidad

(9) _____ les dimos juguetes (10) _____ los niños pobres en el hospital.

	Student Edition/Teacher's Edition		Ancillaries
	Page #	Activity	
Vocabulary	p. 429 p. 439	Supplementary Pre-AP* Activity Supplementary Pre-AP* Activity	*Go Online:* Self-test *Assessment Program:* Prueba 9A-2, pp. 231–232
Listening	p. 432 p. 436 p. 440	Supplementary Pre-AP* Activity Act. 14 Supplementary Pre-AP* Activity	*Video Program* Chapter 4B *Video Teacher's Guide* Chapter 4B *Writing, Audio & Video Workbook:* Act. 9, p. 175 *Pre-AP* Resource Book:* p. 92
Reading	p. 440	Supplementary Pre-AP* Activity	*MindPoint Quiz Show* *TPR Stories:* ¡Demasiada tele!, p. 127 *Realidades* para hispanohablantes: Lectura 1, p. 342 *Realidades* para hispanohablantes: Lectura 2, p. 344 *Pre-AP* Resource Book:* pp. 92–93

Speaking	p. 429
	p. 443
		Supplementary Pre-AP* Activity
		Presentación oral
			TPR Stories: Personalized Mini-situations,
			  pp. 123–126
			Realidades para hispanohablantes: Presentación
			  oral, p. 347
			Teacher's Resource Book, Temas 5–9:
			  Communicative Activity 9A-2, pp. 232–233
			Teacher's Resource Book, Temas 5–9: Situation
			  cards, p. 234
			Assessment Program: Parte II, Hablar, p. 238
			Pre-AP* Resource Book: p. 92

Writing	p. 429 p. 432 p. 436 p. 439 p. 440	Supplementary Pre-AP* Activity Supplementary Pre-AP* Activity Act. 14 Supplementary Pre-AP* Activity Supplementary Pre-AP* Activity	*Writing, Audio & Video Workbook:* Act. 13, p. 179 *Reading and Writing for Success:* Test 17, pp. 51–53 *Realidades* para hispanohablantes: Act. M, p. 343 *Realidades* para hispanohablantes: Act. O, p. 345 *Go Online:* Internet Link Activity *ExamView:* Pre-AP* Question Bank *Assessment Program:* Parte II, Escribir, p. 237 *Pre-AP* Resource Book:* pp. 92–93

	Student Edition/Teacher's Edition		Ancillaries
	Page #	Activity	
Vocabulary	p. 453	Supplementary Pre-AP* Activity	*Go Online:* Self-test Assessment Program: Prueba 9B-2, pp. 243–244
Listening	p. 460	Differentiated Instruction: Advanced Learners/Pre-AP*	*Video Program* Chapter 9B *Video Teacher's Guide* Chapter 9B *Writing, Audio & Video Workbook:* Act. 9, p. 184 *Pre-AP* Resource Book:* p. 92
	p. 462	Supplemental Pre-AP* Activity	
	p. 465	Differentiated Instruction: Advanced Learners/Pre-AP*	
Reading	p. 454	Act. 4	*Reading and Writing for Success:* Test 18, pp. 54–56 *MindPoint Quiz Show* *TPR Stories:* El regalo de los Reyes Magos, p. 130 *Realidades* para hispanohablantes: Lectura 1, p. 362 *Realidades* para hispanohablantes: Lectura 2, p. 364 *Pre-AP* Resource Book:* pp. 92–93
Speaking	p. 453	Supplementary Pre-AP* Activity	*Teacher's Resource Book, Temas 5–9:* Communicative Activity 9B-1, pp. 254–255 *Teacher's Resource Book, Temas 5–9:* Situation cards, p. 258 *Assessment Program:* Parte II, Hablar, p. 250 *Pre-AP* Resource Book:* p. 92
	p. 454	Act. 4	
	p. 460	Differentiated Instruction: Advanced Learners/Pre-AP*	
	p. 465	Supplemental Pre-AP* Activity	
Writing	p. 460	Differentiated Instruction: Advanced Learners/Pre-AP*	*Writing, Audio & Video Workbook:* Act. 13, p. 188 *Reading and Writing for Success:* Test 18, pp. 54–56 *Realidades* para hispanohablantes: Act. O, p. 363 *Realidades* para hispanohablantes: Presentación escrita, p. 367 *Go Online:* Internet Link Activity *ExamView:* Pre-AP* Question Bank *Assessment Program:* Parte II, Escribir, p. 250 *Pre-AP* Resource Book:* pp. 92–93
	p. 462	Supplemental Pre-AP* Activity	
	p. 465	Supplemental Pre-AP* Activity	
	p. 467	Presentación escrita	

Teacher Activity 1
Listening Comprehension

Use the first portion of the reading *La invasión del ciberspanglish*, p. 464 of the **Realidades** Student Textbook, to engage students in the Dictogloss activity on p. 14. (Read aloud the first two paragraphs on p. 464, not the entire reading.) Once students have completed the steps to the Dictogloss activity, have them open their texts to p. 464, read the entire passage aloud with a partner, then work as a class to answer the *¿Comprendes?* questions.

Teacher Activity 2
Formal Oral Presentation

1. Have students watch the video for *Capítulo* 9B. (See **Realidades** Teacher's Resource Book, p. 251.)

2. Have students read *A sus teclados, listos a navegar* on p. 456 of the **Realidades** Student Textbook.

3. Next, have students prepare a one-minute talk about the pros and cons of communicating via traditional methods (telephone, mail) vs. cyber methods. The amount of preparation time can vary, but should not be longer than three or four minutes. Students should be encouraged to make an outline of the presentation rather than try to write it out word for word. They should try to provide examples from the text and video sources as part of their argument.

4. Students are then allowed one minute to record their presentations, or they may make their presentations to a group of three or four students.

5. In groups of three or four, students should listen to each recording (or hear each presentation) and discuss the content and quality using the scoring guidelines on p. 45.

Teacher Activity 3
Evaluating with Rubrics

The teacher should make three photocopies of each student's written work for Student Activity 3 on the next page. Place students in groups of four. Distribute copies of the scoring guidelines found on p. 45. (Since this is a writing task, the *Fluency* category on the bottom row can be ignored at this time.) Distribute the copies of the students' work within each group. Have each student read his or her writing aloud to the group, one piece at a time, and discuss the content and quality of each writing piece using the scoring guidelines. Each group may select one sample to share with the whole class.

Student Activity 1
Paragraph Completion

Directions: Read the following passage, completing the blanks with a word in Spanish that is logical and grammatically correct. You must spell and accent the word correctly.

Muchos mayors tienen miedo (1) _____ navegar en la Red. Para ellos, comunicarse tan rápidamente es complicado. Saben (2) _____ la Red sirve (3) _____ escribirles a sus familiares (4) _____ recibir fotos digitales, pero la tecnología es algo fuera de su generación. Una pareja, los Señores Romero, acaba (5) _____ tomar un curso para estar en línea. Quieren poder comunicarse (6) _____ sus hijos (7) _____ viven en España actualmente. Para ellos, la Red es (8) _____ manera más rápida y más barata de comunicación a otro país.

Student Activity 2
Paragraph Completion

Directions: Read the following passage, completing the blanks with the form of the word in parenthesis that is grammatically correct. You must spell and accent the word correctly.

Hoy en día, los salones de chat (1) _____ (servir) para muchos jóvenes como (2) _____ (el) manera favorita de comunicación con los amigos. Un salón de chat también (3) _____ (poder) ser una oportunidad de (4) _____ (conocer) a (5) _____ (otro) gente. Algunos padres (6) _____ (creer) que los salones de chat (7) _____ (ser) para buscar información pero no para hablar con amigos. Es verdad que los jóvenes (8) _____ (necesitar) tener cuidado y no (9) _____ (deber) compartir información personal con los desconocidos. Como los salones de chat no (10) _____ (costar) nada, los jóvenes creen que es más barato hablar por la Red que aumentar los gastos celulares.

Student Activity 3
Informal Writing

Write an e-mail to a classmate to tell him or her about a movie you just saw. Give the title, describe the main characters, and tell about the main plot points. Tell your friend if you liked the movie or not, and why. Suggested writing time: 10 minutes.

PRENTICE HALL

Realidades

Level 2
Resource Support

	Student Edition/Teacher's Edition		Ancillaries
	Page #	**Activity**	
Vocabulary	p. 20 p. 23	Supplemental Pre-AP* Activity Act. 6	*Go Online:* Self-test
Listening	pp. 20–21 p. 35	Videohistoria Supplemental Pre-AP* Activity	*Video Program* Chapter 1A *Video Teacher's Guide* Chapter 1A *Writing, Audio & Video Workbook:* Act. 2, pp. 6–7 *Pre-AP* Resource Book:* p. 99
Reading	p. 30 p. 33 p. 35	Act. 18 Act. 23 Supplemental Pre-AP* Activity	*MindPoint Quiz Show* *TPR Stories:* Juanito el ocupado, p. 10 *TPR Stories:* El elefante sin memoria, p. 16 *Realidades* para hispanohablantes: Act. K, p. 20 *Realidades* para hispanohablantes: Lectura 1, pp. 22–23 *Realidades* para hispanohablantes: Lectura 2, pp. 24–25 *Pre-AP* Resource Book:* pp. 98–99
Speaking	p. 20 p. 22 p. 35 p. 37	Supplemental Pre-AP* Activity Differentiated Instruction, Advanced Learners/Pre-AP* Supplemental Pre-AP* Activity Presentación oral	*Assessment Program:* Examen de 1A, Parte II, Hablar, p. 22 *Teacher's Resource Book, Para empezar–Tema 4:* Communicative Activity 1A-1, pp. 30–31 *Teacher's Resource Book, Para empezar–Tema 4:* Situation cards, p. 34 *Realidades* para hispanohablantes: Presentación oral, p. 27 *TPR Stories:* pp. 11–15 *Pre-AP* Resource Book:* pp. 98–99
Writing	p. 30 p. 33 p. 22 p. 30 p. 35	Act. 18 Act. 23 Differentiated Instruction, Advanced Learners/Pre-AP* Supplemental Pre-AP* Activity Supplemental Pre-AP* Activity	*Go Online:* Internet Link Activity *Assessment Program:* Examen 1A, Parte II, Escribir, p. 21 *Writing, Audio & Video Workbook:* Act. 13, p.15 *Reading and Writing for Success:* Test 2, pp. 4–6 *ExamView:* Pre-AP* Question Bank *Realidades* para hispanohablantes: Act. K, p. 20 *Realidades* para hispanohablantes: Lectura 1, pp. 22–23 *Realidades* para hispanohablantes: Lectura 2, pp. 24–25 *Pre-AP* Resource Book:* pp. 98–99

© Pearson Education, Inc. All rights reserved.

	Student Edition/Teacher's Edition		Ancillaries
	Page #	Activity	
Vocabulary	p. 48	Supplemental Pre-AP* Activity	*Realidades* para hispanohablantes: Act. B, p. 19 *Go Online*: Self-test *Realidades* para hispanohablantes: Act. P, p. 42
Listening	pp. 48–49 p. 48	Videohistoria Supplemental Pre-AP* Activity	*Writing, Audio & Video Workbook*: Act. 7, p. 19 *Video Program* Chapter 1B *Video Teacher's Guide* Chapter 1B *Pre-AP* Resource Book*: p. 99
Reading	p. 60 p. 61 p. 64	Act. 22 Act. 23 Perspectivas del mundo hispano	*Lecturas* para hispanohablantes: La casa de los azulejos, pp. 10–12 *Realidades* para hispanohablantes: Lectura, pp. 44–45 *Reading and Writing for Success*: Test 19, pp. 57–59 *Go Online*: Internet Link Activity *MindPoint Quiz Show* *TPR Stories*: La vida en Colorado, p. 18 *TPR Stories*: Tito lo hace todo, p. 22 *Realidades* para hispanohablantes: Act. G, pp. 34–35 *Pre-AP* Resource Book*: pp. 98–99
Speaking	p. 57 p. 58 p. 60	Supplemental Pre-AP* Activity Differentiated Instruction: Advanced Learners/Pre-AP* Act. 22	*Assessment Program*: Examen 1B, Parte II, Hablar, p. 36 *Teacher's Resource Book, Para empezar–Tema 4*: Communicative Activity 1B-1, pp. 54–55 *Teacher's Resource Book, Para empezar–Tema 4*: Situation cards, p. 58 *TPR Stories*: pp. 19–21 *Pre-AP* Resource Book*: pp. 98–99
Writing	p. 58 p. 60 p. 63 p. 65	Differentiated Instruction: Advanced Learners/Pre-AP* Act. 22 Supplemental Pre-AP* Activity Presentación escrita	*Writing, Audio & Video Workbook*: Act .13, p. 24 *Reading and Writing for Success*: Test 19, pp. 57–59 *Realidades* para hispanohablantes: Presentación escrita, p. 47 *Assessment Program*: Examen 1B, Parte II, Escribir, pp. 36, 39 *Go Online*: Internet Link Activity *ExamView*: Pre-AP* Question Bank *Realidades* para hispanohablantes: Act. E, p. 33 *Realidades* para hispanohablantes: Act. G, pp. 34–35 *Realidades* para hispanohablantes: Act. M, p. 40 *Pre-AP* Resource Book*: pp. 98–99

Teacher Activity 1
Formal Writing

Have students read *Un anuncio* on p. 61 of the *Realidades* Student Textbook. Students should then write three paragraphs describing how they believe people can remain in good physical condition throughout life citing activities from the reading as examples to support their ideas. Then make three photocopies of each student's written work. Place students in groups of four. Distribute copies of the scoring guidelines found on p. 45. (Since this is a writing task, the *Fluency* category on the bottom row can be ignored at this time.) Distribute the copies of the students' work within each group. Have each student read his or her writing aloud to the group, one piece at a time, and discuss the content and quality of each writing piece using the scoring guidelines. Each group may select one sample to share with the whole class.

Teacher Activity 2
Paragraph Completion

Make a transparency of the following passage. In pairs, have students complete the blanks with a word in Spanish that is logical and grammatically correct. They must spell and accent the word correctly.

Hace dos semanas (1) _____ mi familia y yo vivimos en esta communidad, (2) _____ todavía no conozco (3) _____ nadie. Asisto (4) _____ la secundaria con mis dos hermanos. (5) _____ reglas de esta escuela no son tan estrictas (6) _____ las de nuestra vieja escuela. Como tengo (7) _____ buena voz, voy (8) _____ tratar (9) _____ cantar en el coro. Así espero conocer (10) _____ muchos amigos nuevos.

Teacher Activity 3
Paragraph Completion

Make a transparency of the following passage. In pairs, have students complete the blanks with the form of the word in parenthesis that is grammatically correct. They must spell and accent the word correctly.

Hola Marta,

Después de clase, (1) _____ (querer) hablarte para (2) _____ (saber) lo que (3) _____ (preferir) hacer este sábado. Por la mañana, tengo que ayudar a mi mamá por dos o tres horas, pero después, (4) _____ (poder) pasar tiempo contigo. Debes (5) _____ (levantarse) temprano para cumplir con tus quehaceres también. ¿Qué (6) _____ (pensar) de jugar a los bolos? También podemos (7) _____ (vestirse) muy bien para asistir a un concierto. ¿Tienes (8) _____ (otro) ideas? Me gustaría ir al centro comercial (9) _____ (tanto) como pasar tiempo (10) _____ (charlar) contigo. No sé el mejor plan. Tenemos que pensarlo. Te escribo más tarde en el salón de chat. Hasta luego.

Tu amiga,

Teresa

Student Activity 1
Informal Speaking

Work with a partner to write complete-sentence answers to the following questions. Be sure to verify the correctness of your answers. Then, use the questions (and answers) to play *Preguntas rápidas* (see p. 38) or to prepare for *One minute of questions* (For Levels 1 and 2) (see p. 38).

1. ¿Qué tienes que hacer para tus clases?
   _____

2. ¿Qué se prohíbe en tu escuela?
   _____

3. ¿Cuáles reglas en la escuela que no te gustan?
   _____

4. ¿Con quiénes almuerzas?
   _____

5. ¿A qué hora empiezan tus clases? ¿Es temprano?
   _____

6. ¿Conoces a alguien en tu clase de matemáticas?
   _____

7. ¿Te dan mucha tarea algunos profesores?
   _____

8. ¿Comprendes lo que te dice tu profesor(a) de español?
   _____

9. ¿Quién es tan amable como tú?
   _____

10. ¿Qué piensas de las artes marciales?
    _____

11. ¿Cuánto tiempo hace que conoces a tu mejor amigo(a)?
    _____

12. ¿Cuánto tiempo hace que asistes a tu escuela?
    _____

13. ¿Cuántas hora pasas por día navegando la Red?
    _____

14. ¿Eres miembro(a) de algún club o equipo?
    _____

15. ¿Qué vas a hacer hoy después de las clases?
    _____

16. ¿Sabes jugar algún deporte? ¿Cuál?
    _____

	Student Edition/Teacher's Edition		Ancillaries
	Page #	**Activity**	
Vocabulary	p. 87	Act. 21	*Assessment Program:* Prueba 2A-2, p. 43–44 *Go Online:* Self-test *Realidades* para hispanohablantes: Act. 2A-1, p. 21
Listening	pp. 76–77	Videohistoria	*Writing, Audio & Video Workbook:* Act. 3, pp. 26–27 *Writing, Audio & Video Workbook:* Act. 7, p. 29 *Writing, Audio & Video Workbook:* Act. 8, p. 30 *Video Program* Chapter 2A *Video Teacher's Guide* Chapter 2A *Pre-AP* Resource Book:* p. 102
Reading			*Realidades* para hispanohablantes: Act. 2A-6, p. 24 *MindPoint Quiz Show* *Lecturas* para hispanohablantes: Obatalá y Orula, pp.19–21 *Lecturas* para hispanohablantes: Oda a las papas fritas, p. 23 *TPR Stories:* Las audiciones de Santiago, p. 25 *TPR Stories:* La vida de una actriz, pp. 29–30 *Realidades* para hispanohablantes: Act. N, p. 62 *Realidades* para hispanohablantes: Act. P, p. 64 *Pre-AP* Resource Book:* pp. 102–103
Speaking	p. 76 p. 78 p. 87 p. 91 p. 93	Supplemental Pre-AP* Activity Differentiated Instruction: Advanced Learners/Pre-AP* Act. 21 Supplemental Pre-AP* Activity Presentación oral	*Assessment Program:* Examen 2A, Parte II, Hablar, p. 50 *Teacher's Resource Book, Para empezar–Tema 4:* Communicative Activity 2A-1, pp. 84–85 *Teacher's Resource Book, Para empezar–Tema 4:* Situation cards, p. 88 *Realidades* para hispanohablantes: Presentación oral, p. 67 *TPR Stories:* pp. 26–28 *Pre-AP* Resource Book:* p. 102
Writing	p. 76 p. 85 p. 87	Supplemental Pre-AP* Activity Supplemental Pre-AP* Activity Act. 21	*Writing, Audio & Video Workbook:* Act. 13, p. 34 *Go Online:* Internet Link Activity *ExamView:* Pre-AP* Question Bank *Assessment Program:* Examen 2A, Parte II, Escribir, p. 51 *Realidades* para hispanohablantes: Act. K, p. 60 *Realidades* para hispanohablantes: Act Ñ, p. 63 *Realidades* para hispanohablantes: Act. P, pp. 64–65 *Pre-AP* Resource Book:* pp. 102–103

	Student Edition/Teacher's Edition		Ancillaries
	Page #	**Activity**	
Vocabulary	p. 104	Supplemental Pre-AP* Activity	*Go Online:* Self-test
Listening	pp. 104–105	Videohistoria	*Writing, Audio & Video Workbook:* Act. 2, pp. 35–36
	p. 108	Supplemental Pre-AP* Activity	*Video Program* Chapter 2B
	p. 120	Supplemental Pre-AP* Activity	*Video Teacher's Guide* Chapter 2B
			Pre-AP* Resource Book: p. 102
Reading	p. 108	Supplemental Pre-AP* Activity	*Reading and Writing for Success:* Test 20, pp. 60–62
	p. 120	Supplemental Pre-AP* Activity	*TPR Stories:* Princesita y el agua, p. 31
	p. 120	Perspectivas del mundo hispano	*TPR Stories:* La Tienda "Variedad", pp. 35–36
			MindPoint Quiz Show
			Realidades para hispanohablantes: Act. Q, p. 82
			Realidades para hispanohablantes: Act. V, pp. 84–85
			Pre-AP* Resource Book: p. 103
Speaking	p. 104	Differentiated Instruction: Advanced Learners/Pre-AP*	*Assessment Program:* Examen de 2B, Parte II, Hablar, p. 64
	p.104	Supplemental Pre-AP* Activity	*Teacher's Resource Book, Para empezar–Tema 4:* Communicative Activity 2B-1, pp. 112–113
	p. 117	Act. 24	*Teacher's Resource Book, Para empezar–Tema 4:* Situation cards, p. 116
	p. 120	Supplemental Pre-AP* Activity	*TPR Stories:* pp. 32–34
			Pre-AP* Resource Book, pp. 102–103
Writing	p. 108	Supplemental Pre-AP* Activity	*Assessment Program:* Examen de 2B, Parte II, Escribir, p. 65
	p. 116	Differentiated Instruction: Advanced Learners/Pre-AP*	*Writing, Audio & Video Workbook:* Act. 12, p. 44
	p. 117	Act. 24	*Reading and Writing for Success:* Test 20, pp. 60–62
	p. 121	Presentación escrita	*Realidades* para hispanohablantes: Presentación escrita, p. 87
			Go Online: Internet Link Activity
			ExamView: Pre-AP* Question Bank
			Realidades para hispanohablantes: Acts. R, S, T, U, p. 83
			Realidades para hispanohablantes: Act. V, pp. 84–85
			Pre-AP* Resource Book, pp. 102–103

Teacher Activity 1
Circumlocution

Place students in pairs and provide each one with one of the following lists of words. Allow 4-5 minutes for each individual to write definitions in Spanish for the given words. Next, partners take turns expressing the meaning of the word to each other, with the opposite partner trying to guess the word that is being defined. After the partners have concluded by guessing the words for all of the definitions, allow a few students to share some of the "best" definitions with the class.

Directions: Write a definition in Spanish for each of the following words without using the word or similar root words in the definition.

Student A—List 1		Student B—List 2	
1. lentamente	4. ganga	1. el desodorante	4. flojo
2. toalla	5. mediano	2. despertarse	5. encontrar
3. pedir prestado	6. cuero	3. salon de belleza	6. vivo

Teacher Activity 2
Informal Speaking—Simulated Conversation

Directions for Student Activity 3

1. Make a transparency of the following scenario: Your first-period teacher wants to understand why you arrive late to class almost every day.

    Conversation:
    PROFESOR: Mira, ¿por qué sueles llegar tarde a mi clase?
    ESTUDIANTE: (20-30 second response)
    PROFESOR: ¿A qué hora te despiertas y qué haces después?
    ESTUDIANTE: (20-30 second response)
    PROFESOR: ¿Qué desayunas?
    ESTUDIANTE: (20-30 second response)
    PROFESOR: Pues, ¿cómo piensas resolver el problema?
    ESTUDIANTE: (20-30 second response)
    PROFESOR: De acuerdo. Vamos a ver si la situación se mejora o no.

2. Have students read the conversation framework above, and then prepare (by writing down key words), how they would fill in the following conversation with rich and full responses to the questions. The goal is to provide as much speech as possible in the time provided, rather than to settle on a basic, short appropriate response.

3. Teachers may wish to ask the class to brainstorm together about some possible responses, but ultimately, the preparation should be accomplished individually. The amount of preparation time can vary, but should not be longer than three or four minutes.

4. Students are then allowed to record their conversations. (See Recording and Evaluating on p. 40.) The teacher can be the voice of the *Profesor,* allowing no more than 30 seconds for each response from the students.

5. In groups of three or four, students should listen to each recording and discuss the content and quality using the scoring guidelines on p. 45.

Student Activity 1
Paragraph Completion

Directions: Read the following passage, completing the blanks with a word in Spanish that is logical and grammatically correct. You must spell and accent the word correctly.

Si algún dia vas de compras en (1) _____ país hispanohablante, debes saber (2) _____ tanto la ropa (3) _____ los zapatos tienen diferentes tallas. Un vestido de (4) _____ talla 12, (5) _____ ejemplo, puede ser 46 en España. Además, entre países, a veces (6) _____ tallas son diferentes. (7) _____ zapato de hombre de 91/2 es aproximadamente el 43 en España y el 27 en México. Hay sitios de Web (8) _____ dan (9) _____ conversiones y algunas tiendas también ofrecen tablas (10) _____ conversión. En España, para calcular el número de zapatos de mujer, generalmente añades 30, y para (11) _____ de hombres, añades 33.5.

Student Activity 2
Paragraph Completion

Directions: Read the following passage, completing the blanks with the form of the word in parenthesis that is grammatically correct. You must spell and accent the word correctly.

El mayo pasado, Carlos tuvo la idea de sorprenderle a su mamá para el día de las madres. Primero, (1) _____ (decidir) invitar a (2) _____. (todo) la familia, en secreto, a una fiesta para ella. Le (3) _____ (buscar) una falda de talla mediana de un sólo color. A mamá le (4) _____ (encantar) (5) _____ (este) tipo de faldas. Afortunadamente, (6) _____ (encontrar) una ganga— (7) _____ (escoger) una falda perfecta en liquidación.

El día de la fiesta, Carlos (8) _____ (arreglarse) rápido y (9) _____ (vestirse) de su mejor camisa. Sus hermanos lo (10) _____ (ayudar) a poner la mesa y a preparar (11) _____ (alguno) comida. Mamá (12) _____ (sorprenderse) mucho al ver las preparaciones y les (13) _____ (dar) un fuerte abrazo a sus hijos, y especialmente a Carlos.

	Student Edition/Teacher's Edition		Ancillaries
	Page #	**Activity**	
Vocabulary	p. 132	Supplemental Pre-AP* Activity	*Go Online:* Self-test
Listening	pp. 132–133	Videohistoria	*Assessment Program:* Examen de 3A, Parte II, Escuchar, p. 78
	p. 132	Supplemental Pre-AP* Activity	*Writing, Audio & Video Workbook:* Act. 9, p. 51
			Video Program Chapter 3A
			Video Teacher's Guide Chapter 3A
Reading	p. 140	Supplemental Pre-AP* Activity	*MindPoint Quiz Show*
	p. 146	Supplemental Pre-AP* Activity	*TPR Stories:* ¡Se me olvido!, p. 38
			TPR Stories: La vida sin crema de afeitar, p. 42
			Realidades para hispanohablantes: Act. S, p. 106
			Pre-AP* Resource Book: pp. 106–107
Speaking	p. 132	Supplemental Pre-AP* Activity	*Assessment Program:* Examen de 3A, Parte II, Hablar, p. 79
	p. 140	Supplemental Pre-AP* Activity	*Teacher's Resource Book, Para empezar–Tema 4:* Communicative Activity 3A-2, p. 144
	p. 142	Differentiated Instruction: Advanced Learners/Pre-AP*	*Teacher's Resource Book, Para empezar–Tema 4:* Situation cards, p. 145
	p. 145	Act. 24	*TPR Stories:* pp. 39–41
	p. 149	Presentación oral	*Realidades* para hispanohablantes: Presentación oral, p. 107
			Pre-AP* Resource Book: p. 106
Writing	p. 132	Supplemental Pre-AP* Activity	*Assessment Program:* Examen de 3A, Parte II, Escribir, p. 79
	p. 140	Supplemental Pre-AP* Activity	*Writing, Audio & Video Workbook:* Act. 13, p. 55
	p. 142	Differentiated Instruction: Advanced Learners/Pre-AP*	*Go Online:* Internet Link Activity
	p. 145	Supplemental Pre-AP* Activity	*ExamView:* Pre-AP* Question Bank
	p. 146	Act. 24	*Realidades* para hispanohablantes: Act. P, p. 103
			Realidades para hispanohablantes: Act. S, p. 106
			Pre-AP* Resource Book: pp. 106–107

	Student Edition/Teacher's Edition		Ancillaries
	Page #	Activity	
Vocabulary	p. 160	Supplemental Pre-AP* Activity	*Go Online:* Self-test
Listening	pp. 160–161	Videohistoria	*Video Program* Chapter 3B
			Video Teacher's Guide Chapter 3B
	p. 174	Supplemental Pre-AP* Activity	*Writing, Audio & Video Workbook:* p. 58
Reading	p. 174	Supplemental Pre-AP* Activity	*Lecturas* para hispanohablantes: La Navidad de Miguelito, pp. 30–32
	p. 176	Perspectivas del mundo hispano	*Lecturas* para hispanohablantes: ¡A leer!, pp. 35–36
			Reading and Writing for Success: Test 21, pp. 63–65
			MindPoint Quiz Show
			TPR Stories: Una aventura en la calle, p. 44
			TPR Stories: Manejando con Desi, p. 48
			Realidades para hispanohablantes: Act R, p. 122
			Realidades para hispanohablantes: Act. V, p. 124
			Pre-AP Resource Book:* pp. 106–107
Speaking	p. 160	Supplemental Pre-AP* Activity	*TPR Stories:* pp. 45–47
	p. 169	Supplemental Pre-AP* Activity	*Teacher's Resource Book, Para empezar–Tema 4:* Communicative Activity 3B-1, pp. 168–169
	p. 173	Act. 22	*Teacher's Resource Book, Para empezar–Tema 4:* Situation cards, p. 172
			Assessment Program: Examen de capítulo 3B, Parte II, Hablar, p. 93
			Pre-AP Resource Book:* p. 106
Writing	p. 164	Differentiated Instruction: Advanced Learners/Pre-AP*	*Writing, Audio & Video Workbook:* Act. 13, p. 66
	p. 173	Act. 22	*Reading and Writing for Success:* Test 21, pp. 63–65
	p. 177	Presentación escrita	*Go Online:* Internet Link Activity
			Exam View: Pre-AP* Question Bank
			Assessment Program: Examen de capítulo 3B, Parte II, Escribir, p. 93
			Realidades para hispanohablantes: Act. U, p. 123
			Realidades para hispanohablantes: Act. X, p. 125
			Realidades para hispanohablantes: Presentación escrita, p. 127
			Pre-AP Resource Book:* pp. 106–107

Teacher Activity
Formal Writing

Have students each choose a Spanish-speaking country they would like to visit. From the school library, a classroom reference, or the Internet, they should then find a publication about the country that includes: locations of cultural and historical significance, weather, and currency exchange rate. The publication will be needed in class on the day of the writing exercise.

In class, give students 30-40 minutes to write three paragraphs on the following topic:
- Explain what would be needed to prepare for a trip to [name of country]. Include details about:
- How long of a trip to plan based on the number of sites to see.
- Justify the places you would visit while there based on their cultural and / or historical significance.
- Tell how you would travel to and within the country.
- Describe the clothing you would need to pack based on where you will visit.
- Tell how much money you would need to take and why.
- Describe what you expect to be the highlight of this trip.

Students should cite facts from the publication to support their travel plans.

Next, make three photocopies of each student's written work. Place students in groups of four. Distribute copies of the scoring guidelines found on p. 45. (Since this is a writing task, the *Fluency* category on the bottom row can be ignored at this time.) Distribute the copies of the students' work within each group. Have each student read his or her writing aloud to the group, one piece at a time, and discuss the content and quality of each writing piece using the scoring guidelines. Each group may select one sample to share with the whole class.

Student Activity 1
Paragraph Completion

Directions: Read the following passage, completing the blanks with the form of the word in parenthesis that is grammatically correct. You must spell and accent the word correctly.

Imagina que llegas a casa y no (1) _____ (poder) abrir la puerta. No hay nadie en casa y no puedes entrar. ¿Qué puedes hacer? Esto no es un (2) _____ (grande) problema si vives en un barrio de un país hispanohablante. Aquí (3) _____ (el) vecinos se (4) _____ (conocer) bien. Son (5) _____ (simpático) y se (6) _____ (ayudar). Cuando (7) _____ (olvidarse) las llaves puedes ir a casa de (8) _____ (tu) vecinos. Si pueden, ellos te ayudan a entrar en tu casa. Si tienes hambre, te (9) _____ (dar) algo de comer. Te dejan llamar por teléfono. En (10) _____ (este) países, el barrio es (11) _____ (un) institución. Es como una extensión del hogar.

Student Activity 2
Paragraph Completion

Directions: Read the following passage, completing the blanks with the form of the word in parenthesis that is grammatically correct. You must spell and accent the word correctly.

PAPÁ: ¿Por qué te quedas (1) _____ (dormir) todo el día?

HIJO: (2) _____ (salir) con amigos al cine a las ocho y no quiero (3) _____ (dormirse) durante la película. Por eso, descanso ahora.

PAPÁ: Pero también tienes responsabilidades (4) _____ (familial).

   ¡(5) _____ (venir) acá y (6) _____ (ayudar) a limpiar el garaje! Después, (7) _____ (poner) la mesa para la cena.

HIJO: Pero papá, ¿por qué (8) _____ (tener) que hacerlo todo hoy? ¿No (9) _____ (poder) esperar hasta mañana.

PAPÁ: Eso no. Ya tenemos planes mañana. (10) _____ (hacer) ahora, por favor.

HIJO: Bueno, papa, en seguida. Como no me dejas descansar, me es posible (11) _____ (manejar) el coche al cine en vez de (12) _____ (ir) a pie?

PAPÁ: ¡Ay, qué hijo!

	Student Edition/Teacher's Edition		Ancillaries
	Page #	Activity	
Vocabulary	p. 188	Supplemental Pre-AP* Activity	*Go Online:* Self-test
Listening	pp. 188–189	Videohistoria	*Video Program* Chapter 4A *Video Teacher's Guide* Chapter 4A *Pre-AP* Resource Book:* p. 110
Reading	p. 194 p. 201 p. 203	Differentiated Instruction: Advanced Learners/Pre-AP* Act. 26 Supplemental Pre-AP* Activity	*MindPoint Quiz Show* *TPR Stories:* La educación de Burbuja, p. 52 *TPR Stories:* Magdalena, la mala educada, p. 56 *Realidades* para hispanohablantes: Act. O, p. 144 *Pre-AP* Resource Book:* pp. 110–111
Speaking	p. 201 p. 205	Act. 26 Presentación oral	*TPR Stories:* pp. 53–55 *Teacher's Resource Book, Para empezar–Tema 4:* Communicative Activity 4A-1, pp. 198–199 *Teacher's Resource Book, Para empezar–Tema 4:* Situation cards, p. 201 *Assessment Program:* Examen del capítulo 4A, Parte II, Hablar, p. 107 *Realidades* para hispanohablantes: Presentación oral, p. 147 *Pre-AP* Resource Book:* p. 110
Writing	p. 188 p. 194 p. 197 p. 201	Supplemental Pre-AP* Activity Differentiated Instruction: Advanced Learners/Pre-AP* Supplemental Pre-AP* Activity Act. 26	*Writing, Audio & Video Workbook:* Act. 12, p. 76 *Reading and Writing for Success:* Test 22, pp. 66–67 *Go Online:* Internet Link Activity *ExamView:* Pre-AP* Question Bank *Assessment Program:* Examen del capítulo 4A, Parte II, Escribir, p. 107 *Realidades* para hispanohablantes: Act. Q, p. 145 *Pre-AP* Resource Book:* pp. 110–111

	Student Edition/Teacher's Edition		Ancillaries
	Page #	**Activity**	
Vocabulary			*Go Online:* Self-test
Listening	pp. 214–215	Videohistoria	*Video Program* Chapter 4B
			Video Teacher's Guide Chapter 4B
	p. 221	Supplemental Pre-AP* Activity	*Pre-AP* Resource Book:* p. 110
Reading	p. 228	Supplemental Pre-AP* Activity	*Reading and Writing for Success:* Test 22, pp. 66–68
	p. 230	Perspectivas del mundo hispano	*MindPoint Quiz Show*
			TPR Stories: María, Diego y los gatos, p. 58
			TPR Stories: La boda de Héctor y Marisel, p. 62
			Lecturas para hispanohablantes: Espiral, p. 39
			Lecturas para hispanohablantes: Un terremoto en mi cuarto, pp. 43–44
			Realidades para hispanohablantes: Act. Q, p. 162
			Realidades para hispanohablantes: Act. W, p. 166
			Pre-AP* Resource Book: pp. 110–111
Speaking	p. 214	Supplemental Pre-AP* Activity	*TPR Stories:* pp. 59–61
	p. 226	Act. 19	*Teacher's Resource Book, Para empezar–Tema 4:* Communicative Activity 4B-1, pp. 226–227
			Teacher's Resource Book, Para empezar–Tema 4: Situation cards, p. 231
			Assessment Program: Parte II, Hablar, p. 120
			Pre-AP* Resource Book: p. 110
Writing	p. 214	Supplemental Pre-AP* Activity	*Writing, Audio & Video Workbook:* Act. 4, p. 80
	p. 221	Supplemental Pre-AP* Activity	*Writing, Audio & Video Workbook:* Act. 13, p. 87
	p. 224	Differentiated Instruction: Advanced Learners/Pre-AP*	*Reading and Writing for Success:* Test 22, p. 66
			Go Online: Internet Link Activity
	p. 226	Act. 19	*ExamView:* Pre-AP* Question Bank
	p. 228	Supplemental Pre-AP* Activity	*Assessment Program:* Parte II, Escribir, p. 120
	p. 231	Presentación escrita	*Realidades* para hispanohablantes: Acts. R and S, p. 163
			Realidades para hispanohablantes: Act. W, p. 166
			Realidades para hispanohablantes: Presentación escrita, p. 167
			Pre-AP* Resource Book: pp. 110–111

Teacher Activity 1
Circumlocution

Place students in pairs and provide each one with one of the following lists of words. Allow 4–5 minutes for each individual to write definitions in Spanish for the given words. Next, partners take turns expressing the meaning of the word to each other, with the opposite partner trying to guess the word that is being defined. After the partners have concluded by guessing the words for all of the definitions, allow a few students to share some of the "best" definitions with the class.

Directions: Write a definition in Spanish for each of the following words without using the word or similar root words in the definition.

Student A—List 1	Student B—List 2
1. patio de recreo	1. vecino
2. portarse mal	2. oso de peluche
3. los bloques	3. dinosaurio
4. enorme	4. casarse con
5. recordar	5. despedirse de
6. llorar	6. la reunión

Teacher Activity 2
Listening Comprehension

Use the reading, *El grillo y el jaguar* from p. 202 in the **Realidades** Student Textbook to engage students in the Dictogloss activity on p. 14. It may be necessary to pre-teach some of the unfamiliar vocabulary (*grillo, tenían miedo, se escondieron,* etc.) using TPR or some other means in order to make the story more meaningful. Once students have completed the steps to the Dictogloss activity, have them open their books and read the selection aloud with a partner. Following the paired reading, students should continue working in pairs to answer and discuss the questions in *¿Comprendiste?* and *Y tú ¿qué dices?*

Teacher Activity 3
Reading Comprehension

Make a transparency of the following questions. After reading *El grillo y el jaguar*, pp. 202-203 in the **Realidades** Student Textbook, have students select the most appropriate answer to the following questions.

1. ¿Por qué salió el jaguar de su casa?
   a. Tenía sed.
   b. Tenía miedo.
   c. Le gustaba rugir.

2. ¿Por qué necesitaba el grillo que el jaguar le perdonara?
   a. No se escondió.
   b. No oyó al jaguar.
   c. No saludó al rey.

3. ¿Por qué ganó el grillo la carrera?
   a. Era más rápido que el jaguar.
   b. Era más astuto que al jaguar.
   c. Siguió cantando.

Student Activity 1
Paragraph Completion

Directions: Read the following passage, completing the blanks with a word in Spanish that is logical and grammatically correct. You must spell and accent the word correctly.

Ésta es mi abuela, Nela Toledo. Ella es (1) _____ mamá de mi papá y todos (2) _____ queremos mucho. Ella vive sola (3) _____ San Miguel de Allende, (4) _____ es una pequeña ciudad cerca de Guanajuato. Y mi abuelo...bueno, ni mi abuela ni mi papá querían hablar de él. Era (5) _____ misterio para la familia. Mi abuela tiene muchísimos amigos y (6) _____ de sus mejores amigas es su vecina, Olga. A (7) _____ dos les encanta pasear por la ciudad ir de compras (8) _____ mercado y hablar con (9) _____ vecinos.

Student Activity 2
Paragraph Completion

Directions: Read the following passage, completing the blanks with the form of the word in parenthesis that is grammatically correct. You must spell and accent the word correctly.

GASPAR: ¿Por qué no (1) _____ (venir) a la fiesta de ayer?

ROSA: Porque no me sentía bien.

GASPAR: (2) _____ (ser) una fiesta estupenda. Estaban todos—Raúl Paco, Lucía ....
¡Todos los compañeros de la escuela secundaria! También vi a Roberto. Hace dos años que (3) _____ (vivir) en otra ciudad, pero (4) _____ (regresar) para la fiesta. ¡Qué alegría verlo! Cuando nos vimos, nos quedamos (5) _____ (mirarse) como tontos y luego nos abrazamos emocionados. Pasamos horas contándonos cosas.

ROSA: Vaya, pues yo no recordaba que ustedes (6) _____ (llevarse)
(7) _____ (tanto) bien. Siempre estaban (8) _____ (pelearse).

GASPAR: Bueno, no siempre (9) _____ (estar) de acuerdo en todo, pero
(10) _____ (quererse) mucho.

	Student Edition/Teacher's Edition		Ancillaries
	Page #	**Activity**	
Vocabulary	p. 242	Supplemental Pre-AP* Activity	*Go Online:* Self-test
Listening	pp. 242–243	Videohistoria	*Video Program* Chapter 5A
			Video Teacher's Guide Chapter 5A
	p. 242	Supplemental Pre-AP* Activity	*Writing, Audio & Video Workbook:* Act. 5, p. 91
	p. 249	Supplemental Pre-AP* Activity	*Pre-AP* Resource Book:* p. 114
Reading	p. 253	Act. 20	*MindPoint Quiz Show*
	p. 257	Supplemental Pre-AP* Activity	*TPR Stories:* La leyenda de José María, p. 66
			TPR Stories: Guau, el héroe, p. 70
			Lecturas para hispanohablantes: Act. P, p. 182
			Lecturas para hispanohablantes: Act. T, p. 184
			Pre-AP* Resource Book: pp. 114–115
Speaking	p. 242	Supplemental Pre-AP* Activity	*TPR Stories:* pp. 67–69
	p. 249	Supplemental Pre-AP* Activity	*Teacher's Resource Book, Temas 5–9:* Communicative Activity 5A-1, pp. 14–15
	p. 253	Act. 20	*Teacher's Resource Book, Temas 5–9:* Situation cards, p. 18
	p. 257	Supplemental Pre-AP* Activity	*Assessment Program:* Parte II, Hablar, p. 134
	p. 259	Presentación oral	*Realidades* para hispanohablantes: Presentación oral, p. 187
			Pre-AP* Resource Book: p. 114
Writing	p. 242	Supplemental Pre-AP* Activity	*Writing, Audio & Video Workbook:* Act. 4, p. 90
	p. 250	Differentiated Instruction: Advanced Learners/Pre-AP*	*Writing, Audio & Video Workbook:* Act. 13, p. 97
			Go Online: Internet Link Activity
	p. 257	Supplemental Pre-AP* Activity	*ExamView:* Pre-AP* Question Bank
			Assessment Program: Parte II, Escribir, p. 134
			Realidades para hispanohablantes: Act. S, p. 183
			Realidades para hispanohablantes: Act. W, p. 185
			Pre-AP* Resource Book: pp. 114–115

	Student Edition/Teacher's Edition		Ancillaries
	Page #	**Activity**	
Vocabulary	p. 268	Supplemental Pre-AP* Activity	*Go Online:* Self-test
Listening	pp. 269–269	Videohistoria	*Video Program* Chapter 5B *Video Teacher's Guide* Chapter 5B *Pre-AP* Resource Book:* p. 114
Reading	p. 283 p. 284	Supplemental Pre-AP* Activity Perspectivas del mundo hispano	*Reading and Writing for Success:* Test 23, pp. 69–70 *MindPoint Quiz Show* *TPR Stories:* Alicia la alérgica, p. 72 *TPR Stories:* El día terrible d la curandera, p. 76 *Lecturas* para hispanohablantes: Conversando con un campeón de surfing, pp. 52–54 *Realidades* para hispanohablantes: Act. O, p. 202 *Realidades* para hispanohablantes: Lectura 2, p. 204 *Pre-AP* Resource Book:* pp. 114–115
Speaking	p. 268 p. 281 p. 283	Supplemental Pre-AP* Activity Act. 26 Supplemental Pre-AP* Activity	*TPR Stories:* pp. 73–75 *Lecturas* para hispanohablantes: Conversando con un campeóon de surfing, pp. 52–54 *Teacher's Resource Book, Temas 5–9:* Communicative Activity 5B-1, pp. 40–41 *Teacher's Resource Book, Temas 5–9:* Situation cards, p. 44 *Assessment Program:* Parte II, Hablar, p. 147 *Pre-AP* Resource Book:* p. 114
Writing	p. 272 p. 272 p. 285	Supplemental Pre-AP* Activity Differentiated Instruction: Advanced Learners/Pre-AP* Presentación escrita	*Writing, Audio & Video Workbook:* Act.13, p. 106 *Lecturas* para hispanohablantes: Conversando con un campeón de surfing, pp. 52–54 *Reading and Writing for Success:* Test 23, pp. 69–71 *Go Online:* Internet Link Activity *ExamView:* Pre-AP* Question Bank *Assessment Program:* Parte II, Escribir, p. 147 *Realidades* para hispanohablantes: Act. Q, p. 203 *Realidades* para hispanohablantes: Act. T, p. 205 *Realidades* para hispanohablantes: Presentación escrita, p. 207 *Pre-AP* Resource Book:* p. 115

Teacher Activity 1
Formal Oral Presentation

1. Have students read the *Lectura* on pp. 256-257 of the *Realidades* Student Text Book silently.

2. Next, have students prepare a one-minute news commentary as if they were reporters in the field, citing data from the *Lectura*. The amount of preparation time can vary, but should not be longer than three or four minutes.

3. Students are then allowed one minute to record their presentations, or they may make their presentations to a group of three or four students.

4. In groups of three or four, students should listen to each recording (or hear each presentation) and discuss the content and quality using the scoring guidelines on p. 45.

Teacher Activity 2
Informal Writing

After students have completed Student Activity 2 on the next page, make three photocopies of each student's written work. Place students in groups of four. Distribute copies of the scoring guidelines found on p. 45. (Since this is a writing task, the *Fluency* category on the bottom row can be ignored at this time.) Distribute the copies of the students' work within each group. Have each student read his or her writing aloud to the group, one piece at a time, and discuss the content and quality of each writing piece using the scoring guidelines. Each group may select one sample to share with the whole class.

Student Activity 1
Paragraph Completion

Directions: Read the following passage, completing the blanks with the form of the word in parenthesis that is grammatically correct. You must spell and accent the word correctly.

Ayer visité la sala de emergencia porque (1)_____ (alguno) día quiero ser médica. Ayudé a una enfermera todo el día. Vi michas cosas muy interesantes. Una chica se torció la rodilla esquiando, y por eso le (2) _____ (traer) unas muletas. El médico la examinó y le recetó pastillas para el dolor. (3) _____ (otro) persona se rompió el tobillo y le sacaron (4) _____ (un) radiografías de los huesos. Después le pusieron un yeso porque tenía dos huesos (5) _____ (roto). Unos paramédicos (6) _____ (venir) a la sala de emergencia en una ambulancia con un señor que (7) _____ (tener) un accidente de coche. Dijeron que tenían que hacerle (8) _____ (un) operación de emergencia porque estaba (9) _____ (perder) (10) _____ (mucho) sangre. A veces durante mi visita a la sala de emergencia, (11) _____ (tener) miedo de todo lo que (12) _____ (estar) pasando, pero todavía (13) _____ (querer) ser médica para ayudar a la gente.

Student Activity 2
Informal Writing

Imagine that you are at home recovering from a recent accident. Since you cannot go anywhere or do anything, write a short note to send to a friend in another town to let him or her know:

- What happened to you and when
- What the doctor said
- How long it will take you to recuperate
- What the first thing is that you will do when you are able

	Student Edition/Teacher's Edition		Ancillaries
	Page #	Activity	
Vocabulary			Go Online: Self-test Pre-AP* Resource Book: p. 119
Listening	pp. 296–297 p. 296 p. 308 p. 311	Videohistoria Supplemental Pre-AP* Activity Supplemental Pre-AP* Activity Supplemental Pre-AP* Activity	Video Program Chapter 6A Video Teacher's Guide Chapter 6A Writing, Audio & Video Workbook: Act. 9, p.111 Pre-AP* Resource Book: p. 118
Reading	p. 311	Supplemental Pre-AP* Activity	Reading and Writing for Success: Test 24, pp. 72–74 MindPoint Quiz Show TPR Stories: En busca de una idea, p. 80 TPR Stories: Dora la entrenadora, p. 83 Lecturas para hispanohablantes: Una carta a Dios, pp. 57–59 Lecturas para hispanohablantes: Doña primavera, p. 61 Realidades para hispanohablantes: Act. Q, p. 222 Realidades para hispanohablantes: Act. U, p. 224 Pre-AP* Resource Book: pp. 118–119
Speaking	p. 296 p. 308 p. 309	Supplemental Pre-AP* Activity Supplemental Pre-AP* Activity Act. 22	TPR Stories: pp. 81–82 Teacher's Resource Book, Temas 5–9: Communicative Activity 6A-1, pp. 70–71 Teacher's Resource Book, Temas 5–9: Situation cards, p. 74 Assessment Program: Parte II, Hablar, p. 160 Realidades para hispanohablantes: Presentación oral, p. 227 Pre-AP* Resource Book: pp. 118–119
Writing	p. 296 p. 302 p. 308 p. 309 p. 311	Supplemental Pre-AP* Activity Differentiated Instruction: Advanced Learners/Pre-AP* Supplemental Pre-AP* Activity Act. 22 Supplemental Pre-AP* Activity	Writing, Audio & Video Workbook: Act. 4, p. 108 Writing, Audio & Video Workbook: Act. 12, p. 114 Writing, Audio & Video Workbook: Act. 13, p. 115 Lecturas para hispanohablantes: Una carta a Dios, pp. 57–59 Lecturas para hispanohablantes: Doña primavera, p. 61 Reading and Writing for Success: Test 24, pp. 72–74 Go Online: Internet Link Activity ExamView: Pre-AP* Question Bank Assessment Program: Parte II, Escribir, p. 159 Realidades para hispanohablantes: Act. S, p. 223 Realidades para hispanohablantes: Act. W, p. 225 Pre-AP* Resource Book: pp. 118–119

Realidades 2

Capítulo 6B

Pre-AP* Resource Chart

	Student Edition/Teacher's Edition		Ancillaries
	Page #	Activity	
Vocabulary	p. 323	Supplemental Pre-AP* Activity	*Go Online:* Self-test *Pre-AP* Resource Book:* p. 119
Listening	pp. 322–323	Videohistoria	*Video Program* Chapter 6B *Video Teacher's Guide* Chapter 6B
	p. 334	Supplemental Pre-AP* Activity	*Writing, Audio & Video Workbook:* Act. 8, p. 120
	p. 336	Supplemental Pre-AP* Activity	*Writing, Audio & Video Workbook:* Act. 9, p. 121 *Pre-AP* Resource Book:* p. 118
Reading	p. 334	Differentiated Instruction: Advanced Learners/Pre-AP*	*MindPoint Quiz Show* *TPR Stories:* La película más violenta, p. 85
	p. 336	Supplemental Pre-AP* Activity	*TPR Stories:* Manuela y Manuel, p. 89
	p. 338	Perspectivas del mundo hispano	*Lecturas* para hispanohablantes: Qué hacer frente a un huracán, pp. 62–64 *Reading and Writing for Success:* Test 24, pp. 72–74 *Realidades* para hispanohablantes: Act. Ñ, p. 242 *Realidades* para hispanohablantes: Act. Q, p. 244 *Pre-AP* Resource Book:* pp. 118–119
Speaking	p. 323	Supplemental Pre-AP* Activity	*TPR Stories:* pp. 86–88
	p. 336	Supplemental Pre-AP* Activity	*Teacher's Resource Book, Temas 5–9:* Communicative Activity 6B-1, pp. 96–97 *Teacher's Resource Book, Temas 5–9:* Situation cards, p. 100 *Assessment Program:* Parte II, Hablar, p. 173 *Pre-AP* Resource Book:* pp. 118–119
Writing	p. 324	Differentiated Instruction: Advanced Learners/Pre-AP*	*Writing, Audio & Video Workbook:* Act. 4, p. 118 *Writing, Audio & Video Workbook:* Act. 13, p. 125
	p. 330	Act. 16	*Lecturas* para hispanohablantes: Qué hacer frente a un huracán, pp. 62–64
	p. 336	Supplemental Pre-AP* Activity	*Go Online:* Internet Link Activity
	p. 339	Presentación escrita	*ExamView:* Pre-AP* Question Bank *Assessment Program:* Parte II, Escribir, p. 173 *Realidades* para hispanohablantes: Act. P, p. 243 *Realidades* para hispanohablantes: Act. S, p. 245 *Realidades* para hispanohablantes: Presentación escrita, p. 247 *Pre-AP* Resource Book:* pp. 118–119

Teacher Activity 1
Circumlocution

Place students in groups of 3 or 4. Copy and cut apart the following four sets of words / clues, giving each student one set of the answers for the crossword puzzle in Student Activity 1 on the next page. Have students practice circumlocution skills in Spanish by engaging them in the Group Crossword Practice as outlined on p. 43.

Horizontal
1. metió un gol
5. galán
6. competir
7. se trata de
10. nos volvemos
14. extraterrestre

Horizontal
16. me enojé
17. dicho
18. hizo el papel de
19. dormirse
21. fracaso

Vertical
2. estar enamorado de
4. devuelto
5. se aburren
6. concurso
8. robó
9. matar
11. puesto

Vertical
12. tener éxito
13. argumento
15. escena
20. entrevista
22. reina
23. aplaudiste

Teacher Activity 2
Paragraph Completion

Make a transparency of the following passage. Alone or in pairs, have students complete the blanks with a word in Spanish that is logical and grammatically correct. They must spell and accent the word correctly.

En muchas películas de otros países el diálogo de la película aparece (1) _____ inglés en la parte de abajo de la pantalla. Con estos subtítulos (2) _____ más fácil comprender el argumento (3) _____ la película. Cuando hay subtítulos, es importante concentrarse un poco más y observar (4) _____ expresiones y los movimientos de los actores. (5) _____ bueno es que es más interesante ver la película en versión original con subtítulos.

(6) _____ solución para que el público pueda comprender una película es sustituir el diálogo original (7) _____ una nueva grabación del diálogo en el idioma del país. Algunas personas prefieren ver las películas en versión original, con subtítulos, porque comprenden el idioma de la película y pueden escuchar (8) _____ voz verdadera de los actores y los sonidos de la ambientación. (9) _____ otras personas les gusta leer los subtítulos porque, cuando los leen, pueden aprender un poco del idioma original de la película. Y otras dicen que no (10) _____ gusta el doblaje porque pierden el tono y la entonación de los actores.

Student Activity 1
Circumlocution

Directions: Taking turns, explain the vocabulary words on the answer sheet you have been given to the members of your group using Spanish only. You should not use any forms of the word as you try to explain what your word is. Be sure to use "horizontal" and "vertical" plus the number of the word in the puzzle to help your group members locate the correct placement of the word.

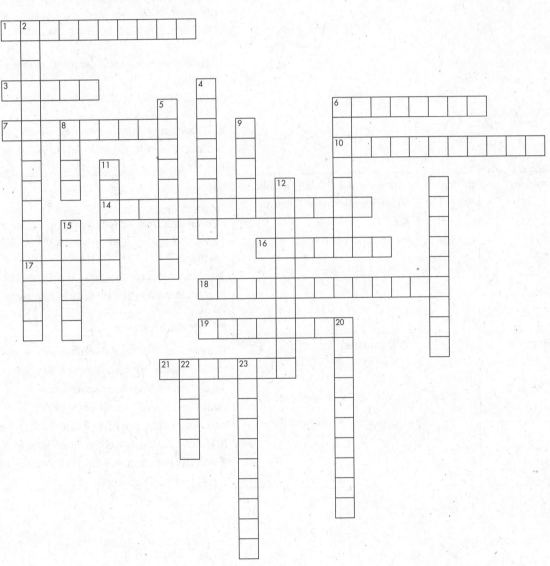

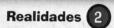
	Student Edition/Teacher's Edition		Ancillaries
	Page #	Activity	
Vocabulary	p. 350	Supplemental Pre-AP* Activity	*Go Online:* Self-test
Listening	pp. 350–351	Videohistoria	*Video Program* Chapter 7A *Video Teacher's Guide* Chapter 7A
Reading			*MindPoint Quiz Show* *TPR Stories:* La comida deliciosa puede ser peligrosa, p. 92 *TPR Stories:* Patricia Pamplona y la cena perfecta, p. 96 *Lecturas* para hispanohablantes: Cuaderno de tareas, pp. 68–70 *Lecturas* para hispanohablantes: Recuerdo infantil, p. 72 *Realidades* para hispanohablantes: Act. N, p. 262 *Realidades* para hispanohablantes: Act. P, p. 264 *Pre-AP* Resource Book:* pp. 122–123
Speaking	p. 350 p. 361 p. 363 p. 367	Supplemental Pre-AP* Activity Supplemental Pre-AP* Activity Act. 18 Presentación oral	*TPR Stories:* pp. 93–95 *Teacher's Resource Book, Temas 5–9:* Communicative Activity 7A-1, pp. 126–127 *Teacher's Resource Book, Temas 5–9:* Situation cards, p. 130 *Assessment Program:* Parte II, Hablar, p. 186 *Realidades* para hispanohablantes: Presentación oral, p. 267 *Pre-AP* Resource Book:* p. 122
Writing	p. 356 p. 361 p. 365	Differentiated Instruction: Advanced Learners/Pre-AP* Act. 18 Supplemental Pre-AP* Activity	*Writing, Audio & Video Workbook:* Act. 4, p. 128 *Writing, Audio & Video Workbook:* Act. 13, p. 135 *Go Online:* Internet Link Activity *ExamView:* Pre-AP* Question Bank *Assessment Program:* Parte II, Escribir, p. 186 *Realidades* para hispanohablantes: Act. O, p. 263 *Realidades* para hispanohablantes: Act. Q, p. 265 *Pre-AP* Resource Book:* pp. 122–123

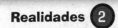
	Student Edition/Teacher's Edition		Ancillaries
	Page #	Activity	
Vocabulary	p. 376	Supplemental Pre-AP* Activity	*Go Online:* Self-test
Listening	pp. 376–377	Videohistoria	*Video Program* Chapter 7B
	p. 384	Differentiated Instruction: Advanced Learners/Pre-AP*	*Video Teacher's Guide* Chapter 7B
	p. 391	Differentiated Instruction: Advanced Learners/Pre-AP*	*Writing, Audio & Video Workbook:* Act. 8, p. 141
Reading	p. 392	Perspectivas del mundo hispano	*Reading and Writing for Success:* Test 25, pp. 75–77
			MindPoint Quiz Show
			TPR Stories: Un picnic en el parque, p. 98
			TPR Stories: La sencillez del cámping, p. 102
			Lecturas para hispanohablantes: Asignatura pendiente, pp. 73–74
			Realidades para hispanohablantes: Act. O, p. 282
			Realidades para hispanohablantes: Act. R, p. 284
			Pre-AP Resource Book:* pp. 122–123
Speaking	p. 376	Supplemental Pre-AP* Activity	*Teacher's Resource Book, Temas 5–9:* Communicative Activity 7B-1, pp. 152–153
	p. 384	Differentiated Instruction: Advanced Learners/Pre-AP*	*Teacher's Resource Book, Temas 5–9:* Situation cards, p. 156
	p. 389	Act. 25	*TPR Stories:* pp. 99–101
			Assessment Program: Parte II, Hablar, p. 199
			Pre-AP Resource Book:* p. 122
Writing	p. 382	Differentiated Instruction: Advanced Learners/Pre-AP*	*Writing, Audio & Video Workbook:* Act. 13, p. 145
	p. 389	Act. 25	*Reading and Writing for Success:* Test 25, pp. 75–77
	p. 391	Differentiated Instruction: Advanced Learners/Pre-AP*	*Go Online:* Internet Link Activity
	p. 393	Presentación escrita	*ExamView:* Pre-AP* Question Bank
			Assessment Program: Parte II, Escribir, p. 199
			Realidades para hispanohablantes: Act. Q, p. 283
			Realidades para hispanohablantes: Act. T, p. 285
			Realidades para hispanohablantes: Presentación escrita, p. 287
			Pre-AP Resource Book:* pp. 122–123

Teacher Activity
Informal Writing

Have students imagine that they just went on a family picnic and outing. They should write an e-mail to a friend describing the event. After students have completed their writing, make three photocopies of each student's written work. Place students in groups of four. Distribute copies of the scoring guidelines found on p. 45. (Since this is a writing task, the *Fluency* category on the bottom row can be ignored at this time.) Distribute the copies of the students' work within each group. Have each student read his or her writing aloud to the group, one piece at a time, and discuss the content and quality of each writing piece using the scoring guidelines. Each group may select one sample to share with the whole class.

Student Activity 1
Paragraph Completion

Directions: Read the following passage, completing the blanks with a word in Spanish that is logical and grammatically correct. You must spell and accent the word correctly.

ANA:　Me parece (1) _____ el sabor de la comida siempre es mejor al aire libre. No hay

　　(2) _____ mejor que el pollo asado. Me encanta (3) _____ olor. ¡Y el maíz a la parilla

　　es fantástico!

BETO:　Y no hay nada peor que las hormigas y las moscas caminando (4) _____ la comida.

　　¡Qué asco! (5) _____ molestan mucho. En el comedor no hay insectos.

JULIA:　Es (6) _____ difícil preparar la comida con leña. Si llueve (7) _____ sábado, el suelo

　　estará mojado. Es más fácil preparar la cena en la cocina. ¡Y en casa no va (8) _____

　　llover!

ANA:　Es más informal y divertido comer al aire libre. Después de comer, podemos dar una

　　caminata (9) _____ hablar alrededor del fuego. Será más especial. Y podemos

　　vestirnos (10) _____ ropa más cómoda.

Student Activity 2
Paragraph Completion

Directions: Read the following passage, completing the blanks with the form of the word in parenthesis that is grammatically correct. You must spell and accent the word correctly.

Para celebrar su aniversario, Héctor (1) _____ (hacer) una reservación para llevar a

su señora, Carmen, a un restaurante donde se (2) _____ (servir) camarones a la

parilla. Caminaron por la Calle Valdés para llegar allí. El restaurante (3) _____ (ser)

bien interesante, decorado de ollas, sartenes y utensilios para cocinar. Los (4) _____

(sentar) en una mesa cerca del balcón con una vista de la plaza. Héctor y Carmen (5)

_____ (el) dos pidieron un plato de mariscos (6) _____ (hervir). De postre,

probaron unas frutas (7) _____ (fresco). Antes de (8) _____ (salir) del

restaurante, Carmen le dijo a Hector, «No (9) _____ (olvidarse) de dejarle al

camarero una buena propina, pero no le (10) _____ (dar) demasíado.»

	Student Edition/Teacher's Edition		Ancillaries
	Page #	Activity	
Vocabulary			*Go Online:* Self-test
			Pre-AP* Resource Book: p. 126
			Pre-AP* Resource Book: p. 127
Listening	pp. 404–405	Videohistoria	*Video Program* Chapter 8A
			Video Teacher's Guide Chapter 8A
	p. 406	Differentiated Instruction: Advanced Learners/Pre-AP*	*Pre-AP* Resource Book:* p. 126
	p. 408	Supplemental Pre-AP* Activity	
	p. 419	Supplemental Pre-AP* Activity	
Reading	p. 406	Differentiated Instruction: Advanced Learners/Pre-AP*	*MindPoint Quiz Show*
			TPR Stories: Álvaro aburrido, p. 106
	p. 419	Supplemental Pre-AP* Activity	*TPR Stories:* El viejero infeliz (Primera parte), p. 110
	p. 419	Act. 19	*Lecturas* para hispanohablantes: Paula, pp. 76–78
			Lecturas para hispanohablantes: Buenos hotdogs, pp. 80–81
			Realidades para hispanohablantes: Act. O, p. 302
			Realidades para hispanohablantes: Act. R, p. 304
			Pre-AP* Resource Book: pp. 126–127
Speaking	p. 419	Act. 19	*TPR Stories:* pp. 107–109
	p. 419	Supplemental Pre-AP* Activity	*Teacher's Resource Book, Temas 5–9:* Communicative Activity 8A-1, pp. 182–183
	p. 421	Presentación oral	*Teacher's Resource Book, Temas 5–9:* Situation cards, p. 186
			Assessment Program: Parte II, Hablar, p. 212
			Realidades para hispanohablantes: Presentación oral, p. 307
			Pre-AP* Resource Book: pp. 126–127
Writing	p. 404	Supplemental Pre-AP* Activity	*Writing, Audio & Video Workbook:* Act. 13, p. 155
	p. 406	Differentiated Instruction: Advanced Learners/Pre-AP*	*Go Online:* Internet Link Activity
			ExamView: Pre-AP* Question Bank
	p. 408	Supplemental Pre-AP* Activity	*Assessment Program:* Parte II, Escribir, p. 212
	p. 419	Act. 19	*Realidades* para hispanohablantes: Act. Q, p. 303
			Realidades para hispanohablantes: Act. R, p. 305
			Pre-AP* Resource Book: pp. 126–127

	Student Edition/Teacher's Edition		Ancillaries
	Page #	**Activity**	
Vocabulary			*Go Online:* Self-test *Pre-AP* Resource Book:* p. 126 *Pre-AP* Resource Book:* p. 127
Listening	pp. 428–429	Videohistoria	*Video Program* Chapter 8B *Video Teacher's Guide* Chapter 8B *Pre-AP* Resource Book:* p. 126
	p. 428	Supplemental Pre-AP* Activity	
	p. 437	Supplemental Pre-AP* Activity	
	p. 442	Supplemental Pre-AP* Activity	
Reading	p. 428	Supplemental Pre-AP* Activity	*Reading and Writing for Success:* Test 26, pp. 78–80 *Teacher's Resource Book, Temas 5–9:* Communicative Activity 8B-2, pp. 210–211 *MindPoint Quiz Show* *TPR Stories:* La vida buena en San Juan, p. 112 *TPR Stories:* El viajero infeliz (Segunda parte), p. 117 *Lecturas para hispanohablantes:* Port Aventura, pp. 82–84 *Realidades para hispanohablantes:* Act. Ñ, p. 322 *Realidades para hispanohablantes:* Act. Q, p. 324 *Pre-AP* Resource Book:* p. 127
	p. 441	Act. 21	
	p. 444	Perspectivas del mundo hispano	
Speaking	p. 428	Supplemental Pre-AP* Activity	*TPR Stories:* pp. 113–116 *Teacher's Resource Book, Temas 5–9:* Communicative Activity 8B-2, pp. 210–211 *Teacher's Resource Book, Temas 5–9:* Situation cards, p. 212 *Assessment Program:* Parte II, Hablar, p. 120 *Pre-AP* Resource Book:* pp. 126–127
	p. 437	Supplemental Pre-AP* Activity	
	p. 441	Act. 21	
	p. 442	Supplemental Pre-AP* Activity	
Writing	p. 428	Supplemental Pre-AP* Activity	*Writing, Audio & Video Workbook:* Act. 4, p. 158 *Writing, Audio & Video Workbook:* Act. 13, p. 165 *Reading and Writing for Success:* Test 27, pp. 78–80 *Go Online:* Internet Link Activity *ExamView:* Pre-AP* Question Bank *Assessment Program:* Parte II, Escribir, p. 120 *Realidades para hispanohablantes:* Act. P, p. 323 *Realidades para hispanohablantes:* Act. S, p. 325 *Realidades para hispanohablantes:* Presentación escrita, p. 327 *Pre-AP* Resource Book:* pp. 126–127
	p. 437	Supplemental Pre-AP* Activity	
	p. 438	Differentiated Instruction: Advanced Learners/Pre-AP*	
	p. 441	Act. 21	
	p. 445	Presentación escrita	

Teacher Activity 1
Circumlocution

Place students in groups of 3 or 4. Cut apart the following sets of words, giving each student one set of the answers for the crossword puzzle in Student Activity 1 on the next page. Have students practice circumlocution skills in Spanish by engaging them in the Group Crossword Practice as outlined on p. 43.

Horizontal
6. pasillo
8. habitación
9. extranjero
12. aduanera
14. Castillo
18. cortés
19. bote de vela

Vertical
1. cajero
2. puerta de embarque
3. planear
4. duró
5. hizo escala
7. de ida y vuelta
10. ruido

Horizontal
21. propina
23. abordaste
24. tal vez
25. registrar
26. sugerimos
27. regatear

Vertical
11. facturé
13. bello
15. siguiente
16. pasajero
17. conseguí
20. disfrutar de
22. retraso

Teacher Activity 2
Paragraph Completion

Make a transparency of the following passage. Alone or in pairs, have students complete the blanks with a word in Spanish that is logical and grammatically correct. They must spell and accent the word correctly.

Las playas de Torremolinos son estupendas. Todas parecen una tarjeta postal. (1) _____ disfrutar (2) _____ todo, es necesario (3) _____ pasen al menos dos días allí. En Torremolinos pueden navegar, hacer surf de vela, (4) _____ montar una moto acuática. Hay actividades para toda la familia. Su habitación está en un edificio histórico (5) _____ siglo dieciocho. (6) _____ entrar, a su derecha está la recepción. En la recepción hay (7) _____ foto de los reyes y muchas cosas típicas (8) _____ España, como artesanías y cuadros. El hotel (9) _____ famoso porque es tradicional y moderno al mismo tiempo: al lado de la recepción hay un cajero automático. El restaurante del hotel es (10) _____ de los mejores en Madrid.

Student Activity 1
Circumlocution

Directions: Taking turns, explain the vocabulary words on the answer sheet you have been given to the members of your group using Spanish only. You should not use any forms of the word as you try to explain what your word is. Be sure to use "horizontal" and "vertical" plus the number of the word in the puzzle to help your group members locate the correct placement of the word.

	Student Edition/Teacher's Edition		Ancillaries
	Page #	Activity	
Vocabulary	p. 454 p. 469	Supplemental Pre-AP* Activity Supplemental Pre-AP* Activity	*Go Online:* Self-test
Listening	pp. 454–455 p. 460	Videohistoria Differentiated Instruction: Advanced Learners/Pre-AP*	*Video Program* Chapter 9A *Video Teacher's Guide* Chapter 9A *Pre-AP* Resource Book:* pp. 130–131
Reading	p. 463	Supplemental Pre-AP* Activity	*MindPoint Quiz Show* *TPR Stories:* Algún día seré..., p. 120 *TPR Stories:* Algún día seré...(segunda parte), p. 125 *Lecturas* para hispanohablantes: Ficción, pp. 88–89 *Lecturas* para hispanohablantes: Aprender el inglés, p. 91 *Realidades* para hispanohablantes: Act. O, p. 342 *Realidades* para hispanohablantes: Act. R, p. 344 *Pre-AP* Resource Book:* pp. 130–131
Speaking	p. 454 p. 467 p. 469 p. 471	Supplemental Pre-AP* Activity Act. 25 Supplemental Pre-AP* Activity Presentación oral	*TPR Stories:* pp. 121–124 *Teacher's Resource Book, Temas 5–9:* Communicative Activity 9A-2, pp. 240–241 *Teacher's Resource Book, Temas 5–9:* Situation cards, p. 242 *Assessment Program:* Parte II, Hablar, p. 238 *Realidades* para hispanohablantes: Presentación oral, p. 347 *Pre-AP* Resource Book:* pp. 130–131
Writing	p. 460 p. 463 p. 467 p. 469	Act. 25 Supplemental Pre-AP* Activity Differentiated Instruction: Advanced Learners/Pre-AP* Supplemental Pre-AP* Activity	*Writing, Audio & Video Workbook:* Act. 4, p. 168 *Writing, Audio & Video Workbook:* Act. 13, p. 175 *Go Online:* Internet Link Activity *ExamView:* Pre-AP* Question Bank *Assessment Program:* Parte II, Escribir, p. 238 *Realidades* para hispanohablantes: Act. P, p. 343 *Realidades* para hispanohablantes: Act. T, p. 345 *Pre-AP* Resource Book:* pp. 130–131

	Student Edition/Teacher's Edition		Ancillaries
	Page #	**Activity**	
Vocabulary	p. 478	Supplemental Pre-AP* Activity	*Go Online:* Self-test
	p. 482	Differentiated Instruction: Advanced Learners/Pre-AP*	
Listening	pp. 478–479	Videohistoria	*Video Program* Chapter 9B
			Video Teacher's Guide Chapter 9B
	p. 491	Supplemental Pre-AP* Activity	*Pre-AP* Resource Book:* pp. 130–131
Reading	p. 493	Supplemental Pre-AP* Activity	*Reading and Writing for Success:* Test 27, pp. 81–83
	p. 494	Perspectivas del mundo hispano	*MindPoint Quiz Show*
			TPR Stories: El superhéroe del futuro, p. 127
			TPR Stories: El club de ecología, pp. 128–129
			Lecturas para hispanohablantes: Lo hispano es bello, pp. 93–94
			Realidades para hispanohablantes: Act. O, p. 362
			Realidades para hispanohablantes: Act. R, p. 364
			Pre-AP* Resource Book: pp. 130–131
Speaking	p. 478	Supplemental Pre-AP* Activity	*Teacher's Resource Book, Temas 5–9:* Communicative Activity 9B-1, pp. 264–265
	p. 491	Supplemental Pre-AP* Activity	*Teacher's Resource Book, Temas 5–9:* Situation cards, p. 268
	p. 493	Supplemental Pre-AP* Activity	*Assessment Program:* Parte II, Hablar, p. 251
			Pre-AP* Resource Book: pp. 130–131
Writing	p. 482	Differentiated Instruction: Advanced Learners/Pre-AP*	*Writing, Audio & Video Workbook*: Act.13, p. 184
	p. 490	Act. 22	*Reading and Writing for Success:* Test 27, pp. 81–83
	p. 491	Supplemental Pre-AP* Activity	*Go Online:* Internet Link Activity
	p. 495	Presentación escrita	*ExamView:* Pre-AP* Question Bank
			Assessment Program: Parte II, Escribir, p. 250
			Realidades para hispanohablantes: Act. Q, p. 363
			Realidades para hispanohablantes: Act. T, p. 365
			Realidades para hispanohablantes: Presentación escrita, p. 367
			Pre-AP* Resource Book: pp. 130–131

Teacher Activity 1
Formal Oral Presentation

1. Have students listen to Audio Activity 7 on p. 169 in the *Realidades* Writing, Audio & Video Workbook.

2. Next, have students prepare a one-minute talk based on *Mi vida hoy y en el futuro* found on p. 471 of the *Realidades* Student Textbook. Like the teens speaking in Activity 7, students should give reasons for making the career choice that they present. The amount of preparation time can vary, but should not be longer than three or four minutes.

3. Students are then allowed one minute to record their presentations, or they may make their presentations to a group of three or four students.

4. In groups of three or four, students should listen to each recording (or hear each presentation) and discuss the content and quality using the scoring guidelines on p. 45.

Teacher Activity 2
Formal Writing

Have students read *Animales en peligro de extinción* on p. 483 of the *Realidades* Student Textbook as well as *La contaminación acústica* on p. 489 of the *Realidades* Student Textbook. They should also listen to Audio Activity 8 on p. 179 of the *Realidades* Writing, Audio & Video Workbook. Students should then write four paragraphs describing what they believe to be the most serious global environmental problem and propose solutions for resolving that problem. They should cite the two readings and audio text mentioned above as examples of ways to resolve environmental problems.

Then make three photocopies of each student's written work. Place students in groups of four. Distribute copies of the scoring guidelines found on p. 45. (Since this is a writing task, the *Fluency* category on the bottom row can be ignored at this time.) Distribute the copies of the students' work within each group. Have each student read his or her writing aloud to the group, one piece at a time, and discuss the content and quality of each writing piece using the scoring guidelines. Each group may select one sample to share with the whole class.

Teacher Activity 3
Informal Writing

1. Have students imagine that they are spending a week away from home doing community service work. They should write a postcard to their parents telling them what they have been doing while on volunteer assignment.

2. After students have completed this activity, make three photocopies of each student's written work. Place students in groups of four. Distribute copies of the scoring guidelines found on p. 45. (Since this is a writing task, the *Fluency* category on the bottom row can be ignored at this time.) Distribute the copies of the students' work within each group. Have each student read his or her writing aloud to the group, one piece at a time, and discuss the content and quality of each writing piece using the scoring guidelines. Each group may select one sample to share with the whole class.

Student Activity 1
Informal Speaking

Work with a partner to write complete-sentence answers to the following questions. Be sure to verify the correctness of your answers. Then, use the questions (and answers) to play *Preguntas rápidas* (see p. 38) or to prepare for *One minute of questions* (For Levels 1 and 2) (see p. 38).

1. ¿Te sugieren tus profesores que estudies durante las vacaciones?

2. ¿Les gusta a tus padres que vayas al extranjero?

3. ¿Insiste tu amigo(a) en que le mandes una tarjeta postal?

4. ¿Cuánto tiempo dura un vuelo a España?

5. ¿Te diviertes mucho viajando por bote de vela?

6. ¿Es bueno que visites los sitios históricos?

7. ¿Adónde viajarás el verano próximo?

8. ¿Asistirás a la universidad después del colegio?

9. ¿Cómo te ganarás la vida en el futuro?

10. ¿Tendrás que estudiar muchos años para tu carrera futura?

11. ¿Seguirás una carrera militar?

12. ¿Será importante que hagamos mejores leyes para el medio ambiente?

13. Si reciclamos más, ¿podremos reducir la basura en el mundo?

14. ¿Dudas que haya soluciones fáciles para el medio ambiente?

15. ¿A qué hora saldrás de la escuela esta tarde?

16. ¿Cómo recomiendas que se resuelva el problema de la guerra?

Level 3
Resource Support

	Student Edition/Teacher's Edition		Ancillaries
	Page #	Activity	
Vocabulary	p. 23	Supplemental Pre-AP* Activity	*Assessment Program:* Examen 1, Vocabulario y gramática 1, p. 20 *Assessment Program:* Examen 2: Vocabulario y gramática, p. 29 *Go Online:* Self-test
Listening	p. 38 p. 56	Supplemental Pre-AP* Activity Supplemental Pre-AP* Activity	*Video Program* Chapter 1 *Video Teacher's Guide* Chapter 1 *Writing, Audio & Video Workbook:* Act. 1, p. 8 *Pre-AP* Resource Book,* pp. 135–136
Reading	p. 38	Supplemental Pre-AP* Activity	*MindPoint Quiz Show* *Lecturas* para hispanohablantes: La vida, *p. 13* *Lecturas* para hispanohablantes: Viajes, pp. 15–16 *Reading and Writing for Success:* Test 28, pp. 84–87 *Pre-AP* Resource Book:* pp. 135–136
Speaking	p. 23 p. 41 p. 42 p. 43 p. 44 p. 51 p. 56	Supplemental Pre-AP* Activity Act. 35 Differentiated Instruction: Advanced Learners/Pre-AP* Act. 38 Supplemental Pre-AP* Activity Presentación oral Supplemental Pre-AP* Activity	*Assessment Program:* Examen 1, Hablar, p. 33 *Teacher's Resource Book:* Situation cards, p. 41 *Realidades* para hispanohablantes: Act. Z, p. 37 *Realidades* para hispanohablantes: Presentación oral, p. 38 *Lecturas* para hispanohablantes: Después de leer, pp. 12, 14, 16 *Pre-AP* Resource Book,* pp. 135–136
Writing	p. 23 p. 34 p. 36 p. 41 p. 42 p. 43 p. 44 p. 53 p. 56	Supplemental Pre-AP* Activity Supplemental Pre-AP* Activity Differentiated Instruction: Advanced Learners/Pre-AP* Act. 35 Differentiated Instruction: Advanced Learners/Pre-AP* Act. 38 Supplemental Pre-AP* Activity Presentación escrita Supplemental Pre-AP* Activity	*Go Online:* Internet Link Activity *Assessment Program:* Examen 1, Escribir, p. 33 *Writing, Audio & Video Workbook:* Act. 12, p. 18 *Writing, Audio & Video Workbook:* Act. 13, p. 19 *Realidades* para hispanohablantes: Act. Q, p. 27 *Realidades* para hispanohablantes: Presentación escrita, p. 39 *Lecturas* para hispanohablantes: Ampliación, pp. 12, 14, 16 *Reading and Writing for Success:* Test 28, pp. 84–87 *ExamView:* Pre-AP* Question Bank *Pre-AP* Resource Book:* p. 135

Teacher Activity 1
Informal Speaking—Simulated Conversation

1. Allow students one minute to prepare to record the conversation. For earlier *temas*, teachers may wish to allow more preparation time. However, allowing too much preparation time will lead to students' writing the script of what they want to say, and subsequently reading it. The purpose of the preparation time is to get a sense of the conversation and to generally gather thoughts.

2. Students should record their conversations. (See Recording and Evaluating on p. 40.) (See also "Administering the *Examen del capítulo* Speaking Proficiency Test" on p. T66 of the *Realidades* Assessment Program.) The teacher can be the voice of the other person in the conversation, allowing no more than 30 seconds for each response from students.

3. In groups of three or four, students should listen to each recording and discuss the content and quality using the scoring guidelines on p. 45. Teachers may also consider using the "Speaking and Writing Rubrics for the *Examen del capítulo*" available in the *Realidades* Assessment Program front matter. Near the end of *Realidades* 3, teachers might wish to begin using adapted versions of the official AP* Spanish Language Scoring Guidelines for the informal speaking task found at: apcentral.collegeboard.com/spanlang.

Teacher Activity 2
Formal Writing

For each of the Formal Writing Student Activities, there are recommend readings as well as a recommended listening selection. Students should:

1. Listen to the indicated audio selection, taking notes as they listen.

2. Complete the two reading selections silently.

3. Prepare a formal written essay citing information from the audio and reading sources. By the end of the academic year, students should be able to write approximately 200 words.

Once students have finished writing, make three photocopies of each student's written work. Place students in groups of four. Distribute copies of the scoring guidelines found on p. 45. (Since this is a writing task, the *Fluency* category on the bottom row can be ignored at this time.) Distribute the copies of the students' work within each group. Have each student read his or her writing aloud to the group, one piece at a time, and discuss the content and quality of each writing piece using the scoring guidelines. Each group may select one sample to share with the whole class, as time permits. Near the end of *Realidades* 3, teachers might wish to begin using adapted versions of the official AP* Spanish Language Scoring Guidelines for the formal writing task found at: apcentral.collegeboard.com/spanlang.

Note: Continue to consider and to bring to students' attention the many writing tips offered in the *Realidades* Student Textbook as well as in the "Preparing to Write an Essay" section of this Pre-AP* Resource Book.

Student Activity 1
Informal Speaking—Simulated Conversation

Directions: You will now participate in a simulated telephone conversation before which you will have 45 seconds to read the outline of the conversation. During that time, plan how you will respond by making brief notes to yourself. Do not try to write out your answers, as there will not be sufficient time, and the purpose of this exercise is to strengthen your ability to engage in sustained conversations in Spanish. After the preparation time ends, the phone conversation will begin. When it is your turn to speak, you will have 30 seconds to respond. Use your 30 seconds to give an appropriate response, using up the allocated time as fully as possible.

Scenario: You just returned from a two-week family vacation. Your friend, Nico, has called to ask if you enjoyed your trip.

NICO: ¿Qué tal, amigo? Hace mucho que no nos hablamos. ¿Cómo estás?

TÚ: _____

NICO: Pues, cuéntame algo de tus vacaciones. ¿Cuál fue la mejor cosa que hiciste?

TÚ: _____

NICO: ¿Te aburriste en algún momento?

TÚ: _____

NICO: ¡Qué va! ¿Cuándo vamos a vernos? ¿Quieres hacer algo mañana?

TÚ: _____

NICO: Perfecto. Hasta entonces. Adiós.

Student Activity 2
Formal Writing

Directions: First, you will hear an audio recording. You should take notes as you listen. Next, you will read the print articles. You will have a maximum of 15 minutes to accomplish these steps. Then, you will have 45 minutes to write a well-organized, formal essay on the topic below. Be sure to use information from all three sources to support your ideas in your essay, and cite the sources appropriately as they are used. This essay is not intended to be a summary of the three sources, but rather, an opportunity for you to synthesize these sources into your own ideas.

Audio Source: Video Script, *Los deportes en el mundo hispano*, Capítulo 1 (*Realidades* TRB, p. 33)

Reading Source 1: *Parques nacionales de América del Sur* (*Realidades* Student Textbook, p. 27)

Reading Source 2: *El Camino de Santiago* (*Realidades* Student Textbook, pp. 48-49)

Topic: Explique el valor y los beneficios de viajar al extranjero.

	Student Edition/Teacher's Edition		Ancillaries
	Page #	**Activity**	
Vocabulary	p. 73	Supplemental Pre-AP* Activity	*Realidades para hispanohablantes:* Act. B, p.19 *Assessment Program:* Prueba 2–2, pp. 39–40 *Assessment Program:* Prueba 2–6, p. 49 *Go Online:* Self-test
Listening	p. 73 p. 74 p. 92 p. 102	Supplemental Pre-AP* Activity Supplemental Pre-AP* Activity Supplemental Pre-AP* Activity Supplemental Pre-AP* Activity	*Writing, Audio & Video Workbook:* Act. 4, p. 24 *Writing, Audio & Video Workbook:* Act. 5, p. 25 *Video Program* Chapter 2; *Video Teacher's Guide* Chapter 2 *Pre-AP* Resource Book:* pp. 138–139
Reading	p. 75	Act. 12	*Lecturas para hispanohablantes:* Alguna vez, pp. 19–20; Niña, p. 23; El museo de joyas del bosque lluvioso, pp. 24–26 *Realidades para hispanohablantes:* Lectura, pp. 44–45 *Reading and Writing for Success:* Test 29, pp. 88–90 *Go Online:* Internet Link Activity *MindPoint Quiz Show* *Teacher's Resource Book:* Communicative Activity 2–2, pp. 77–78 *Pre-AP* Resource Book:* pp. 138–139
Speaking	p. 73 p. 74 p. 84 p. 92 p. 93 p. 97 p. 102	Supplemental Pre-AP* Activity Supplemental Pre-AP* Activity Supplemental Pre-AP* Activity Supplemental Pre-AP* Activity Supplemental Pre-AP* Activity Presentación oral Supplemental Pre-AP* Activity	*Assessment Program:* Examen del capítulo 2, Parte D, Hablar, p. 56 *Teacher's Resource Book:* Communicative Activity 2–2, pp. 77–78 *Teacher's Resource Book:* Situation cards, p. 83 *Realidades para hispanohablantes:* Presentación oral, p. 70 *Lecturas para hispanohablantes:* Después de leer y Ampliación, pp. 23, 26 *Pre-AP* Resource Book:* pp. 138–139
Writing	p. 75 p. 76 p. 84 p. 86 p. 92 p. 93 p. 98 p. 102	Act.12 Differentiated Instruction: Advanced Learners/Pre-AP* Supplemental Pre-AP* Activity Supplemental Pre-AP* Activity Supplemental Pre-AP* Activity Supplemental Pre-AP* Activity Presentación escrita Supplemental Pre-AP* Activity	*Writing, Audio & Video Workbook:* Act. 9, p. 29 *Writing, Audio & Video Workbook:* Act. 13, p. 33 *Reading and Writing for Success:* Test 19, pp. 57–59 *Realidades para hispanohablantes:* Act. BB, p. 69; Presentación escrita, p. 71 *Lecturas para hispanohablantes:* Ampliación, p. 21 *Assessment Program:* Examen del capítulo 2, Parte C, p. 56 *Go Online:* Internet Link Activity *ExamView:* Pre-AP* Question Bank *Pre-AP* Resource Book:* pp. 138–139

Teacher Activity 1
Formal Speaking—Oral Presentation

For each of the Oral Presentation Student Activities, there is a recommend reading and listening selection. Students should:

1. Listen to the indicated audio selection, taking notes as they listen.

2. Complete the reading selection silently.

3. Prepare an oral presentation citing information from the audio and reading sources.

4. After the audio selection, allow students no more than 10 minutes to complete the reading selection and prepare the oral presentation. Students should not try to script every word of the presentation, but rather make notes about ideas they wish to express, noting key vocabulary expressions, conjugations, etc.

5. Students are then allowed two minutes to record their presentations, or they may make their presentations to a group of three or four students, and occasionally to the whole class.

6. Recordings are the preferred method of presentation, as this will allow students, in groups of three or four, to listen to each recording (or hear each presentation) and discuss the content and quality using the scoring guidelines on p. 45. Teachers may also consider using the "Speaking and Writing Rubrics for the *Examen del capítulo* available in the *Realidades* Assessment Program front matter. Near the end of *Realidades* 3, teachers might wish to begin using adapted versions of the official AP* Spanish Language Scoring Guidelines for the formal speaking task found at: apcentral.collegeboard.com/spanlang.

Teacher Activity 2
Informal Writing

After students have completed the Informal Writing task, make three photocopies of each student's written work. Place students in groups of four. Distribute copies of the scoring guidelines found on p. 45. (Since this is a writing task, the *Fluency* category on the bottom row can be ignored at this time.) Distribute the copies of the students' work within each group. Have each student read his or her writing aloud to the group, one piece at a time, and discuss the content and quality of each writing piece using the scoring guidelines. Each group may select one sample to share with the whole class. Near the end of *Realidades* 3, teachers might wish to begin using adapted versions of the official AP* Spanish Language Scoring Guidelines for the informal writing task found at: apcentral.collegeboard.com/spanlang.

Student Activity 1
Paragraph Completion

Directions: Read the following passage, completing the blanks with a word in Spanish that is logical and grammatically correct. You must spell and accent the word correctly.

María de los Remedios Varo y Uranga nació (1) _____ 16 de diciembre de 1908 en Angelés, un pequeño pueblo (2) _____ norte de Barcelona. Era hija (3) _____ Rodrigo Varo y de Ignacia Uranga. Su padre era ingeniero. Construía canales. A causa de su trabajo, Rodrigo llevaba (4) _____ su familia por muchas partes de España y del Norte de América. Desde joven, a Remedios (5) _____ gustaba pintar. Como otros artistas y escritores españoles de su generación, ella viajó (6) _____ París en 1930 en búsqueda de nuevas ideas. Allí, encontró una fuente (7) _____ inspiración en el movimiento surrealista. Los surrealistas trataron (8) _____ expresar imágines del subconsciente. En 1936, a causa de la Guerra Civil española, Remedios tuvo (9) _____ buscar refugio en México. Allí, Remedios creó algunas de las obras más originales (10) _____ la pintura moderna.

Student Activity 2
Formal Speaking—Oral Presentation

Imagine that you must give a formal presentation on the topic of art and inspiration. Tell the class what sort of art would you like to express (music, dance, painting, sculpture, etc.) and why. Be sure to explain what you would use for your inspiration. To prepare for your presentation:

1. Listen to the Video Script, *El arte en el mundo hispano*, *Capítulo 2*. (**Realidades** TRB p. 74)

2. Read *Entrevista con Dina Bursztyn*. (**Realidades** Student Textbook, p. 70)

3. Prepare an outline of the presentation, noting key vocabulary words and ideas. Be sure to cite information and/or examples from the reading as well as from the audio portion of this activity. (Do not try to write an entire script. You will have 10 minutes to complete steps 2 and 3.)

4. Make a live presentation to your classmates, or record your oral presentation, as directed by your teacher. The maximum presentation length is two minutes. You should use all the time allowed giving as rich and full a presentation as possible.

Student Activity 3
Informal Writing

Write an e-mail to your friend inviting him or her to go with you to visit your favorite art museum on Sunday afternoon. Let your friend know:

- What he or she can expect to see there
- Why you love to visit this particular museum
- What time you would like to go

You have 10 minutes to complete this task. Write as complete a response as possible, using rich details and appropriate language.

	Student Edition/Teacher 's Edition		Ancillaries
	Page #	**Activity**	
Vocabulary	p. 129	Supplemental Pre-AP* Activity	*Assessment Program:* Prueba 3–2, pp. 61–62
			Assessment Program: Prueba 3–7, pp. 71–72
			Go Online: Self-test
Listening	p. 115	Supplemental Pre-AP* Activity	*Video Program* Chapter 3
	p. 121	Supplemental Pre-AP* Activity	*Video Teacher's Guide* Chapter 3
	p. 148	Supplemental Pre-AP* Activity	*Pre-AP* Resource Book:* pp. 141–142
Reading	p. 139	Act. 40	*Realidades* para hispanohablantes: Act. 2A-6, p. 24
	p. 148	Supplemental Pre-AP* Activity	*MindPoint Quiz Show*
			Reading and Writing for Success: Test 30, pp. 91–94
			Lecturas para hispanohablantes: El diario a diario, p. 29; Tiempo libre, p. 31; De los periódicos, p. 34
			Pre-AP* Resource Book: pp. 141–142
Speaking	p. 115	Supplemental Pre-AP* Activity	*Assessment Program:* Examen del capítulo 3, Hablar, p. 80
	p. 121	Supplemental Pre-AP* Activity	*Teacher's Resource Book:* Communicative Activity 3–4, pp. 123–124
	p. 124	Act. 17	
	p. 129	Supplemental Pre-AP* Activity	*Teacher's Resource Book:* Situation cards, p. 125
	p. 134	Differentiated Instruction: Advanced Learners/Pre-AP*	*Realidades* para hispanohablantes: Act. GG, p. 101; Presentación oral, p. 102
	p. 137	Supplemental Pre-AP* Activity	*Lecturas* para hispanohablantes: Después de leer, pp. 29, 32, 34
	p. 139	Presentación oral	
	p. 143	Act. 40	*Pre-AP* Resource Book:* pp. 141–142
	p. 148	Supplemental Pre-AP* Activity	
Writing	p. 115	Supplemental Pre-AP* Activity	*Writing, Audio & Video Workbook:* Act. 7, p. 41
	p. 122	Differentiated Instruction: Advanced Learners/Pre-AP*	*Writing, Audio & Video Workbook:* Act. 8, p. 42
			Writing, Audio & Video Workbook: Act. 13, p. 47
	p. 124	Act. 17	*Teacher's Resource Book:* Communicative Activity 3–4, pp. 124–125
	p. 134	Differentiated Instruction: Advanced Learners/Pre-AP*	*Realidades* para hispanohablantes: El español en el mundo del trabajo, p. 93
	p. 137	Supplemental Pre-AP* Activity	*Realidades* para hispanohablantes: Presentación escrita, p. 103
	p. 144	Presentación escrita	
	p. 148	Supplemental Pre-AP* Activity	*Lecturas* para hispanohablantes: Ampliación, pp. 29, 32, 34
			Go Online: Internet Link Activity
			ExamView: Pre-AP* Question Bank
			Assessment Program: Examen 3, Escribir, p. 80
			Pre-AP* Resource Book: pp. 141–142

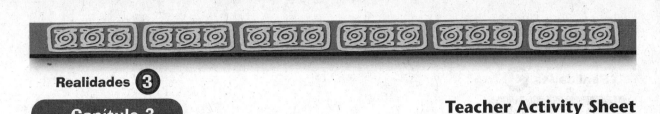

Teacher Activity 1
Informal Speaking—Simulated Conversation

1. Allow students one minute to prepare to record the conversation. For earlier *temas,* teachers may wish to allow more preparation time. However, allowing too much preparation time will lead to students' writing the script of what they want to say, and subsequently reading it. The purpose of the preparation time is to get a sense of the conversation and to generally gather thoughts.

2. Students should record their conversations. (See Recording and Evaluating on p. 40.) (See also "Administering the *Examen del capítulo* Speaking Proficiency Test" on p. T66 of the *Realidades* Assessment Program.) The teacher can be the voice of the other person in the conversation, allowing no more than 30 seconds for each response from the students.

3. In groups of three or four, students should listen to each recording and discuss the content and quality using the scoring guidelines on p. 49. Teachers may also consider using the "Speaking and Writing Rubrics for the *Examen del capítulo*" available in the *Realidades* Assessment Program front matter. Near the end of *Realidades* 3, teachers might wish to begin using adapted versions of the official AP* Spanish Language Scoring Guidelines for the informal speaking task found at: apcentral.collegeboard.com/spanlang.

Teacher Activity 2
Formal Writing

For each of the Formal Writing Student Activities, there are recommend readings as well as a recommended listening selection. Students should:

1. Listen to the indicated audio selection, taking notes as they listen.

2. Complete the two reading selections silently.

3. Prepare a formal written essay citing information from the audio and reading sources. By the end of the academic year, students should be able to write approximately 200 words.

Once students have finished writing, make three photocopies of each student's written work. Place students in groups of four. Distribute copies of the scoring guidelines found on p. 45. (Since this is a writing task, the *Fluency* category on the bottom row can be ignored at this time.) Distribute the copies of the students' work within each group. Have each student read his or her writing aloud to the group, one piece at a time, and discuss the content and quality of each writing piece using the scoring guidelines. Each group may select one sample to share with the whole class, as time permits. Near the end of *Realidades* 3, teachers might wish to begin using adapted versions of the official AP* Spanish Language Scoring Guidelines for the formal writing task found at: apcentral.collegeboard.com/spanlang.

Note: Continue to consider and to bring to students' attention the many writing tips offered in the *Realidades* Student Textbook as well as in the "Preparing to Write an Essay" section of this Pre-AP* Resource Book.

Student Activity 1
Informal Speaking—Simulated Conversation

Directions: You will now participate in a simulated telephone conversation and will have 45 seconds to read the outline of the conversation. During that time, plan how you will respond by making brief notes to yourself. Do not try to write out your answers, as there will not be sufficient time, and the purpose of this exercise is to strengthen your ability to engage in sustained conversations in Spanish. After the preparation time ends, the phone conversation will begin. When it is your turn to speak, you will have 30 seconds to respond. Use your 30 seconds to give an appropriate response, using up the allocated time as fully as possible.

Scenario: You and your classmate, Lisa, are assigned to give a talk to a group of elementary students next week about health and fitness. Lisa calls you to begin to plan your presentation.

LISA: Hola, amigo(a). Quisiera hablarte sobre nuestra presentación a los estudiantes de la escuela elemental. ¿Tienes ideas?

TÚ: _____

LISA: ¿Qué tipos de ejercicios y actividades debemos recomendarles?

TÚ: _____

LISA: ¿Cuáles aspectos de la dieta quieres presentar?

TÚ: _____

LISA: Bien. ¿Y qué te parece demostrarles algunos ejercicios físicos?

TÚ: _____

LISA: Perfecto. Me gusta este plan. Nos vemos mañana.

TÚ: _____

Student Activity 2
Formal Writing

Directions: First, you will hear an audio recording. You should take notes as you listen. Next, you will read the print articles. You will have a maximum of 15 minutes to accomplish these steps. Then, you will have 45 minutes to write a well-organized, formal essay on the topic below. Be sure to use information from all three sources to support your ideas in your essay, and cite the sources appropriately as they are used. This essay is not intended to be a summary of the three sources, but rather, an opportunity for you to synthesize these sources into your own ideas.

Audio Source: Audio Activity 1 (*Realidades* TRB, p. 111)

Reading Source 1: *Conexiones: Las ciencias* (*Realidades* Student Textbook, p. 124)

Reading Source 2: *¡Cambia tus hábitos!* (*Realidades* Student Textbook, pp. 146-148)

Topic: Explique la importancia de una dieta nutritiva y equilibrada.

	Student Edition/Teacher's Edition		Ancillaries
	Page #	Activity	
Vocabulary	p. 162	Supplemental Pre-AP* Activity	*Assessment Program:* Prueba 4–2, pp. 85–86
	p. 177	Supplemental Pre-AP* Activity	*Assessment Program:* Prueba 4–6, p. 94
			Go Online: Self-test
Listening	p. 162	Supplemental Pre-AP* Activity	*Writing, Audio & Video Workbook:* Act. 4, p. 52
	p. 164	Differentiated Instruction: Advanced Learners/Pre-AP*	*Video Program* Chapter 4
			Video Teacher's Guide Chapter 4
	p. 177	Supplemental Pre-AP* Activity	*Pre-AP* Resource Book:* pp. 144–145
	p. 192	Supplemental Pre-AP* Activity	
Reading	p. 173	Act. 21	*Reading and Writing for Success:* Test 31, pp. 95–97
			Lecturas para hispanohablantes: Apocalipsis, p. 37; Génesis, p. 38; Niño del futuro, p. 40; Los teseros ocultos del fondo del mar, pp. 42–43
			MindPoint Quiz Show
			Pre-AP* Resource Book: pp. 144–145
Speaking	p. 162	Supplemental Pre-AP* Activity	*Assessment Program:* Examen del capítulo 4, Hablar, p. 102
	p. 164	Differentiated Instruction: Advanced Learners/Pre-AP*	*Teacher's Resource Book:* Situation cards, p. 166
	p. 171	Supplemental Pre-AP* Activity	*Realidades* para hispanohablantes: Act. Z, p. 133
	p. 173	Act. 21	*Realidades* para hispanohablantes: Presentación oral, p. 134
	p. 177	Supplemental Pre-AP* Activity	*Lecturas* para hispanohablantes: Después de leer, pp. 37, 38, 40
	p. 189	Presentación oral	
	p. 192	Supplemental Pre-AP* Activity	*Pre-AP* Resource Book:* pp. 144–145
Writing	p. 162	Supplemental Pre-AP* Activity	*Assessment Program:* Examen del capítulo 4, Escribir, p. 102
	p. 164	Differentiated Instruction: Advanced Learners/Pre-AP*	*Writing, Audio & Video Workbook:* Act. 9, p. 57
	p. 171	Supplemental Pre-AP* Activity	*Writing, Audio & Video Workbook:* Act. 13, p. 61
	p. 173	Act. 21	*Reading and Writing for Success:* Test 20, pp. 60–62
	p. 178	Differentiated Instruction: Advanced Learners/Pre-AP*	*Realidades* para hispanohablantes: Fondo cultural, p. 123
	p. 182	Act. 34	*Realidades* para hispanohablantes: Presentación escrita, p. 135
	p. 183	Supplemental Pre-AP* Activity	*Lecturas* para hispanohablantes: Ampliación, pp. 37, 38, 40, 44
	p. 190	Presentación escrita	*Go Online:* Internet Link Activity
	p. 192	Supplemental Pre-AP* Activity	*ExamView:* Pre-AP* Question Bank
			Pre-AP* Resource Book: pp. 144–145

Teacher Activity 1
Formal Speaking—Oral Presentation

For each of the Oral Presentation Student Activities, there is a recommend reading as well as a recommended listening selection. Students should:

1. Listen to the indicated audio selection, taking notes as they listen.

2. Complete the reading selection silently.

3. Prepare an oral presentation citing information from the audio and reading sources.

4. After the audio selection, allow students no more than 10 minutes to complete the reading selection and prepare the oral presentation. Students should not try to script every word of the presentation, but rather make notes about ideas they wish to express, noting key vocabulary expressions, conjugations, etc.

5. Students are then allowed two minutes to record their presentations, or they may make their presentations to a group of three or four students, and occasionally to the whole class.

6. Recordings are the preferred method of presentation, as this will allow students, in groups of three or four, to listen to each recording (or hear each presentation) and discuss the content and quality using the scoring guidelines on p. 45. Teachers may also consider using the "Speaking and Writing Rubrics for the *Examen del capítulo* available in the *Realidades* Assessment Program front matter. Near the end of *Realidades* 3, teachers might wish to begin using adapted versions of the official AP* Spanish Language Scoring Guidelines for the formal speaking task found at: apcentral.collegeboard.com/spanlang.

Teacher Activity 2
Informal Writing

After students have completed the Informal Writing task, make three photocopies of each student's written work. Place students in groups of four. Distribute copies of the scoring guidelines found on p. 45. (Since this is a writing task, the *Fluency* category on the bottom row can be ignored at this time.) Distribute the copies of the students' work within each group. Have each student read his or her writing aloud to the group, one piece at a time, and discuss the content and quality of each writing piece using the scoring guidelines. Each group may select one sample to share with the whole class. Near the end of *Realidades* 3, teachers might wish to begin using adapted versions of the official AP* Spanish Language Scoring Guidelines for the informal writing task found at: apcentral.collegeboard.com/spanlang.

Student Activity 1
Paragraph Completion

Directions: Read the following passage, completing the blanks with a word in Spanish that is logical and grammatically correct. You must spell and accent the word correctly.

Cuando hay problemas o conflictos en una familia, (1) _____ mejor es tratar (2) _____ resolver (3) _____ problemas. Los conflictos ocurren cuando hay diferencias de opinión (4) _____ los miembros de la familia. Entonces, todos tienen que colaborar para reconciliarse, o sea, para hacer (5) _____ paces. Hay (6) _____ evitar las peleas entre los miembros de la familia. Se puede discutir, pero sin insultar ni acusar (7) _____ nadie de algo que no hizo. Si algún miembro de la familia (8) _____ porta mal, es decir, su comportamiento es malo, debemos tratar de (9) _____ haga caso, porque eso pueder romper la paz o la armonia familiar. Y más que nada, cada uno debe pensar (10) _____ los demás y no sólo en sí mismo, para tener una bonita relación.

Student Activity 2
Formal Speaking—Oral Presentation

Imagine that you must give a formal presentation for your Spanish class on the topic of friendship. You must tell the class why you believe that lasting friendships are important. To prepare for your presentation:

1. Listen to the Video Script, *Una amistad entre hermanos, Capítulo 4.* (*Realidades* TRB. p.158)

2. Read *La amistad.* (*Realidades* Student Textbook, p. 70)

3. Prepare an outline of the presentation, noting key vocabulary words and ideas. Be sure to cite information and / or examples from the reading as well as from the audio portion of this activity. (Do not try to write an entire script. You will have 10 minutes to complete steps 2 and 3.)

4. Make a live presentation to your classmates, or record your oral presentation, as directed by your teacher. The maximum presentation length is two minutes. You should use all the time allowed giving as rich and full a presentation as possible.

Student Activity 3
Informal Writing

You and your best friend just had a big disagreement. Write a short letter to your local newspaper's advice column. In your letter:

- Explain both sides of the disagreement.
- Tell why you think you are right.
- Ask what you should do to resolve this conflict.

You have 10 minutes to complete this task. Write as complete a response as possible, using rich details and appropriate language.

	Student Edition/Teacher's Edition		Ancillaries
	Page #	Activity	
Vocabulary	p. 209 p. 223	Supplemental Pre-AP* Activity Supplemental Pre-AP* Activity	*Assessment Program:* Prueba 5–2, pp. 107 *Assessment Program:* Prueba 5–6, pp. 116–117 *Go Online:* Self-test
Listening	p. 209 p. 219	Supplemental Pre-AP* Activity Supplemental Pre-AP* Activity	*Assessment Program:* Examen del capítulo 5, Escuchar, p. 125 *Video Program* Chapter 5 *Video Teacher's Guide* Chapter 5 *Pre-AP* Resource Book:* pp. 147–148
Reading	p. 241	Supplemental Pre-AP* Activity	*MindPoint Quiz Show* *Reading and Writing for Success:* Test 32, pp. 98–100 *Teacher's Resource Book:* Communicative Activity 5–1, pp. 200–201 *Lecturas* para hispanohablantes: Como un escolar sencillo, pp. 47–49; Canción, p. 51; Poeta y músico del pueblo, pp. 52–54 *Pre-AP* Resource Book:* pp. 147–148
Speaking	p. 209 p. 218 p. 228 p. 231 p. 235 p. 241	Supplemental Pre-AP* Activity Act. 20 Differentiated Instruction: Advanced Learners/Pre-AP* Act. 39 Presentación oral Supplemental Pre-AP* Activity	*Assessment Program:* Examen del capítulo 5, Hablar, p. 124 *Teacher's Resource Book:* Communicative Activity 5–1, pp. 200–201 *Teacher's Resource Book:* Situation cards, p. 208 *Realidades* para hispanohablantes: Act. DD, p. 165 *Realidades* para hispanohablantes: Presentación oral, p. 166 *Lecturas* para hispanohablantes: Después de leer, pp. 49, 51, 54 *Pre-AP* Resource Book:* pp. 147–148
Writing	p. 209 p. 210 p. 218 p. 219 p. 223 p. 227 p. 231 p. 236	Supplemental Pre-AP* Activity Differentiated Instruction: Advanced Learners/Pre-AP* Act. 20 Supplemental Pre-AP* Activity Supplemental Pre-AP* Activity Supplemental Pre-AP* Activity Act. 39 Presentación escrita	*Assessment Program:* Examen del capítulo 5, Escribir, p. 124 *Writing, Audio & Video Workbook:* Act. 9, p. 71 *Writing, Audio & Video Workbook:* Act. 13, p. 75 *Realidades* para hispanohablantes: Act. Ñ, p. 150 *Realidades* para hispanohablantes: El español en la comunidad, p. 161 *Realidades* para hispanohablantes: Presentación escrita, p. 167 *Lecturas* para hispanohablantes: Ampliación, pp. 49, 51, 54 *Go Online:* Internet Link Activity *ExamView:* Pre-AP* Question Bank *Pre-AP* Resource Book:* pp. 147–148

Teacher Activity 1
Informal Speaking—Simulated Conversation

1. Allow students one minute to prepare to record the conversation. For earlier *temas,* teachers may wish to allow just a bit more preparation time. However, allowing too much preparation time will lead to students' writing the script of what they want to say, and subsequently reading it. The purpose of the preparation time is to get a sense of the conversation and to generally gather thoughts.

2. Students should record their conversations. (See Recording and Evaluating on p. 40.) (See also "Administering the *Examen del capítulo* Speaking Proficiency Test" on p. T66 of the *Realidades* Assessment Program.) The teacher can be the voice of the other person in the conversation, allowing no more than 30 seconds for each response from the students.

3. In groups of three or four, students should listen to each recording and discuss the content and quality using the scoring guidelines on p. 45. Teachers may also consider using the "Speaking and Writing Rubrics for the *Examen del capítulo*" available in the *Realidades* Assessment Program front matter. Near the end of *Realidades* 3, teachers might wish to begin using adapted versions of the official AP* Spanish Language Scoring Guidelines for the informal speaking task found at: apcentral.collegeboard.com/spanlang.

Teacher Activity 2
Formal Writing

For each of the Formal Writing Student Activities, there are recommend readings as well as a recommended listening selection. Students should:

1. Listen to the indicated audio selection, taking notes as they listen.

2. Complete the 2 reading selections silently.

3. Prepare a formal written essay citing information from the audio and reading sources. By the end of the academic year, students should be able to write approximately 200 words.

Once students have finished writing, make three photocopies of each student's written work. Place students in groups of four. Distribute copies of the scoring guidelines found on p. 45. (Since this is a writing task, the *Fluency* category on the bottom row can be ignored at this time.) Distribute the copies of the students' work within each group. Have each student read his or her writing aloud to the group, one piece at a time, and discuss the content and quality of each writing piece using the scoring guidelines. Each group may select one sample to share with the whole class, as time permits. Near the end of *Realidades* 3, teachers might wish to begin using adapted versions of the official AP* Spanish Language Scoring Guidelines for the formal writing task found at: apcentral.collegeboard.com/spanlang.

Note: Continue to consider and to bring to students' attention the many writing tips offered in the *Realidades* Student Textbook as well as in the "Preparing to Write an Essay" section of this Pre-AP* Resource Book.

Student Activity 1

Informal Speaking—Simulated Conversation

Directions: You will now participate in a simulated face-to-face conversation. You will have 45 seconds to read the outline of the conversation. During that time, plan how you will respond by making brief notes to yourself. Do not try to write out your answers, as there will not be sufficient time, and the purpose of this exercise is to strengthen your ability to engage in sustained conversations in Spanish. After the preparation time ends, the conversation will begin. When it is your turn to speak, you will have 30 seconds to respond. Use your 30 seconds to give an appropriate response, using up the allocated time as fully as possible.

Scenario: You have been invited to interview as a sales associate in a large department store by the store manager, Señora Robles.

SEÑORA ROBLES: Bienvenido(a), Señor(ita). ¿Quiere sentarse? Me llamo Señora Robles y soy gerente del almacén.

TÚ: _____

SEÑORA ROBLES: ¿Por qué quiere Ud. trabajar de dependiente(a) aquí?

TÚ: _____

SEÑORA ROBLES: ¿En su opinión, cuales son las características necesarias para tener éxito en este trabajo?

TÚ: _____

SEÑORA ROBLES: ¿Cuáles habildades y expereiencias previas tiene Ud.?

TÚ: _____

SEÑORA ROBLES: Bueno. Gracias por su tiempo. Haremos nuestra decision dentro de una semana.

TÚ: _____

Student Activity 2

Formal Writing

Directions: First, you will hear an audio recording. You should take notes as you listen. Next, you will read the print articles. You will have a maximum of 15 minutes to accomplish these steps. Next, you will have 45 minutes to write a well-organized, formal essay on the topic below. Be sure to use information from all three sources to support your ideas in your essay, and cite the sources appropriately as they are used. This essay is not intended to be a summary of the three sources, but rather, an opportunity for you to synthesize these sources into your own ideas.

Audio Source: Video Script: *Un voluntario en la comunidad*, Capítulo 5 (*Realidades* TRB, p. 199)

Reading Source 1: *Profesores voluntarios por la paz, los derechos humanos y el medio ambiente* (*Realidades* Student Textbook, p. 230)

Reading Source 2: *Vuelta de hoja* (*Realidades* Student Textbook, p. 241)

Topic: Explique los beneficios del trabajo voluntario par la sociedad y también para el individuo que lo hace.

	Student Edition/Teacher's Edition		Ancillaries
	Page #	**Activity**	
Vocabulary	p. 254	Supplemental Pre-AP* Activity	*Go Online:* Self-test
	p. 268	Supplemental Pre-AP* Activity	*Assessment Program:* Prueba 6–2, pp. 129–130
			Assessment Program: Prueba 6–6, p. 139
			Realidades para hispanohablantes: Ampliación del lenguaje, Act. N-Ñ, p. 185
Listening	p. 254	Supplemental Pre-AP* Activity	*Video Program* Chapter 6
	p. 268	Supplemental Pre-AP* Activity	*Video Teacher's Guide* Chapter 6
	p. 277	Act. 38	*Pre-AP* Resource Book:* pp. 150–151
Reading			*Lecturas* para hispanohablantes: Balada de los dos abuelos, p. 57; La casa donde me decían poldita, pp. 60–61; El espejo de dos culturas, pp. 63–65
			Reading and Writing for Success: Test 33, pp. 101–103
			MindPoint Quiz Show
			Pre-AP* Resource Book: pp. 150–151
Speaking	p. 260	Differentiated Instruction, Advanced Learners/Pre-AP*	*Teacher's Resource Book:* Communicative Activity 6–2, p. 245
	p. 263	Supplemental Pre-AP* Activity	*Teacher's Resource Book:* Situation cards, p. 249
	p. 265	Act. 19	*Realidades* para hispanohablantes: Act. BB, p. 197; Advanced Presentación oral, p. 198
	p. 270	Differentiated Instruction: Learners/Pre-AP*	*Lecturas* para hispanohablantes: Después de leer, pp. 58, 62, 66
	p. 276	Supplemental Pre-AP* Activity	*Assessment Program:* Examen del capítulo 6, Hablar, p. 146
	p. 277	Act. 38	*Pre-AP* Resource Book:* pp. 150–151
	p. 281	Presentación oral	
	p. 286	Supplemental Pre-AP* Activity	
Writing	p. 254	Supplemental Pre-AP* Activity	*Writing, Audio & Video Workbook:* Act. 9, p. 85
	p. 265	Act. 19	*Writing, Audio & Video Workbook:* Act. 13, p. 89
	p. 277	Act. 38	*Reading and Writing for Success:* Test 21, pp. 63–65
	p. 283	Presentación escrita	*Realidades* para hispanohablantes: Presentación escrita, p. 199
	p. 286	Supplemental Pre-AP* Activity	*Lecturas* para hispanohablantes: Ampliación, pp. 58, 62, 66
			Go Online: Internet Link Activity
			ExamView: Pre-AP* Question Bank
			Assessment Program: Examen del capítulo 6, Escribir, p. 146
			Pre-AP* Resource Book: pp. 150–151

Teacher Activity 1
Formal Speaking—Oral Presentation

For each of the Oral Presentation Student Activities, there is a recommend reading as well as a recommended listening selection. Students should:

1. Listen to the indicated audio selection, taking notes as they listen.

2. Complete the reading selection silently.

3. Prepare an oral presentation citing information from the audio and reading sources.

4. After the audio selection, allow students no more than 10 minutes to complete the reading selection and prepare the oral presentation. Students should not try to script every word of the presentation, but rather make notes about ideas they wish to express, noting key vocabulary expressions, conjugations, etc.

5. Students are then allowed two minutes to record their presentations, or they may make their presentations to a group of three or four students, and occasionally to the whole class.

6. Recordings are the preferred method of presentation, as this will allow students, in groups of three or four, to listen to each recording (or hear each presentation) and discuss the content and quality using the scoring guidelines on p. 45. Teachers may also consider using the "Speaking and Writing Rubrics for the *Examen del capítulo* available in the *Realidades* Assessment Program front matter. Near the end of *Realidades* 3, teachers might wish to begin using adapted versions of the official AP* Spanish Language Scoring Guidelines for the formal speaking task found at: apcentral.collegeboard.com/spanlang.

Teacher Activity 2
Informal Writing

After students have completed the Informal Writing task, make three photocopies of each student's written work. Place students in groups of four. Distribute copies of the scoring guidelines found on p. 45. (Since this is a writing task, the *Fluency* category on the bottom row can be ignored at this time.) Distribute the copies of the students' work within each group. Have each student read his or her writing aloud to the group, one piece at a time, and discuss the content and quality of each writing piece using the scoring guidelines. Each group may select one sample to share with the whole class. Near the end of *Realidades* 3, teachers might wish to begin using adapted versions of the official AP* Spanish Language Scoring Guidelines for the informal writing task found at: apcentral.collegeboard.com/spanlang.

Student Activity 1
Paragraph Completion

Directions: Read the following passage, completing the blanks with a word in Spanish that is logical and grammatically correct. You must spell and accent the word correctly.

Al graduarse del colegio (1) _____ de la Universidad, los estudiantes tienen muchas responsabilidades. Entre ellas, pueden seguir sus estudios o comenzar una carrera. Hoy en día hay muchas opciones. (2) _____ puede seguir (3) _____ carrera tradicional, como (4) _____ de ser médico, peluquero o cocinero, pero el future también nos traerá trabajos que aún no (5) _____ han descubierto. La tecnología ha hecho esto posible.

La tecnología no sólo ha creado nuevos trabajos (6) _____ todas partes del mundo, sino (7) _____ también ha creado nuevos medios de comunicación (8) _____ el Internet y nos ha dado muchas maneras (9) _____ expresar (10) _____ creatividad.

Student Activity 2
Formal Speaking—Oral Presentation

Imagine that you must give a formal presentation to the hiring committee at a company where you would like to work. You must tell the committee why you believe you are the ideal candidate for the company and what interests you about working there. To prepare:

1. Listen to the Video Script, *La tecnología en la carrera de un profesional, Capítulo* 6. (*Realidades* TRB, p. 242)

2. Read *A primera vista 2.* (*Realidades* Student Textbook, pp. 266-67)

3. Prepare an outline of the presentation, noting key vocabulary words and ideas. Be sure to cite information and/or examples from the reading as well as from the audio portion of this activity. (Do not try to write an entire script. You will have 10 minutes to complete steps 2 and 3.)

4. Make a live presentation to your classmates, or record your oral presentation, as directed by your teacher. The maximum presentation length is two minutes. You should use all the time allowed giving as rich and full a presentation as possible.

Student Activity 3
Informal Writing

You were just accepted to your first college choice. In 10 minutes, write an e-mail to your grandparents telling them:

• Where you were accepted

• Why you want to attend this college or university

• What you will study there

• What you hope to do after you graduate.

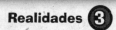
	Student Edition/Teacher's Edition		Ancillaries
	Page #	**Activity**	
Vocabulary	p. 301	Supplemental Pre-AP* Activity	*Go Online:* Self-test
			Assessment Program: Prueba 7–2, pp. 151–152
			Assessment Program: Prueba 7–5, pp. 159–160
Listening	p. 304	Supplemental Pre-AP* Activity	*Video Program* Chapter 7
	p. 320	Supplemental Pre-AP* Activity	*Video Teacher's Guide* Chapter 7
			Pre-AP* Resource Book: pp. 153–154
Reading	p. 307	Act. 13	*MindPoint Quiz Show*
	p. 304	Supplemental Pre-AP* Activity	*Reading and Writing for Success:* Test 34, pp. 104–106
	p. 312	Supplemental Pre-AP* Activity	*Teacher's Resource Book:* Communicative Activity 7–3, pp. 288–289
	p. 331	Supplemental Pre-AP* Activity	
			Lecturas para hispanohablantes: Oda al tomate, p. 69; Los pequeños objetos, p. 72; Mestizaje artesano, pp. 74–75
			Pre-AP* Resource Book: pp. 153–154
Speaking	p. 301	Supplemental Pre-AP* Activity	*Teacher's Resource Book:* Communicative Activity 7–2, p. 287
	p. 307	Act. 13	
	p. 304	Supplemental Pre-AP* Activity	*Teacher's Resource Book:* Communicative Activity 7–3, pp. 288–289
	p. 306	Differentiated Instruction: Learners/Pre-AP*	*Realidades* para hispanohablantes: Act. CC, p. 229
	p. 312	Supplemental Pre-AP* Activity	*Realidades* para hispanohablantes: Advanced Presentación oral, p. 23
	p. 320	Supplemental Pre-AP* Activity	
	p. 320	Differentiated Instruction: Advanced Learners/Pre-AP*	*Lecturas* para hispanohablantes: Después de leer, pp. 70, 73, 76
	p. 323	Act. 34	*Teacher's Resource Book:* Situation cards, p. 292
	p. 327	Presentación oral	*Assessment Program:* Examen del capítulo 7, Hablar, p. 167
	p. 331	Supplemental Pre-AP* Activity	*Pre-AP* Resource Book:* pp. 153–154
Writing	p. 306	Differentiated Instruction: Advanced Learners/Pre-AP*	*Writing, Audio & Video Workbook:* Act. 9, p. 99
			Writing, Audio & Video Workbook: Act. 13, p. 103
	p. 307	Act. 13	*Reading and Writing for Success:* Test 34, pp. 104–106
	p. 312	Supplemental Pre-AP* Activity	
	p. 320	Differentiated Instruction: Learners/Pre-AP*	*Realidades* para hispanohablantes: Advanced Presentación escrita, p. 231
	p. 323	Act. 34	*Lecturas* para hispanohablantes: Ampliación, pp. 70, 73, 76
	p. 328	Presentación escrita	*Go Online:* Internet Link Activity
			ExamView: Pre-AP* Question Bank
			Assessment Program: Examen del capítulo 7, Escribir, p. 167
			Pre-AP* Resource Book: pp. 153–154

Teacher Activity 1
Informal Speaking—Simulated Conversation

1. Allow students one minute to prepare to record the conversation. For earlier *temas,* teachers may wish to allow just a bit more preparation time. However, allowing too much preparation time will lead to students' writing the script of what they want to say, and subsequently reading it. The purpose of the preparation time is to get a sense of the conversation and to generally gather thoughts.

2. Students should record their conversations. (See Recording and Evaluating on p. 40.) (See also "Administering the *Examen del capítulo* Speaking Proficiency Test" on p. T66 of the ***Realidades*** Assessment Program.) The teacher can be the voice of the other person in the conversation, allowing no more than 30 seconds for each response from the students.

3. In groups of three or four, students should listen to each recording and discuss the content and quality using the scoring guidelines on p. 45. Teachers may also consider using the "Speaking and Writing Rubrics for the *Examen del capítulo*" available in the ***Realidades*** Assessment Program front matter. Near the end of ***Realidades*** 3, teachers might wish to begin using adapted versions of the official AP* Spanish Language Scoring Guidelines for the informal speaking task found at: apcentral.collegeboard.com/spanlang.

Teacher Activity 2
Formal Writing

For each of the Formal Writing Student Activities, there are recommend readings as well as a recommended listening selection. Students should:

1. Listen to the indicated audio selection, taking notes as they listen.

2. Complete the two reading selections silently.

3. Prepare a formal written essay citing information from the audio and reading sources. By the end of the academic year, students should be able to write approximately 200 words.

Once students have finished writing, make three photocopies of each student's written work. Place students in groups of four. Distribute copies of the scoring guidelines found on p. 45. (Since this is a writing task, the *Fluency* category on the bottom row can be ignored at this time.) Distribute the copies of the students' work within each group. Have each student read his or her writing aloud to the group, one piece at a time, and discuss the content and quality of each writing piece using the scoring guidelines. Each group may select one sample to share with the whole class, as time permits. Near the end of ***Realidades*** 3, teachers might wish to begin using adapted versions of the official AP* Spanish Language Scoring Guidelines for the formal writing task found at: apcentral.collegeboard.com/spanlang.

Note: Continue to consider and to bring to students' attention the many writing tips offered in the ***Realidades*** Student Textbook as well as in the "Preparing to Write an Essay" section of this Pre-AP* Resource Book.

Student Activity 1
Paragraph Completion

Directions: Read the following passage, completing the blanks with the form of the word in parenthesis that is grammatically correct. You must spell and accent the word correctly.

El personaje más famoso de la literatura (1) _____ (español) es Don Quijote de la Mancha, (2) _____ (el) protagonista de la novela del mismo nombre que (3) _____ (escribir) Miguel de Cervantes. La historia cuenta que el Quijote leyó (4) _____ (tanto) libros sobre caballeros andantes, que un día perdió el juicio y decidió ser uno de ellos. En la época en que él vive (el siglo XVII) ya no (5) _____ (haber) caballeros andantes, pero en su imaginación, el Quijote ve a las sirvientas como princesas, las posadas como castillos, y los molinos como gigantes contra (6) _____ (el) que tiene que pelear. El conflicto entre la fantasía del Quijote y la realidad (7) _____ (producir) situaciones (8) _____ (cómico) que hacen reír.

Student Activity 2
Informal Speaking—Simulated Conversation

Directions: You will now participate in a simulated conversation. You will have 45 seconds to read the outline of the conversation. During that time, plan how you will respond by making brief notes to yourself. Do not try to write out your answers, as there will not be sufficient time, and the purpose of this exercise is to strengthen your ability to engage in sustained conversations in Spanish. After the preparation time ends, the conversation will begin. When it is your turn to speak, you will have 30 seconds to respond. Use your 30 seconds to give an appropriate response, using up the allocated time as fully as possible.

Scenario: A writer for your school newspaper, Miguel, is preparing an article about strange and weird occurrences in students' lives. Tell him your story about the most unusual thing that has ever happened to you.

MIGUEL: Como lo sabes, entrevisto a varios compañeros de clase para saber algo de los eventos más extraños de sus vidas. ¿Cuándo y dónde ocurrió lo más raro de tu vida?

TÚ: _____

MIGUEL: ¿Y qué pasó?

TÚ: _____

MIGUEL: ¿Hay manera de explicar lo que ocurrió?

TÚ: _____

MIGUEL: ¿Cómo te sentías?

TÚ: _____

MIGUEL: Pues, gracias por contármelo. Espero que leas el artículo cuando se publique.

TÚ: (Despídete.)

	Student Edition/Teacher's Edition		Ancillaries
	Page #	**Activity**	
Vocabulary	p. 346 p. 356	Supplemental Pre-AP* Activity Supplemental Pre-AP* Activity	*Go Online:* Self-test *Assessment Program:* Prueba 8–2, pp. 173–174 *Assessment Program:* Prueba 8–5, pp. 181–182
Listening	p. 356	Supplemental Pre-AP* Activity	*Video Program* Chapter 8 *Video Teacher's Guide* Chapter 8 *Pre-AP* Resource Book:* pp. 156–157

Reading	p. 362
	p. 366
		Supplemental Pre-AP* Activity
		Act. 30
			Reading and Writing for Success: Test 35,
			  pp. 107–109
			MindPoint Quiz Show
			Lecturas para hispanohablantes: Memorias,
			  pp. 79–80
			Lecturas para hispanohablantes: Yo voy soñando
			  caminos..., p. 83
			Lecturas para hispanohablantes: Un boom
			  llamado trekking, pp. 84–86
			Pre-AP Resource Book:* pp. 156–157

Speaking	p. 348
	
	p. 353
	p. 354
	p. 356
	p. 366
	p. 373
	p. 379
		Differentiated Instruction:
		  Advanced Learners/Pre-AP*
		Act. 15
		Supplemental Pre-AP* Activity
		Act. 30
		Presentación oral
		Supplemental Pre-AP* Activity
		Supplemental Pre-AP* Activity
			Teacher's Resource Book: Situation cards, p. 333
			Realidades para hispanohablantes: Act. AA, p. 261
			Realidades para hispanohablantes: Presentación
			  oral, p. 262
			Lecturas para hispanohablantes: Después de leer,
			  pp. 81, 86
			Assessment Program: Examen del capítulo 8,
			  Hablar, p. 189
			Pre-AP Resource Book:* pp. 156–157

Writing	p. 346
	p. 348
	
	p. 353
	p. 354
	p. 362
	p. 364
	
	p. 375
		Supplemental Pre-AP* Activity
		Differentiated Instruction,
		  Advanced Learners/Pre-AP*
		Supplemental Pre-AP* Activity
		Act. 15
		Supplemental Pre-AP* Activity
		Differentiated Instruction:
		  Advanced Learners/Pre-AP*
		Presentación escrita
			Writing, Audio & Video Workbook: Act. 8, p. 112
			Writing, Audio & Video Workbook: Act. 13, p. 117
			Realidades para hispanohablantes: Fondo
			  cultural, p. 252
			Realidades para hispanohablantes: Presentación
			  escrita, p. 263
			Lecturas para hispanohablantes: Ampliación,
			  pp. 81, 83, 86
			Go Online: Internet Link Activity
			ExamView: Pre-AP* Question Bank
			Assessment Program: Examen del capítulo 8,
			  Escribir, p. 189
			Pre-AP Resource Book:* pp. 156–157

Teacher Activity 1
Formal Speaking—Oral Presentation

For each of the Oral Presentation Student Activities, there is a recommend reading as well as a recommended listening selection. Students should:

1. Listen to the indicated audio selection, taking notes as they listen.

2. Complete the reading selection silently.

3. Prepare an oral presentation citing information from the audio and reading sources.

4. After the audio selection, allow students no more than 10 minutes to complete the reading selection and prepare the oral presentation. Students should not try to script every word of the presentation, but rather make notes about ideas they wish to express, noting key vocabulary expressions, conjugations, etc.

5. Students are then allowed two minutes to record their presentations, or they may make their presentations to a group of three or four students, and occasionally to the whole class.

6. Recordings are the preferred method of presentation, as this will allow students, in groups of three or four, to listen to each recording (or hear each presentation) and discuss the content and quality using the scoring guidelines on p. 45. Teachers may also consider using the "Speaking and Writing Rubrics for the *Examen del capítulo* available in the *Realidades* Assessment Program front matter. Near the end of *Realidades* 3, teachers might wish to begin using adapted versions of the official AP* Spanish Language Scoring Guidelines for the formal speaking task found at: apcentral.collegeboard.com/spanlang.

Teacher Activity 2
Informal Writing

After students have completed the Informal Writing task, make three photocopies of each student's written work. Place students in groups of four. Distribute copies of the scoring guidelines found on p. 45. (Since this is a writing task, the *Fluency* category on the bottom row can be ignored at this time.) Distribute the copies of the students' work within each group. Have each student read his or her writing aloud to the group, one piece at a time, and discuss the content and quality of each writing piece using the scoring guidelines. Each group may select one sample to share with the whole class. Near the end of *Realidades* 3, teachers might wish to begin using adapted versions of the official AP* Spanish Language Scoring Guidelines for the informal writing task found at: apcentral.collegeboard.com/spanlang.

Student Activity 1
Paragraph Completion

Directions: Read the following passage, completing the blanks with a word in Spanish that is logical and grammatically correct. You must spell and accent the word correctly.

Desde (1) _____ se fundó Buenos Aires en 1536, allí se han mezclado distintas culturas, religiones y tradiciones. Aunque (2) _____ idioma oficial de Argentina es el español, en la ciudad hay barrios en (3) _____ que más se hablan el italiano, el inglés, el yiddish, el ruso o el árabe y donde se pueden ver mezquitas, sinagogas, (4) _____ iglesias. Anteriormente, la mayoría (5) _____ los inmigrantes que llegaban a Buenos aires venían de Europa, pero en los últimos tiempos la mayoría ha llegado de otros países latinoamericanos, sobre todo (6) _____ Bolivia.

　　Esta inmigración de diferentes grupos étnicos ha hecho de Buenos Aires una ciudad multicultural y cosmopolita. En algunos casos los inmigrantes se han asimilado a la manera de vivir del lugar. Por ejemplo, aunque muchos hablan (7) _____ propias lenguas, la mayoría habla también español.

　　También (8) _____ puede encontrar en un mismo barrio se practican las religiones judía, cristiana, y musulmana, y se comen platos (9) _____ vienen de muchos lugares como la pasta de Italia o los guisos de España.

Student Activity 2
Formal Speaking—Oral Presentation

Imagine that you must give a formal presentation describing your favorite city in the world. Include in your presentation a brief description of the city including its location, what historical influences have served to shape this city, and why you like to go there. To prepare:

1. Listen to the Video Script, *Unas herencias ricas*, Capítulo 8. (*Realidades* TRB, p. 325)

2. Read *Mi herencia africana*. (*Realidades* Student Textbook, p. 362)

Prepare an outline of the presentation, noting key vocabulary words and ideas. Be sure to cite information and/or examples from the reading as well as from the audio portion of this activity. (Do not try to write an entire script. You will have 10 minutes to complete steps 2 and 3.) Make a live presentation to your classmates, or record your oral presentation, as directed by your teacher. The maximum presentation length is two minutes. You should use all the time allowed giving as rich and full a presentation as possible.

Student Activity 3
Informal Writing

You won a weekend trip with your family to your favorite city on a radio contest. In 10 minutes, write a postcard to your friend back home describing to him (or her):

- All the things you have seen in a short time
- What historical sites are in this city
- What restaurants you have visited
- The quality of your hotel

	Student Edition/Teacher's Edition		Ancillaries
	Page #	Activity	
Vocabulary	p. 392 p. 407	Supplemental Pre-AP* Activity Supplemental Pre-AP* Activity	*Go Online:* Self-test *Assessment Program:* Prueba 9–2, pp. 195–196 *Assessment Program:* Prueba 9–6, pp. 204–205
Listening	p. 400	Supplemental Pre-AP* Activity	*Video Program* Chapter 9 *Video Teacher's Guide:* Chapter 9 *Pre-AP* Resource Book:* pp. 159–160

Reading	p. 400
	p. 403
	p. 407
	p. 415
	p. 423
		Supplemental Pre-AP* Activity ·
		Act. 19
		Supplemental Pre-AP* Activity
		Act. 36
		Supplemental Pre-AP* Activity
			Reading and Writing for Success: Test 36,
			  pp. 110–112
			Lecturas para hispanohablantes: Usos y abusos
			  del paraguas, pp. 89–90
			Lecturas para hispanohablantes: La tarara, p. 92
			Lecturas para hispanohablantes: El cubano de la
			  . moda, pp. 94–96
			Pre-AP* Resource Book: pp. 159–160

Speaking	p. 392
	p. 400
	p. 402
	
	p. 403
	p. 407
	p. 412
	
	p. 419
	p. 423
		Supplemental Pre-AP* Activity
		Supplemental Pre-AP* Activity
		Differentiated Instruction:
		  Advanced Learners/Pre-AP*
		Act. 19
		Supplemental Pre-AP* Activity
		Differentiated Instruction:
		  Advanced Learners/Pre-AP*
		Presentación oral
		Supplemental Pre-AP* Activity
			Teacher's Resource Book: Communicative Activity
			  9–2, p. 368
			Teacher's Resource Book: Situation cards, p. 372
			Realidades para hispanohablantes: Act. M, p. 279
			Realidades para hispanohablantes: Act. AA, p. 293
			Realidades para hispanohablantes: Presentación
			  oral, p. 294
			Lecturas para hispanohablantes: Después de leer,
			  pp. 90, 92, 96
			Assessment Program: Examen del capítulo 9,
			  Hablar, p. 211
			Pre-AP* Resource Book: p. 159

Writing	p. 402
	
	p. 403
	p. 407
	p. 412
	
	p. 415
	p. 415
	p. 421
	p. 423
		Differentiated Instruction:
		  Advanced Learners/Pre-AP*
		Act. 19
		Supplemental Pre-AP* Activity
		Differentiated Instruction:
		  Advanced Learners/Pre-AP*
		Supplemental Pre-AP* Activity
		Act. 36
		Presentación escrita
		Supplemental Pre-AP* Activity
			Writing, Audio & Video Workbook: Act. 9, p. 127
			Writing, Audio & Video Workbook: Act. 10, p. 128
			Writing, Audio & Video Workbook: Act. 13, p. 131
			Teacher's Resource Book: Communicative Activity
			  9–2, p. 368
			Realidades para hispanohablantes: Fondo
			  cultural, p. 274
			Realidades para hispanohablantes: Act. M, p. 279
			Realidades para hispanohablantes: Presentación
			  escrita, p. 295
			Lecturas para hispanohablantes: Ampliación,
			  pp. 90, 92, 96
			Go Online: Internet Link Activity
			ExamView: Pre-AP* Question Bank
			Assessment Program: Examen del capítulo 9,
			  Escribir, p. 211
			Pre-AP* Resource Book: pp. 159–160

Teacher Activity 1
Informal Speaking—Simulated Conversation

1. Allow students one minute to prepare to record the conversation. For earlier *temas,* teachers may wish to allow just a bit more preparation time. However, allowing too much preparation time will lead to students' writing the script of what they want to say, and subsequently reading it. The purpose of the preparation time is to get a sense of the conversation and to generally gather thoughts.

2. Students should record their conversations. (See Recording and Evaluating on p. 36.) (See also "Administering the *Examen del capítulo* Speaking Proficiency Test" on p. T66 of the *Realidades* Assessment Program.) The teacher can be the voice of the other person in the conversation, allowing no more than 30 seconds for each response from the students.

3. In groups of three or four, students should listen to each recording and discuss the content and quality using the scoring guidelines on p. 49. Teachers may also consider using the "Speaking and Writing Rubrics for the *Examen del capítulo*" available in the *Realidades* Assessment Program front matter. Near the end of *Realidades* 3, teachers might wish to begin using adapted versions of the official AP* Spanish Language Scoring Guidelines for the informal speaking task found at: apcentral.collegeboard.com/spanlang.

Teacher Activity 2
Formal Writing

For each of the Formal Writing Student Activities, there are recommend readings as well as a recommended listening selection. Students should:

1. Listen to the indicated audio selection, taking notes as they listen.

2. Complete the two reading selections silently.

3. Prepare a formal written essay citing information from the audio and reading sources. By the end of the academic year, students should be able to write approximately 200 words.

Once students have finished writing, make three photocopies of each student's written work. Place students in groups of four. Distribute copies of the scoring guidelines found on p. 49. (Since this is a writing task, the *Fluency* category on the bottom row can be ignored at this time.) Distribute the copies of the students' work within each group. Have each student read his or her writing aloud to the group, one piece at a time, and discuss the content and quality of each writing piece using the scoring guidelines. Each group may select one sample to share with the whole class, as time permits. Near the end of *Realidades* 3, teachers might wish to begin using adapted versions of the official AP* Spanish Language Scoring Guidelines for the formal writing task found at: apcentral.collegeboard.com/spanlang.

Note: Continue to consider and to bring to students' attention the many writing tips offered in the *Realidades* Student Textbook as well as in the "Preparing to Write an Essay" section of this Pre-AP* Resource Book.

Student Activity 1
Paragraph Completion

Directions: Read the following passage, completing the blanks with the form of the word in parenthesis that is grammatically correct. You must spell and accent the word correctly.

A menos que (1) _____ (alguno) actividades humanas (2) _____ (disminuir), muchos de los animales desaparecerán de nuestro planeta. Tenemos que parar el excesivo uso de los aerosoles y otros productos químicos para no (3) _____ (dañar) más la capa de ozono. Y tenemos que protestar contra las fábricas que siguen (4) _____ (echar) desperdicios en nuestros ríos. Aunque los dueños de las fábricas sin duda (5) _____ (saber) que esto es ilegal, algunos no dejan de hacerlo. Por eso, a menos que el gobierno les (6) _____ (empezar) a dar multas altas, estas personas no dejarán de contaminar los ríos. Si el gobierno hubiera creado leyes apropiadas hace varios años, (7) _____ (haber) menos problemas hoy. Es nuestra responsabilidad cuidar y proteger el planeta en que vivimos. No podemos disminuir la contaminación sin (8) _____ (hacer) un esfuerzo. Si todos hiciéramos un esfuerzo, (9) _____ (producirse) muchos cambios positivos.

Student Activity 2
Formal Writing

Directions: First, you will hear an audio recording. You should take notes as you listen. Next, you will read the print articles. You will have a maximum of 15 minutes to accomplish these steps. Next, you will have 45 minutes to write a well-organized, formal essay on the topic below. Be sure to use information from all three sources to support your ideas in your essay, and cite the sources appropriately as they are used. This essay is not intended to be a summary of the three sources, but rather, an opportunity for you to synthesize these sources into your own ideas.

Audio Source: Video Script, *Exploremos la naturaleza fascinante*, Capítulo 9 (***Realidades*** TRB, p. 365)

Reading Source 1: *Victoria parcial para las ballenas* (***Realidades*** Student Textbook, p. 415)

Reading Source 2: *Galápagos: el encuentro con la naturaleza* (***Realidades*** Student Textbook, p. 416)

Topic: Explique como se puede establecer un balance entre las necesidades económicas y la protección del medio ambiente.

	Student Edition/Teacher's Edition		Ancillaries
	Page #	**Activity**	
Vocabulary	p. 439	Supplemental Pre-AP* Activity	*Go Online:* Self-test *Assessment Program:* Prueba 10–2, pp. 217–218 *Assessment Program:* Prueba 10–6, pp. 226–227
Listening	p. 450 p. 461 p. 471	Supplemental Pre-AP* Activity Supplemental Pre-AP* Activity Supplemental Pre-AP* Activity	*Video Program* Chapter 10 *Video Teacher's Guide* Chapter 10 *Pre-AP* Resource Book:* pp. 162–163

Reading	p. 450
	p. 461
	p. 461
	p. 471
		Supplemental Pre-AP* Activity
		Supplemental Pre-AP* Activity
		Act. 39
		Supplemental Pre-AP* Activity
			Reading and Writing for Success: Test 37,
			    pp. 113–115
			MindPoint Quiz Show
			Lecturas para hispanohablantes: Motivos de la
			    gimnasia sueca, pp. 98–100; Loa del fut-bol,
			    pp. 103–104; Indurain cumple, pp. 106–107
			Pre-AP* Resource Book: pp. 162–163

Speaking	p. 446
	p. 447
	p. 450
	p. 465
	p. 460
	p. 461
	p. 461
	p. 471
		Supplemental Pre-AP* Activity
		Act. 17
		Supplemental Pre-AP* Activity
		Presentación oral
		Supplemental Pre-AP* Activity
		Supplemental Pre-AP* Activity
		Act. 39
		Supplemental Pre-AP* Activity
			Lecturas para hispanohablantes: Conversando
			    con un campeón de surfing, pp. 52–54
			Teacher's Resource Book: Communicative Activity
			    10–4, pp. 413–414
			Teacher's Resource Book: Situation cards, p. 415
			Realidades para hispanohablantes: Act. BB, p. 325
			Realidades para hispanohablantes: Presentación
			    oral, p. 326
			Lecturas para hispanohablantes: Después de leer,
			    pp. 101, 105, 108
			Assessment Program: Examen del capítulo 10,
			    Hablar, p. 234
			Pre-AP* Resource Book: pp. 162–163

Writing	p. 439
	p. 444
	
	p. 446
	p. 447
	p. 461
	p. 466
		Supplemental Pre-AP* Activity
		Differentiated Instruction:
		    Advanced Learners/Pre-AP*
		Supplemental Pre-AP*
		Activity 17
		Act. 39
		Presentación escrita
			Writing, Audio & Video Workbook: Act.13, p. 145
			Lecturas para hispanohablantes: Ampliación,
			    pp. 101, 105, 108
			Reading and Writing for Success: Test 23,
			    pp. 69–71
			Realidades para hispanohablantes: Act. S, p. 315
			Realidades para hispanohablantes: Presentación
			    escrita, p. 327
			Go Online: Internet Link Activity
			ExamView: Pre-AP* Question Bank
			Assessment Program: Examen del capítulo 10,
			    Escribir p. 234
			Pre-AP* Resource Book: pp. 162–163

Teacher Activity 1
Formal Speaking—Oral Presentation

For each of the Oral Presentation Student Activities, there is a recommend reading as well as a recommended listening selection. Students should

1. Listen to the indicated audio selection, taking notes as they listen.

2. Complete the reading selection silently.

3. Prepare an oral presentation citing information from the audio and reading sources.

4. After the audio selection, allow students no more than 10 minutes to complete the reading selection and prepare the oral presentation. Students should not try to script every word of the presentation, but rather make notes about ideas they wish to express, noting key vocabulary expressions, conjugations, etc.

5. Students are then allowed two minutes to record their presentations, or they may make their presentations to a group of three or four students, and occasionally to the whole class.

6. Recordings are the preferred method of presentation, as this will allow students, in groups of three or four, to listen to each recording (or hear each presentation) and discuss the content and quality using the scoring guidelines on p. 45. Teachers may also consider using the "Speaking and Writing Rubrics for the *Examen del capítulo*" available in the *Realidades* Assessment Program front matter. Near the end of *Realidades* 3, teachers might wish to begin using adapted versions of the official AP* Spanish Language Scoring Guidelines for the formal speaking task found at: apcentral.collegeboard.com/spanlang.

Teacher Activity 2
Informal Writing

After students have completed the Informal Writing task, make three photocopies of each student's written work. Place students in groups of four. Distribute copies of the scoring guidelines found on p. 45. (Since this is a writing task, the *Fluency* category on the bottom row can be ignored at this time.) Distribute the copies of the students' work within each group. Have each student read his or her writing aloud to the group, one piece at a time, and discuss the content and quality of each writing piece using the scoring guidelines. Each group may select one sample to share with the whole class. Near the end of *Realidades* 3, teachers might wish to begin using adapted versions of the official AP* Spanish Language Scoring Guidelines for the informal writing task found at: apcentral.collegeboard.com/spanlang.

Student Activity 1
Paragraph Completion

Directions: Read the following passage, completing the blanks with the form of the word in parenthesis that is grammatically correct. You must spell and accent the word correctly.

Yo no quería hablar, porque pensé que (1) _____ (ir) a llamar a mi padre como algunos profesores lo hacían cuando (2) _____ (estar) enojados. Pero el profesor me hizo (3) _____ (otro) preguntas y entonces le (4) _____ (contar) todo. También le dije que podía hacer mis tareas, pero que no tenía mis cuadernos, porque (5) _____ (ser) bien pobres y mi papá no podía comprar y que, años atrás, ya mi papá me (6) _____ (querer) sacar de la escuela porque no podía hacer ese gasto más. Y que con mucho sacrificio y esfuerzo había yo podido llegar hasta el sexto curso. Pero no era que mi papá no (7) _____ (querer), sino porque no podía, porque, incluso, a pesar de toda la creencia que había en Pulacayo de que a la mujer no se le debía enseñar a leer, mi papa siempre quiso que (8) _____ (saber) por lo menos eso.

Student Activity 2
Formal Speaking—Oral Presentation

Imagine that you must give a formal presentation discussing the importance of keeping children safe from all harm. Include in your presentation a brief description of the threats children face, what steps can be taken to protect children's rights, and how all citizens can make a difference in the improvement of protecting children. To prepare:

1. Listen to Audio Activity #1. (*Realidades* TRB, p. 401)

2. Read *El gobierno y los derechos de la niñez*. (*Realidades* Student Textbook, p. 439)

3. Prepare an outline of the presentation, noting key vocabulary words and ideas. Be sure to cite information and / or examples from the reading as well as from the audio portion of this activity. (Do not try to write an entire script. You will have 10 minutes to complete steps 2 and 3.)

4. Make a live presentation to your classmates, or record your oral presentation, as directed by your teacher. The maximum presentation length is two minutes. You should use all the time allowed giving as rich and full a presentation as possible.

Student Activity 3
Informal Writing

Your family just got a new puppy. E-mail your friend telling him (or her):

• What sort of dog you have and what it looks like

• What your puppy likes to do

• All the things you plan to do to take good care of your new pet.

You have 10 minutes to complete this task. Write as complete a response as possible, using rich details and appropriate language.

Pre-AP* Resources

Listservs

The following electronic resources are helpful to language teachers and curriculum developers. To subscribe to a listserv, send a message with no subject line as follows:

Subscribe [name of listserv] your first name your last name
For example: subscribe FLTEACH Abraham Lincoln

FLTEACH

- FLTEACH is a forum for discussion among foreign language educators.
  listserv@listserv.acsu.buffalo.edu

SLART-L

- A listserv that focuses on second language acquisition research and teaching.
  listserv@cunyvm.cuny.edu

Web Sites

The number of Web sites of interest to Pre-AP* foreign language educators is too large to list. Below are some places to begin.

http://www.2nse.org

- The National Spanish Examinations, sponsored by AATSP, administered each spring as a competitive measure of students' abilities in Spanish. Provides excellent multiple-choice testing practice for beginning through advanced students in the areas of listening, reading, and cloze passage completion.

http://www.aatsp.org

- The American Association of Teachers of Spanish & Portuguese Web site contains links to teacher resources, publications, conferences, and other important information for Spanish teachers.

apcentral.collegeboard.com

- A free Web site that offers up–to–date information about both the AP* Spanish Language and AP* Spanish Literature exams, as well as a special section dedicated to Pre-AP* World Languages and Cultures. It also contains an extensive list of links to Web sites dedicated to Spanish instruction.

http://www.puzzlemaker.com

- A free service that is useful for quickly creating printable crossword puzzles.

Bibliography*

Díaz, José M. *Listening Comprehension Skills for Intermediate and Advanced Students*. White Plains, NY: Longman Publishing Group, 1995.

- The cassettes and workbook provide an integrated approach by building the vocabulary necessary for comprehension and testing comprehension with multiple-choice listening exercises.

Díaz, José M., and María F. Nadel. *¡En Marcha! A Complete Grammar Review with Web Site*. Boston, MA: Pearson Prentice Hall, 2001.

- *¡En Marcha!* provides additional intermediate-level practice with specific grammatical concepts.

Reading and Writing for Success. Boston, MA: Pearson Prentice Hall, 2001.

- The Grade 8 and Grade 10 Assessments provide intermediate level multiple-choice reading comprehension practice and topics for directed writing.

Walqui-Van Lier, Aída, Ruth A. Barraza, and Mary Ann Dellinger. *Sendas literarias*. Boston, MA: Pearson Prentice Hall, 2005.

- This textbook offers additional practice with reading and pre-reading activities.

*For ordering information on any of the Pearson Prentice Hall products, visit our online catalog at www.PHSchool.com.

Preguntas rápidas
Additional Activities

Here are some additional activities incorporating the bank of *preguntas rápidas* to be found on pp. 166–168.

Daily Practice

Use the questions as warm-up or end-of-class activities, for team competitions, or simply as a break in the middle of class. Take a question from the bank of *preguntas rápidas* on pp. 166–168 and ask the class to respond. Ask for volunteers or call on students randomly. Award participation points on students' ability to answer questions. On any particular day you will not have all students participate, but by doing this activity on a regular basis, you can involve many students and give credit for their participation. As the semester or year progresses and you continue to add questions to the bank, you will keep recycling information from earlier chapters. As students begin Spanish 2, 3, or 4, bring out the banks of questions from the previous level(s) and use these to recycle questions from year to year.

La silla caliente

Periodically have students sit on the "hot seat" to answer questions. This activity can be done as a small group activity or in front of the entire class. If the activity is done in small groups, the teacher will divide the bank of questions among the different groups and then rotate the sets of questions from group to group throughout the time allotted. The student who is on the hot seat is asked several questions by other students or the teacher. By using the bank of *preguntas rápidas* on pp. 166–168, the student may answer questions taken from several chapters. Students can be evaluated on how well they are able to respond. After one student has sat on the "hot seat" to answer several questions, another student takes the spot and begins to answer questions. This activity can be also used as a competition in which students attempt to be the student who is able to answer most questions correctly before being "eliminated."

Preguntas rápidas—*Realidades* 1

1. ¿Qué tiempo hace en el invierno?
2. ¿Qué te gusta hacer en junio?
3. Según tu familia, ¿cómo eres?
4. ¿Qué estudias en la primera hora?
5. En tu escuela, ¿quién enseña la clase de arte?
6. ¿Cuál es tu almuerzo favorito?
7. ¿Qué frutas te gustan más?
8. ¿Crees que la pizza es buena o mala para la salud? ¿Por qué?
9. ¿Qué ejercicio haces con las piernas?
10. Cuando vas de compras, ¿adónde vas?
11. ¿Adónde vas los fines de semana?
12. ¿Qué deportes te gustan más?
13. ¿Qué vas a hacer mañana a las ocho de la noche?
14. Describe a una persona de tu familia o de otra familia.
15. ¿Qué te gusta hacer durante una fiesta de cumpleaños?
16. ¿Quiénes vienen más a tu casa? ¿Qué traen ellos?
17. ¿Qué te gusta pedir en un restaurante?
18. ¿De qué colores son los libros y las carpetas que tienes?
19. ¿Qué posesiones tienes en tu dormitorio? ¿De qué colores son?
20. ¿Ayudas mucho o poco en casa? ¿Cuáles son tus quehaceres?
21. Para ti, ¿cuáles son los tres peores quehaceres?
22. ¿Qué ropa llevas en el verano?
23. ¿Cuáles son tres artículos de ropa que te gustaría comprar?
24. ¿Para quiénes compras regalos? ¿Qué tipo de regalos compras?
25. ¿Qué deportes practicaste el año pasado?
26. Para el cumpleaños de tu mejor amigo(a), ¿qué compraste?
27. ¿Adónde te gustaría ir de vacaciones? ¿Qué te gustaría hacer?
28. ¿Cuándo fuiste a ver una obra de teatro en tu comunidad o en tu escuela? ¿Te gustó?
29. ¿Qué lugares puedes visitar en tu comunidad?
30. ¿Qué cosas reciclan Uds. en casa?
31. ¿Qué podemos hacer para tener un barrio más limpio?
32. ¿Qué hiciste el verano pasado?
33. ¿Qué hizo la gente de tu comunidad el año pasado para ayudar a las víctimas de un desastre?
34. ¿Qué clase de programas de televisión ves más?
35. ¿Qué sabes crear en la computadora?
36. Si necesitas ayuda con la computadora, ¿a quién pides ayuda?

Preguntas rápidas—*Realidades 2*

1. ¿Qué actividades te gusta hacer en tus clases?
2. ¿Qué reglas de la escuela te gustan (o no te gustan)?
3. ¿Qué te gusta más, ser miembro de un club o participar en un deporte? ¿Por qué?
4. ¿Cuáles son las actividades más populares en tu escuela? ¿Por qué son populares?
5. ¿Cómo te preparas para un evento especial? ¿Qué haces primero?
6. ¿Qué ropa y accesorios te pones para ir a una fiesta o un baile?
7. Describe la ropa que está de moda ahora.
8. ¿En qué tienda o almacén puedes encontrar gangas? ¿Cómo son los precios allí?
9. ¿Cuándo compraste un regalo recientemente? ¿Dónde lo compraste?
10. ¿Qué tipo de tiendas y servicios hay en el centro de tu comunidad?
11. ¿Qué haces para ganar dinero? ¿Te gusta el trabajo?
12. ¿Cuál fue tu día más divertido del mes pasado? ¿Por qué?
13. ¿Qué debe hacer un joven para aprender las reglas y señales de tráfico?
14. Explica cómo se va de tu casa a la escuela.
15. ¿Con qué juguetes te gustaba jugar de pequeño(a)?
16. De niño(a), ¿cómo eras?
17. En tu comunidad, ¿en qué días festivos hay fuegos artificiales?
18. ¿Cuándo te reúnes con tus parientes? ¿Dónde se reúnen Uds.?
19. ¿Cuántos años tenías cuando aprendiste a caminar?
20. Para ti, ¿quién es un héroe o una heroína? ¿Por qué?
21. ¿Qué tipo de desastres naturales afecta tu comunidad o región?
22. ¿Qué hora era cuando te levantaste hoy?
23. ¿Cómo te sientes cuando un(a) enfermero(a) te pone una inyección?
24. Cuando tienes dolor de cabeza o estómago, ¿qué haces para sentirte mejor?
25. ¿Te lastimaste alguna vez cuando estabas practicando un deporte o haciendo otra actividad?
26. ¿Qué clase de programa te interesa ver más en la televisión?
27. ¿Quién es tu jugador(a) profesional favorito(a)? ¿En qué deporte compite?
28. ¿Qué es más importante en una película, mucha acción o personajes interesantes? ¿Por qué?
29. ¿Qué película en el cine va a tener mucho éxito este año?
30. ¿Cómo se prepara tu comida favorita?
31. ¿Qué comida picante te gusta más (o menos)?
32. ¿Adónde has viajado? ¿Qué hiciste para planear el viaje?
33. ¿Qué recomiendas que haga un turista cuando acaba de llegar a un país extranjero?
34. ¿Qué serás algún día? ¿Cómo sera un día típico para ti?
35. ¿Qué clases estudiarás en la universidad?
36. ¿Cuáles son algunos de los problemas ecológicos de tu región?

Preguntas rápidas—*Realidades* 3

1. ¿Qué aspectos de la naturaleza de tu region te impresionan más?

2. ¿Qué parque nacional te gustaría visitar? ¿Qué actividades al aire libre puedes hacer allí?

3. Describe el lugar más bello adónde fuiste.

4. ¿Qué atletas de habla hispana conoces? ¿Qué hacen ellos?

5. ¿Qué juegos y actividades hacías de niño(a)? ¿Con quién los hacías?

6. Describe una obra de arte que está en la escuela o en tu casa.

7. ¿Qué o quién te inspiró a pintar o dibujar algo? Cuenta la experiencia.

8. Describe tu disco compacto o canción favorito.

9. Piensa en un momento en que quisiste hacer algo pero no pudiste. Cuenta la experiencia.

10. ¿Qué artista influyó más en el arte o la música de los jóvenes de hoy? ¿Cómo?

11. Explícale a un amigo cómo preparar una receta favorita tuya.

12. Diles a unos jóvenes lo que deben hacer para mantener la salud.

13. ¿Qué debe hacer una persona para reducir el estrés?

14. ¿Cuáles son los beneficios de hacer ejercicio?

15. Para ti, ¿cuáles son las cualidades más importantes que debe tener un(a) profesora(a)?

16. Piensa en una amistad o relación familiar tuya. Descríbela.

17. ¿Qué debe hacer una familia para evitar o resolver conflictos?

18. Tú y tu amigo(a) se pelearon. ¿Qué pueden hacer para reconciliarse?

19. ¿Qué requisitos se solicitan generalmente en un anuncio clasificado?

20. ¿Qué consejos puedes dar a un(a) estudiante que busca un trabajo de tiempo parcial?

21. En tu opinión, ¿cuáles son las responsabilidades de los ciudadanos?

22. ¿Qué habilidades o conocimientos tienes que puedes usar para mejorar tu comunidad?

23. ¿Piensas seguir la misma carrera que tiene una persona de tu familia? ¿Por qué?

24. ¿Cuál es un sueño que quieres realizar?

25. En tu opinión, ¿cuáles serán los mejores avances tecnológicos que verás en el futuro?

26. Describe un monumento, estatua o lugar arqueológico que conoces.

27. Describe un fenómeno o misterio inexplicable que te interesa.

28. ¿Qué culturas han contribuido a la cultura de tu región? Explica qué contribuciones han hecho.

29. Explícale a un(a) nuevo(a) estudiante de otro país lo que puede hacer para integrarse a la cultura de tu región.

30. Piensa en un problema del medio ambiente. Describe el problema y lo que se puede hacer para protegerlo.

31. ¿Cuáles serán los problemas más graves si la población del mundo sigue creciendo?

32. ¿Qué situación del mundo te preocupa más? ¿Por qué?

33. ¿Qué derechos debe garantizar el gobierno para los ciudadanos?

34. ¿Crees que existe la igualdad entre los hombres y las mujeres? Explica.

35. ¿Qué tipos de discriminación existían en tu comunidad hace 50 años? Explica.

36. Describe una manifestación en que tú u otra persona has participado.

Para empezar
Student Activity 1

(1) días; (2) llamo; (3) fecha; (4) número
entre 1 y 31; (5) enero, febrero, etc.; (6) Soy;
(7) lunes, . . . viernes; (8) número entre 1
y 30, cuarto, media; (9) profesor;
(10) ¿Cuántas?

Tema 2
Student Activity 1

(1) b; (2) c; (3) b

Student Activity 2

(1) Tengo; (2) serio; (3) estoy; (4) tercera;
(5) estricta; (6) está; (7) hablamos; (8) está;
(9) contenta; (10) trabajamos;
(11) estudiamos; (12) enseña

Tema 3
Teacher Activity 3

(1) trabajo; (2) hago; (3) levanto; (4) camino;
(5) Prefiero; (6) frescas; (7) muchos; (8) fría;
(9) favorita; (10) encantan; (11) italianas;
(12) gustan

Tema 4
Teacher Activity 2

(1) a; (2) a; (3) c

Teacher Activity 3

A. **Respuestas posibles:** (1) la, una, mi;
(2) muy, etc.; (3) de; (4) le; (5) de; (6) El, este;
(7) al; (8) para; (9) ir; (10) a; (11) estar

B. **Respuestas posibles:**(1) en, para; (2) los;
(3) las; (4) este, el; (5) no; (6) porque;
(7) que; (8) a, para

Tema 5
Student Activity 1

(1) mi; (2) voy, vamos; (3) favorito; (4) pedir;
(5) pide; (6) cumplo; (7) celebrar; (8) vienen;
(9) muchos; (10) nueva

Tema 5
Student Activity 2

Respuestas posibles: (1) por; (2) vienes;
vas; (3) que; (4) está, vive; (5) porque; (6) es;
(7) le; (8) de; (9) sus, mis; (10) saco,
sacamos; (11) qué

Tema 6
Teacher Activity 3

Respuestas posibles: (1) pon; (2) las;
(3) que; (4) están; (5) estoy; (6) si; (7) está;
(8) arreglar, limpiar, etc.

Student Activity 1

(1) c; (2) c; (3) a

Tema 7
Student Activity 2

Respuestas posibles: (1) regalaron; (2) ese;
(3) compré; (4) negros; (5) Pagué;
(6) quedan; (7) gustan; (8) vender;
(9) puedo, podré; (10) otros; (11) estos

Tema 8
Student Activity 2

(1) c; (2) a; (3) b

Student Activity 3

Respuestas posibles: (1) fuimos, viajamos;
(2) gastó, pagó; (3) de; (4) a; (5) tiene;
(6) Son, parecen; (7) para, en; (8) un, medio;
(9) donde; (10) a

Tema 9
Student Activity 1

Respuestas posibles: (1) de; (2) que;
(3) para; (4) o, y; (5) de; (6) con;
(7) que, quienes; (8) la, una

Student Activity 2

Respuestas posibles: (1) sirven; (2) la;
(3) puede; (4) conocer; (5) otra; (6) creen;
(7) son; (8) necesitan; (9) deben;
(10) cuestan

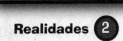
Tema 1
Teacher Activity 2
Respuestas posibles: (1) que; (2) y, pero; (3) a; (4) a; (5) las; (6) como; (7) una; (8) a; (9) de; (10) a

Teacher Activity 3
(1) quiero; (2) saber; (3) prefieres; (4) puedo; (5) levantarte; (6) piensas; (7) vestirnos; (8) otras; (9) tanto; (10) charlando

Tema 2
Student Activity 1
Respuestas posibles: (1) un; (2) que; (3) como; (4) la; (5) por; (6) las; (7) un; (8) que; (9) las; (10) de; (11) el, los

Student Activity 2
(1) decidió; (2) toda; (3) buscó; (4) encanta; (5) este; (6) encontró; (7) escogió; (8) se arregló; (9) se vistió; (10) ayudaron; (11) alguna; (12) se sorprendió; (13) dio

Tema 3
Student Activity 1
(1) puedes; (2) gran; (3) los; (4) conocen; (5) simpáticos; (6) ayudan; (7) te olvidas; (8) tus; (9) dan; (10) estos; (11) una

Student Activity 2
Respuestas posibles: (1) durmiendo; (2) salgo; (3) dormirme; (4) familiales; (5) ven; (6) ayúdame; (7) pon; (8) tengo, tenemos; (9) puedo, podemos; (10) Hazlo; (11) manejar; (12) ir

Tema 4
Student Activity 1
Respuestas posibles: (1) la; (2) la; (3) en, cerca de; (4) que; (5) un; (6) una; (7) las; (8) al; (9) los, sus

Tema 4
Student Activity 2
Respuestas posibles: (1) viniste; (2) Fue; (3) vive; (4) regresó; (5) mirándonos; (6) se llevaban; (7) tan; (8) peleándose; (9) estábamos; (10) nos queríamos

Teacher Activity 3
(1) a; (2) c; (3) b

Tema 5
Student Activity 1
Respuestas posibles: (1) algún; (2) traje, trajo, trajeron; (3) otra; (4) unas; (5) rotos; (6) vinieron; (7) tuvo; (8) una; (9) perdiendo; (10) mucha; (11) tenía; (12) estaba; (13) quiero

Tema 6
Teacher Activity 2
Respuestas posibles: (1) en; (2) es; (3) de; (4) las; (5) Lo; (6) Una, La, Otra; (7) por; (8) la; (9) A; (10) les

Tema 7
Student Activity 1
Respuestas posibles: (1) que; (2) nada, sabor, comida, plato; (3) el; (4) en, sobre, encima de, por; (5) me, nos; (6) muy, más, bien, algo; (7) el; (8) a; (9) o, y; (10) de, con

Student Activity 2
(1) hizo; (2) sirven; (3) era; (4) sentaron; (5) los; (6) hervidos; (7) frescas; (8) salir; (9) te olvides; (10) des

Tema 8
Teacher Activity 2
Respuestas posibles: (1) Para; (2) de; (3) que; (4) y, o; (5) del; (6) al; (7) una; (8) de; (9) es; (10) uno

Capítulo 2
Student Activity 1
(1) el; (2) al; (3) de; (4) a; (5) le; (6) a; (7) de; (8) de; (9) que; (10) de

Capítulo 4
Student Activity 1
(1) lo; (2) de; (3) los, esos; (4) entre; (5) las; (6) que; (7) a; (8) se; (9) que; (10) en

Capítulo 6
Student Activity 1
(1) o; (2) Uno, se; (3) una, la; (4) el; (5) se; (6) en, para, por; (7) que; (8) como; (9) de; (10) la, alguna, nuestra

Capítulo 7
Student Activity 1
(1) española; (2) el; (3) escribió; (4) tantos; (5) hay; (6) los; (7) produce; (8) cómicas

Capítulo 8
Student Activity 1
(1) que; (2) el; (3) los; (4) e; (5) de; (6) de; (7) sus; (8) se; (9) que

Capítulo 9
Student Activity 1
(1) algunas; (2) disminuyan; (3) dañar; (4) echando; (5) saben; (6) empiece; (7) habría (8) hacer; (9) se producirían

Capítulo 10
Student Activity 1
(1) ir; (2) estaban; (3) otras; (4) conté; (5) éramos; (6) había querido; (7) quería, quisiera; (8) supiera, supiéramos